ARCHITECTURES OF SPATIAL JUSTICE

ARCHITECTURES OF SPATIAL JUSTICE

DANA CUFF

THE MIT PRESS
CAMBRIDGE, MASSACHUSETTS
LONDON, ENGLAND

The MIT Press would like to thank the anonymous peer reviewers who provided comments on drafts of this book. The generous work of academic experts is essential for establishing the authority and quality of our publications. We acknowledge with gratitude the contributions of these otherwise uncredited readers.

This book was set in Arnhem by the MIT Press. Printed and bound in the United States of America.

Library of Congress Cataloging-in-Publication Data

Names: Cuff, Dana, 1953- author.
Title: Architectures of spatial justice / Dana Cuff.
Description: Cambridge, Massachusetts : The MIT Press, [2023] | Includes bibliographical references and index.
Identifiers: LCCN 2022017784 (print) | LCCN 2022017785 (ebook) | ISBN 9780262545211 (paperback) | ISBN 9780262373593 (epub) | ISBN 9780262373609 (pdf)
Subjects: LCSH: Architecture--Human factors. | Architecture and society. | Social justice.
Classification: LCC NA2542.4 .C84 2023 (print) | LCC NA2542.4 (ebook) | DDC 720.1/03--dc23/eng/20220720
LC record available at https://lccn.loc.gov/2022017784
LC ebook record available at https://lccn.loc.gov/2022017785

10   9   8   7   6   5   4   3   2   1

To the students and colleagues who have joined me in making cityLAB a place to imagine changing the world and to the next generation of architects who will make that happen

CONTENTS

1

ARCHITECTURE AT THE HEART OF SPATIAL JUSTICE

Architecture has never been more relevant to the most pressing problems facing contemporary life. State violence, the pandemic, and environmental collapse brought on by climate change have exposed systemic inequities in populations worldwide. Architects and urbanists must confront how their own actions contribute to racism and global warming and in what ways they can change their practices. While a substantial body of literature about design for sustainability, resilience, and climate change continues to grow, it generally overlooks the intrinsic connections between design and equity in everyday life. This book's humanistic focus leads to a deceptively simple question: Can architecture embody principles of spatial justice? Even as the answer to this question must somehow be "yes," architecture is almost unimaginable without privilege and its concomitant historic and structural biases. Interrogating two fundamental conditions of architecture reveals the field's capacity to work toward spatial justice. The first is architecture's relation to the public, and the second is architecture's dependence on capital. By examining practices that reimagine these two conditions and upend disciplinary conventions, architecture's limitations and potentials become apparent.

One example serves to spotlight the question of spatial justice in architecture. In 2020, a few months into the coronavirus pandemic, it became apparent that the physical environment—its design, accessibility, distribution, and functionality—played a significant role in the disease. Racial disparities, dangers facing those in care facilities, and economic inequities were tied to life-threatening spatial risks borne disproportionately by essential workers in health care, food and agriculture, and transportation and delivery.[1] Rather than focusing on these critical concerns, by June of 2020 architecture firms and journals were broadcasting touchless office design for tech workers, acoustic separation for at-home Zoom sessions, ways that cities could accommodate fitness training, and private indoor and outdoor "safe" spaces.[2] The degree to which this narrative elevates privilege and ignores those already dispossessed demonstrates how far ethics have been supplanted by economies. Implicit in a post-COVID world are buildings and cities designed for architecture's current clients, where any common realm would necessarily be fashioned from private solutions. Architects look for opportunities where capital has already accumulated, or they escape through utopian fictions. Less easily imagined are alternative futures that architecture might make possible, written by and about, designed for and with, and subsidized by and for the public.

Charles Moore's 1965 claim that "you have to pay for the public life" has only grown more true over the past sixty years.[3] In contrast to his idea of "public-ness as a sort of by-product of real estate planning and development," this book contributes to recent movements that insist that architects contend with their discipline's centuries-old structural problems, and that we do so through the *res publica* within the material world of things, particularly architecture itself.[4] It draws together previously disconnected threads from history, theory, and practice to demonstrate that a path forward is in the making that lays the groundwork for much-needed institutional and disciplinary transformation. Rather than write off architecture's capacity to contribute to the collective challenges of our time, *Architectures of Spatial Justice* argues that we have reached a historic tipping point and offers an evidence-laden path toward systemic change, beginning with targeted segments of design practice. That path is constructed from a series of individual steps that lead away from conventional architectural practice while retaining formal and aesthetic goals that not only define the discipline but embody the collective dignity that design attention renders. When architectural design, programming, conceptual integrity, or structural innovation characterize not only places of privilege but also spaces of currently underserved inhabitants, their lives are materially recognized. These steps rely on theory emanating from iterative reflections in architectural scholarship and from the narrative built by linking select design projects produced over the past century. The evidence shaping this book's argument has been systematically accumulated over the past two decades at cityLAB, my design research center at the University of California Los Angeles (UCLA). The lab has undertaken a series of collaborative research initiatives specifically designed to explore architectural agency through alternatives to conventional modes of practice, relations of capital, and relationships to the public. A selection of projects, some from cityLAB and some from practices in Japan, Mexico, and Chile, demonstrate architecture's potential contribution to spatial justice and comprise a series of experimental field tests to investigate six questions:

1. Where can design be leveraged for common good?
2. Do justice ethics invoke radically public architecture?
3. What role do *partnerships of difference* play?
4. Can a project serve as a generative demonstration rather than a singular solution?
5. How can such demonstrations be realized as legible policy?
6. And finally, what momentum do historically critical junctures provide?

These questions guide the structure of the subsequent chapters and conclude with a consideration of whether architecture can destabilize its own long-standing power relations in order to redress past inequities and create the world we want to live in moving forward. The experimental work that opens each chapter embodies an ongoing struggle to cultivate architecture's ethical capacities.

SPATIAL JUSTICE

For architecture, placing spatial justice at the fore requires rethinking the very core of the discipline. Spatial justice is itself an abstraction, as Ed Soja argued in his book *Seeking Spatial Justice*, and a continual process of contestation over rights to the city.[5] Justice has a geography in which the equitable distribution of and access to city resources, services, and amenities are basic human rights that spatial strategies of design and planning can uphold. Obviously, architecture cannot alone solve entrenched problems of injustice. But to take the challenge seriously, architects and planners must give up authorial claims to creativity in favor of collective ones, must destabilize conventional projects and ideas about clients or patrons, must view their labor as generative rather than oriented toward completion, and must leverage the art of architecture for the commons. There have been previous advocates for similar goals, evidence that the architectural discipline provides adequate space for alternative formulations as well as for resistance. Both types of transformation are more possible now because we are at a historic juncture, evident in the growing vocal demands of students, young practitioners, and disenfranchised publics.

Rather than remaking architecture in toto, seeking spatial justice involves strategic mutations that variegate the discipline and practice. The medical profession provides a useful example. While we expect medicine to adapt to the current and future pandemics, cures for other diseases still require research. Likewise, medical solutions like vaccines depend on larger systems for their effectiveness, such as good governance, adequate health insurance, trustworthy information dissemination, and monitoring of variants. Even when those systems aren't working effectively, everyone agrees that the medical profession has a critical role to play. Where is the equivalent collective charge in architecture schools and practices to address the housing crisis or to make material solutions for the Green New Deal? Is it possible for all the individual initiatives around affordable housing or sustainability to coalesce? This book brings to light the extensive remaking of architecture already in motion on a global scale, priming institutional frameworks that can be reinscribed and identifying cumulative effects. Each chapter begins with an exemplary case study, the first and last undertaken by cityLAB's Los Angeles-based practice. LA is an ideal Petri dish for urban and architectural experimentation because its form resists codification and its population is a microcosm of world cities. cityLAB is explicitly embedded in its urban context as a means to test the broader boundaries of architecture's capacity. The indistinct boundary between architectural and urban design is critical to the book and to cityLAB's focus on framing architecture's political agency, which is most readily visible in the collective urban context.

Calls for spatial justice have pushed architecture to a tipping point and offered an opportunity to expand the field's cultural relevance. This historic juncture unsuspectedly began in the United States with the Occupy movement in September 2011, which itself built on anti-government uprisings in the Arab world. The popular resistance launched against egregious income inequality has been criticized for its lack of structured goals, even as it continues to have ripple effects. Both Michael Sorkin and Richard Sennett tied Occupy to architecture and urbanism, emphasizing the ideological implications but leaving to future works (like this one) just how design might materially advance political and economic critiques.[6] Architecture's dominant history of Eurocentric, White, imperial narratives by and about the powerful repress long-standing counternarratives of spatial justice and resistance that constitute an activist genealogy in the field. This book emanates from those counternarratives to demonstrate the significant potential architecture holds for socially just, anti-racist futures. It relies on decades of scholarship by and about marginalized actors in the design disciplines who, like bell hooks and Gloria Anzaldúa, found their voices empowered in that liminal space.[7]

As we honor these activist threads, we must challenge the disciplinary foundations that were strengthened by the turn in the 1980s and 1990s toward *autonomy*, the theory that architectural form is shaped through self-referential history and discourse. In efforts to establish architecture as a field distinct and independent from others, relationships to capital and the public were deemed irrelevant. Spatial justice by contrast reorients the very notion of architecture from a neoliberal, consumer-centered economic model to one of public goods, undermining the opposition set up between social purpose and aesthetics and the association of aesthetics only with superstructure and wealth. That general dichotomy, however it is framed—between art and engineering, aesthetics and utility, function and form—has energized reverberations in architectural thinking at least since the mid-nineteenth century when John Ruskin reserved the term *architecture* for art and ornament versus mere building.[8] The modern movement challenged this elitism in myriad ways, elevating steel, structure, collaboration, and social purpose.[9] But the stubborn core of architecture persists, naturalized by the "suggestive" Tree of Architecture that introduces Bannister Fletcher's 1901 history textbook.[10] The histories that grow from the trunk and leaf out, classical and European, are those that are written; all others wither on lower limbs, including Peruvian, Mexican, Egyptian, and Chinese and Japanese (rolled into one). We know this second group of histories better than he did, but still not well enough.[11] Finding the suppressed lines of inequity means being willing to reclaim the term *architecture* and recuperating the discipline's complex potential to serve, uphold, and advance justice goals. That our history must be imbricated with new textures and repressed stories goes without saying.

What would it mean to imagine, create, and sustain architecture that stands for *spatial justice*, a term meant to embody social as well as environmental entanglements? We would have to resist power relations that seem intrinsic to the profession, not just those imbalances between architect and client, but also those between client and public, between those who can afford architecture and those who cannot. Compared to medicine, which we can at least acknowledge is an unjust system that provides treatment only to those who can afford it (even if we have not remedied it), we have been blind to the fact that well-designed environments, cities, and buildings should be part of the commonweal. Movements like Black Lives Matter or Housing First are founded on the grounds that systemic racism and homelessness implicate all of us. To open architecture more fully to the possibility of spatial justice requires a critical examination of the discipline in relation to the public and to capital as well as to privilege, power, aesthetics, and sociality—that is, a reevaluation of architecture's fundamentals.

COUNTERACTING PRIVILEGE

To imagine architecture without privilege—without its patrons, wealthy clients, well-endowed cultural institutions, and corporate commissions—would seem to erase architecture's entire history. We begin by undoing architecture's Whiteness, meaning the normalization of White racialized identity through which non-White lives are seen as inferior. Such Whiteness (which is not the same as but is related to the predominance of White architects and educators) permeates architecture to such an extent that anti-racist counterpractices are needed to move the discipline, its power structures, and its practices beyond their Eurocentric foundations. It also requires thinking about worlds that are outside neoliberal logics of capital, through "non-political-economic forms of imagining the future."[12] The origins of such thinking can be found in Bernard Rudofsky's *Architecture Without Architects*, which begins by rhetorically erasing the architect. He might have noted that this architecture is also without clients and commissions in the conventional sense, upending the architect's relation to power and privilege. The structures in its photographs are not "mere building"—they are architecture that by implication warrants architects' and architectural historians' attention. Rudofsky brings to light previously overlooked geographies as well as an unimagined future for the field. *Architectures of Spatial Justice* follows Rudofsky's method (but not his content) by bringing to light works of architecture without clients, commissions, and capital and examines whether built environments can be produced without privilege and power. The book describes cityLAB and its sister practices within universities, public agencies, and nonprofits to examine the degree to which they can be liberated from the standard political economy of architecture. The case studies introducing each chapter explain how resources (including funding) are assembled, assessing the benefits and barriers entailed. Conventional architectural firms surviving on project-by-project commissions also offer some examples of how to carve out mission-driven work. All these efforts, therefore, hold the potential to destabilize power relations and seek spatial justice.

Rudofsky romanticized "non-pedigreed architects," the men and women who built a communal architecture "produced not by specialists but by the spontaneous and continuing activity of a whole people with a common heritage, acting within a community of experience."[13] Today we cannot conjure some whole people operating for a homogeneous common good that exists before or outside capitalism's all-encompassing status. The closest (and cautionary) parallel may be circumstances of collective trauma that suppress difference to face an overwhelming singularity. For example, in post-Depression America, public housing was one such operation, however flawed and politically fraught, in which government aimed to support those in need without specific financial return on its investment. Given property's ultimate primacy, it is unsurprising that the material form of state-subsidized affordable housing segregated poor people of color from the private investment in surrounding neighborhoods. Since the mid-twentieth century, if not before, our construct of "the public" has critically imploded because such unified visions patch over genuine differences while barely concealing unequal, underlying power relations. In cities today, the public realm is relegated to infrastructure like streets or open spaces, but even these are increasingly privatized in contexts of public disinvestment.[14] To challenge the uneven distribution of public goods, more democratic and participatory processes have been devised to open access to design and planning over the last seven decades.[15] However laudable, the flaws of participation-in-practice signal its failures within architecture.

In principle, if decision-making is equitable, accessible, and transparent, then all stakeholders' views will be heard and, by definition, the outcome will be equitable. These views have been deeply explored in terms of the "just city."[16] By contrast, the authorial role held by the architect is construed as the primary source of creative imagination and thus the source of good solutions. But these theoretical positions hardly represent actual practices, which are far more complicated; participation is never perfect, and architecture is never the result of a single genius. In the best efforts, partnerships, collaboration, coproduction, and participatory practices are taken as critical constructs to be scrutinized and designed to assure difference is represented. Throughout this book, small and large examples demonstrate the complexity such partnerships bring to the design process and challenge participation's unassailable standing. If participation is insufficient, how can we attend to and uplift collective interests and undo architecture's privileged status? Since architecture's ties to capital (and lots of it, as Mary McLeod notes[17]) are fundamental, professional ethics constrict its duty narrowly to public health and safety. Further public goods, such as inclusive design processes or buildings for the commons, are the responsibility of the client or of regulation. Beyond that, when architects leverage their skills toward truly social goals it is by ingenious or virtuous means. Sometimes, creativity delivers goods beyond the project brief, as when a building pushes past stated environmental goals. A virtuous or humanitarian alternative is for architects to work pro bono, renouncing financial remuneration for some cause. There are many such examples throughout this text, like the volunteer work by architects after disasters or the creative solutions design teachers and their students develop without fees or contracts. Sam Mockbee's Rural Studio at Auburn University operated both ingeniously and voluntarily to design highly affordable houses in West Alabama.[18] The goals of Rural Studio, founded in the early 1990s, went beyond health and safety to deliver well-designed, dignified, and economical buildings to people usually excluded by race and poverty. By comparison, boundaries around professional ethics have been drawn tightly and legalistically, undermining the profession's relevance by refusing to recognize that every building to some degree contributes to the commons.

To uphold spatial justice requires challenging the boundaries around professional ethics and also around the discipline, including the historically canonized discourse about style and aesthetics. One particularly perverse aspect of this discourse is the easy incompatibility constructed between formal objectives and social or environmental goals: "It's not necessarily all that much fun to live in a work of art."[19] For instance, modernism's failures to tie a progressive politics to its aesthetic corroborated the already-inscribed disassociation between the two. Form and stylistics instead speak about architecture's own traditions, leaving modernism so aesthetically independent of sociopolitical critique that it delivered cold, uninhabitable spaces, or that it was a tool of planners to demolish communities of color through so-called "urban renewal." This modern architectural canon excludes work outside the European-American axis, like Lina Bo Bardi's SESC Pompéia Leisure Center in São Paolo, in which formal sophistication exists comfortably with and is enriched by communitarian goals (see figure 2.7). There is neither historical grounds nor intrinsic theoretical bases for separating social (including environmental) goals from formal goals, yet academic architects in particular cling to their autonomy. Professional architects may attract clients by promoting their social agendas, yet they rarely receive awards for the same. When Alejandro Aravena was awarded the 2016 Pritzker Prize, it was a new and perhaps guilty admission that a winning architect could produce noteworthy buildings that prioritized a social agenda. His firm Elemental's work stands in tacit defiance of the unwritten assumptions about award-worthy buildings by its extremely modest materials and budget and its shared authorship with occupants as described in the introduction to chapter 5. Elemental's projects demonstrate that architecture can seek spatial justice and can recognize such a contribution to the discipline.

Architectures of Spatial Justice writes a new history of architectural practice out of a minor literature.[20] The narrative is woven from threads like those of Mockbee, Rudofsky, Bo Bardi, and Aravena, is tested and strengthened through cityLAB's experimentation, and is philosophically indebted to Black cultural critics bell hooks and Cornell West. The result brings into view an agency for architectural work that displaces privilege and privileges social justice. If we are to train a new generation of architectural workers, we must contend with the fact that three-quarters of architectural educators in America are White, including myself. The broad goal for transforming architecture's future must be to diversify the discipline's content, students, and faculty, and for those of us in education to mitigate the harm that Whiteness renders. This is scholarly, personal, aesthetic, and political labor that I, along with many of the architects cited in the following pages, continue to undertake.

BUILDING ARCHITECTURE'S RELEVANCE

In her reflections on a conference she organized in 2000, Joan Ockman discusses the neopragmatist and post-critical projects in architecture at the turn of the millennium. In some ways, this work picks up a strand from that project: the idea that "to partition politics off from philosophy and aesthetics remains impossible in a world in which cultural practices are inseparable from other forms of social and environmental production. No field demonstrates this more dramatically than architecture."[21]

"Ninety percent of the [architecture] students being trained today are being trained to fulfill the needs of late capitalism." What a surprise to learn that when Peter Eisenman made this statement, he was regretting architecture's lost autonomy, when students were trained to think about architecture, not prepare for the job market.[22] Instead, this book considers how architecture as a discipline can step away from fulfilling the needs of late capitalism but also step away from fulfilling the self-interests of autonomy. A third way is for architecture to meet the growing pressure to respond to the twinned global crises of racialized social inequity and environmental destruction. *Architectures of Spatial Justice* is a considered response to that pressure that focuses on the social problematics, which implicate and are intertwined with environmental discrimination.

For the 2021 book and exhibition at New York City's Museum of Modern Art (MoMA) entitled *Reconstructions: Architecture and Blackness in America*, Milton Curry writes in his concluding statement:

Architecture race theory is a new terminology and conceptual frame for a discursive movement that has already begun. It defines a constellation of scholarship and creative work at the forefront of decentering dominant and hegemonic gazes through which modernist and postmodernist theories of architecture have emerged. It defines projective scholarship and creative work that set forth imaginaries of space and form that reposition Black and African Diasporic identities as worthy of inclusion in a new mainstream of architectural discourse. It is a conceptual frame that unabashedly embraces a political, leftist agenda to radically transform institutions and fundamental conceptions of power within the discipline and practice of architecture.[23]

It is in this spirit that this book is written, as a means to explore and explain practices that insist on anti-racism in architecture. Only in this way can we begin to center those voices that have been silenced and those spaces that have been erased, to make the world we all want to live in.

Consider this: in May of 2021, an *Architectural Digest* article singled out forty-nine reality design shows to watch on television, "from classic favorites like *Fixer Upper* to more niche shows like *Desert Flippers*."[24] What could possibly interest viewers enough to sponsor nearly fifty design programs? And these are just the ones the magazine recommends. This is a perverse extension of Hayden White's accusation that scholarship in the field of history has become so remote from the public sphere that laypeople must satisfy their historical curiosity with the

History Channel, the heritage industry, and docudramas, particularly when considering some of life's most pressing questions about environment, violence, or loss.[25] As a measure of a discipline's relevance, White suggests that scholars' research must engage not only other professional scholars but also a wider audience who wants to "use" that knowledge. This comprises a practical history, in contrast to a theoretical or professional history. For White, this means creating better historical narratives out of more ethically rich sources such as the arts, poetry, and literature. Though White was specifically critical of the uses of history, his concern applies broadly to professional narratives that are inaccessible to the public. While a "practical architecture" might seem overly redundant, it underscores the contrast with disciplinary autonomy. The latter mirrors White's "professional past" and the idea of historical study and writing intended for an academic audience. Practical architecture would admit building practices, histories, and efforts that have a public audience and that are useful in opening possible collective futures. Moreover, it would open the built environment to public processes in which urban performativity—that is, how the quotidian city actually operates—is iteratively shaped. Practical architecture's fundamental emphasis on utility and the everyday reflects an intent to transform the status quo rather than serve it. In this sense, practical architecture embodies an inherently activist orientation. Finally, its practicality admits that "mere building" can be as elegant, sophisticated, and worthy of disciplinary inclusion as its professionally produced counterparts.

The design reality shows appeal in part to those outside the design economy by virtue of their largely being unable to purchase design services, in part to those who may want a "how-to" guide to flipping desert homes, for example, and in part to those who can relate to the experience of fixing up a home. More sublime is the Congolese artist-architect Bodys Isek Kingelez, whose work explicitly reverses the professional's idea of educating the layperson. Variously called an artist, architectural sculptor, or urban futurist, Kingelez made extreme models that reimagined the city, especially Kinshasa, as a more beautiful, technologically advanced, idealized, and inspired place. Kingelez and his models were recognized by institutions and shown in the Centre Pompidou in 1989 and in a major show at MoMA in New York in 2018–19. As a friend explained, he didn't

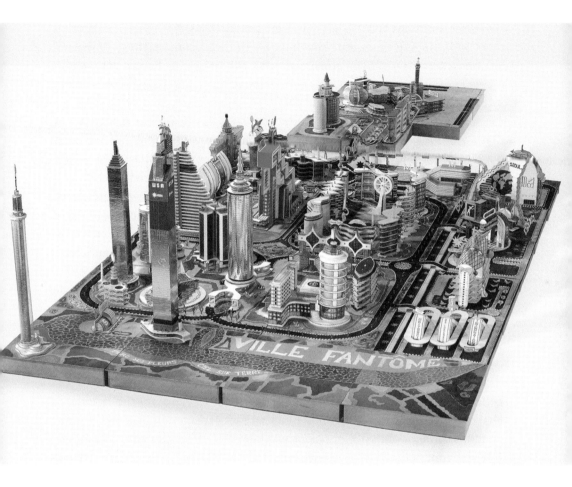

FIGURE 1.1

A model by the artist and architect Bodys Isek Kingelez reimagining his home city of Kinshasa in the Democratic Republic of the Congo. Ville Fantôme, 1996. Paper, paperboard, plastic, 120 × 240 × 580 cm. © Bodys Isek Kingelez. Photo by Maurice Aeschimann, courtesy of the Jean Pigozzi collection of African Art.

expect the buildings or cities he created to be built; instead, "the act of imagining them and bringing them into existence, albeit through maquettes, represents an almost fervent idealism which over time will invariably have its impact on the types of visions that other, less poetic city planners may bring to bear on the future of other African cities."[26]

Such practices are viewed by many architects as outside the discipline, in the case of Kingelez, or beneath it, in the case of the design TV shows. But what does Ville Fantôme have in common with *Desert Flippers*, or either of these with spatial justice? The possible connection is that they are both a version of a practical architecture, giving up on neutrality and objectivity in order to grapple with concerns like the political entrenchment of urban planning, the inequities of property wealth with which architecture is associated, or the contradictions inherent to a speculative market for buildings. If, as is often claimed, architects have abandoned the lion's share of the built environment because it is generic, suburban, or self-built, then it is no wonder that all the people who live in those environments look elsewhere for a practical architecture.

The purpose of this book is twofold: First, to unpack architecture's agency in pursuit of spatial justice. Second, to demonstrate how activist design strategies can move past barriers in order to advance that potential. This is not a redefinition of the discipline but an argument that repressed histories tied to activist practices lend architecture a long overdue relevance for the significant challenges facing cities worldwide today and an articulation of a path toward windows through which other potential dimensions of architecture become visible and admissible. The primary means for doing so are to work through spatial theories of justice, minor and repressed architectural histories, and recent global investigations to demonstrate ways that architecture is already and could be *practicing* spatial justice. To advance actionable, ethical agendas from within the discipline is more of a systemic transformation than a launching of counter or alternative models, which not only let architecture itself off the hook but abandon its significant potential.

Although racial inequality has been unequivocally identified in land and thus in the city, as embodied by spatial segregation, discriminatory zoning, redlining, and property rights,[27] it has been less clear whether the buildings materializing on that land have furthered systemic racism or resisted it. The following chapters scrutinize that divide to reveal it as a false one and show that ties between land and built form are indivisible. Although urban design and landscape architecture have already established their claims on land and its material transformations, architecture has yet to do so. A corollary agenda herein is to demonstrate architecture's responsibility with regard to geographies of injustice alongside its potential agency. This carries forward the work I began in an earlier book, *The Provisional City*, which unpacked architecture's role in past inequities in the context of urban politics.[28] This volume considers how we might redress them.

Architectures of Spatial Justice is part of a growing body of critical literature within and around architecture. The catalogs that accompanied MoMA's exhibitions *Small Scale Big Change* (2010), *Rising Currents* (2011), and *Foreclosed: Rehousing the American Dream* (2012) implicitly argued that established institutions like MoMA and well-known architects could productively engage real-world problems like the inequalities of underserved communities, sea level rise, and the American housing crisis, respectively. Innovative architectural design is a fundamental part of the transformative solutions each volume presents. This book builds on and fills certain gaps within works by authors who adhere to social practice like Tom Finkelpearl as well as those like Jeremy Till who critique architecture as an autonomous discipline and those like Douglas Spencer who view it as a tool of the neoliberal economy. More recent are books that address systemic racism in architectural practice and education, such as Sharon Egretta Sutton's *When Ivory Towers Were Black* about Columbia University (2017) and the important collected volume *Race and Modern Architecture* edited by Irene Cheng, Charles Davis, and Mabel Wilson (2020). From a different perspective, political economic critiques of architecture overlap in some ways with this text. Peggy Deamer's seminal work on architectural labor and Albena Yaneva's 2017 *Five Ways to Make Architecture Political* similarly engage theory to launch new thinking about architecture's relationship to power and its political capacity. Most distinctively, this book integrates urban theory from Ed Soja, Henri Lefebvre, and David Harvey into design theory and practice, particularly through the lens of housing, where architecture is most directly engaged with social justice issues. Its chapters document project-based experiments in practice as well as projects at the margins of the discipline to demonstrate that architecture as spatial justice is well underway. It utilizes a hybrid format between the architectural monograph organized around projects and an architectural history text organized around topics in order to examine the discipline's capacity to advance spatial justice, relying heavily on two decades of my own project-based research, and to offer a comprehensive approach to architecture and spatial justice.

I want to make a distinction between the operations conducted in this book and transformations of expanded and alternative fields with which it might be confused. The "expanded field" model, laid out by art theorist Rosalind Krauss, defined distinct disciplines (in her case, landscape art, sculpture, and architecture) in order to see how they might overlap.[29] Counter-architecture movements define themselves outside the discipline, like community design centers or sustainable development firms that intend to reform the discipline into alternative types of practice to redress some shortcoming. By contrast, in order to define the limits of architecture's rejection of privilege, practical architecture selectively divests itself of several core facets of the discipline such as the separation of formal goals from cultural ones or a reliance on client-driven commissions. To construct practical architecture is to break open the well-defined core of the architectural discipline so that it absorbs and is transformed by what were considered the margins. The margins in architecture are wider and more populous than in most disciplines because the core has been so rigidly defined and maintained.

Architecture's potential for transformation is heightened by a growing awareness of structural racism and other forms of systemic injustice that take shape in the built environment and in the city in particular. This book enters directly into the debates about architecture's role in addressing the growing unhoused population, continued racial segregation, and displacement brought about by gentrification, and it is germane to quandaries about architecture and climate change. The groundbreaking work of numerous architectural practices, including cityLAB, is explained and illustrated as models with the potential to proliferate widely. By challenging conventional roles through history, theory, and contemporary practice, underacknowledged dimensions of architectural agency come to light.

2

LEVERAGING DESIGN

BACKYARD HOMES, CITYLAB, CALIFORNIA

When the architect Roger Sherman and I founded cityLAB in 2006, we'd planned to shape a new kind of practice that could bring architecture to the environmental, political, and cultural realities that had eluded the discipline. I was certain that our discipline had much to offer, in spite of the fact that it had played almost no role in many critical contexts—from earthquake and hurricane recovery, to the growing homelessness crisis, to the vast landscapes that go without formal design: the suburbs, rural regions, and practically all of our everyday environments.

cityLAB launched a design competition called PropX in 2006 to address the housing crisis in Los Angeles, inviting teams of young architects, planners, and real estate developers to invent new policies that would unlock market-driven affordable housing and visualize the housing it would stimulate. One of those teams focused on accessory dwelling units (ADUs) in a project called YIMBY (Yes In My Back Yard), which in turn launched a decade-long series of design research investigations at cityLAB. The PropX initiative involved many of cityLAB's priorities: innovative and investigative design, infill buildings, young practitioners, demonstration projects, urban transformation, and environmental benefits. Most importantly, the initiative aimed to advance spatial justice by unleashing thousands of small affordable housing units.

Much to my surprise, policies already existed in California that nominally permitted secondary units in the City of Los Angeles. However, between

2003—when the most recent "granny flats" legislation was passed to encourage the construction of backyard rental units—and 2010, only eleven building permits had been issued. Our field studies showed that thousands more were illegally built and occupied, particularly in neighborhoods of color. Clearly something was wrong with the policy, and we discovered that, like so much of the postwar built environment, the car had a lot to do with it. cityLAB's research, in keeping with Los Angeles tradition, eventually led back to the car.

Suburban development practices in postwar American cities, often guided by lending requirements, included building a one- or two-car garage, generally at the front of a property. When the granny flats law took effect in 2003, it required on-site parking for up to two more cars in order to add a rental unit, and few lots offered enough space.

We began our Backyard Homes studies in the town of Pacoima, where entire blocks of large lots had been shaped as agricultural parcels at the turn of the century. There, an ecology of informal construction thrived; as many as four unpermitted rental units could be built behind each original house. On the lots, some up to 75 feet wide and 350 feet long, bungalows of about 1,200 square feet sat in front of fenced yards. Behind the yards were vegetable gardens and garages where vehicle repair work or other home-based industries took place. One or two cars might have been parked at the back of the lot or in the driveway but almost never in the garage. Further back on the same lot sat additional units as well as bare land where chickens or goats were sometimes penned. This pattern of using a residential lot to support household economies was identified in other parts of Los Angeles by the historian Becky Nicolaides.[1] To learn all this, we held meetings organized by community groups, visited people's homes, interviewed residents, and followed permit histories, along with more traditional forms of urban history and architectural scholarship. Fieldwork, focus groups, site studies, historical research, and regulatory investigation made up our multi-pronged methodological strategy for gaining a humanistic understanding of neighborhoods and their potential to appropriately ease the housing crisis.

Not long after informal practices revealed the value of extra-large lots for backyard homes, other feasible lot types surfaced, particularly the corner lot and the alley lot. Although conventional wisdom argues that a standard suburban lot

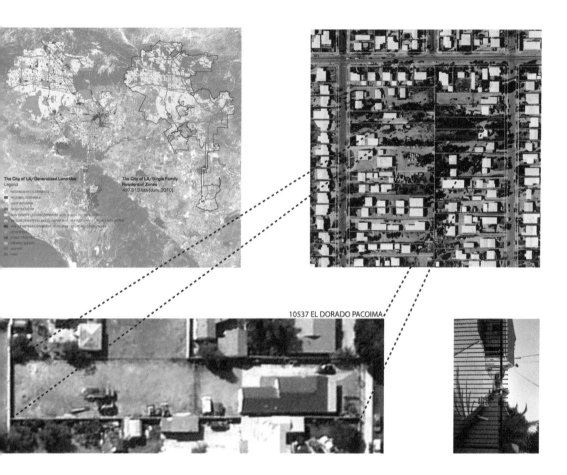

FIGURE 2.1

Backyard Homes potential: from a single lot in Pacoima, to the block of large lots where many accessory dwelling units were built without permits prior to new state legislation, to the Los Angeles map showing its five hundred thousand single-family lots in yellow where accessory dwelling units could be added (2007). Image by Per-Johan Dahl, courtesy of cityLAB.

exists, cityLAB research shows the contrary. Date of land platting, topography, target market, and location within the subdivision all influence lot configuration. We discovered that mid-block lots had little ADU potential unless they were wider than forty feet and had a driveway that led past the existing house. In terms of existing structures, rear-yard garages (usually built before World War II) paired with small original houses created sufficient access and available area for a backyard rental unit, so long as owners had not built substantial home additions. Corner and alley lots allowed for parking without driveways utilizing site area. Our studies led to diagrams of subdivisions characterized by different lot types centering on the three most buildable: large, alley, and corner.

Politics and Community Benefit

For the first seven years of our Backyard Homes initiative, we tried to modify the existing ADU law by working with the Los Angeles City Council so that more homeowners could build legal units. Attempts to make even obviously needed changes were successfully fought by no-growth neighbors in different council districts. For example, an early nineteenth-century firefighting provision based on equipment at the time required a ten-foot-wide "passageway" with no overhead obstructions to every front door on-site. This outdated provision, which essentially prevented large numbers of lots from adding a secondary unit, was invoked to block construction. Neighborhood resistance was effective without being democratic; wealthy, White homeowners were preventing the rest of the city from legalizing secondary units. For several years, we investigated ways that the contestation might be addressed. One strategy leveraged design for a "give-back"; to build an ADU, corner lots could be required to incorporate some community amenity like a "little library," a shady park bench, or a community-oriented business such as childcare or a plant nursery. Alley houses could be required to improve the alleyway according to recent city plans, including re-greening the space with landscape and porous paving, creating lighting and window facades on the alley for public safety, and installing solar energy solutions. We proposed creating provisions to limit construction in neighborhoods where there was concern about the overall number of backyard homes.

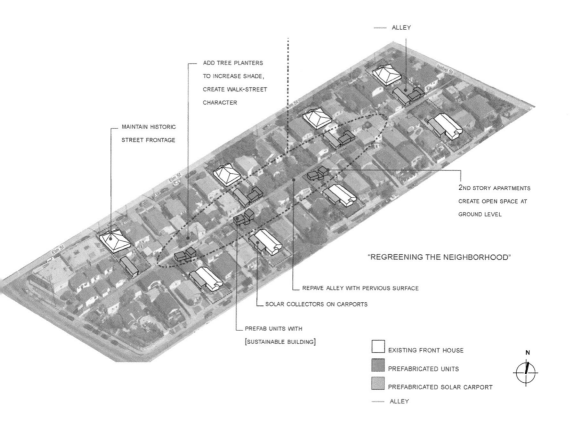

ALLEY

ADD TREE PLANTERS
TO INCREASE SHADE,
CREATE WALK-STREET
CHARACTER

MAINTAIN HISTORIC
STREET FRONTAGE

2ND STORY APARTMENTS
CREATE OPEN SPACE AT
GROUND LEVEL

"REGREENING THE NEIGHBORHOOD"

REPAVE ALLEY WITH PERVIOUS SURFACE

SOLAR COLLECTORS ON CARPORTS

PREFAB UNITS WITH
[SUSTAINABLE BUILDING]

☐ EXISTING FRONT HOUSE

■ PREFABRICATED UNITS

■ PREFABRICATED SOLAR CARPORT

— ALLEY

N

FIGURE 2.2

In a study of alley lots, Kevin Daly Architects developed an accessory dwelling unit proposal that would regreen paved Los Angeles alleyways, make alleys safer, and generate solar power (2009). Courtesy of Kevin Daly Architects.

A grant allowed us and our colleague Dr. Vinit Mukhija to get a better sense of community barriers by surveying the nearly one hundred LA neighborhood associations.[2] Several invited us to come to meetings to discuss the pros and cons of ADUs, where we learned that backyard planting and privacy were principal concerns. Next door neighbors did not want large trees removed or a second-story window looking into their backyard. These meetings produced a significant political insight: backyard homes were neighbor problems, not neighborhood problems. Neighborhood council members voiced concerns about parking, renters, and overcrowding, much of which took the form of discriminatory "othering." The imagined people building and inhabiting secondary units were stigmatized and stereotyped. But after every meeting, some attendees would line up to quietly ask whether their lot was buildable or to describe the difficulty of getting a permit. Even though they would not speak publicly, private individuals wanted a secondary unit for an adult child or aging parents, for a caregiver, to earn rental income, or because they wanted to downsize and stay in the neighborhood. This sparked a new theme: everyone has a backyard home story. To overcome political barriers at the neighborhood scale, we could design new architectural models and new narratives to support them.

The housing crisis in Los Angeles, in California, and in cities across the United States only continued to worsen as our studies progressed. Because of my years of housing research at cityLAB, in fall 2015 I was asked by local state assemblymember Richard Bloom to help put together an informal housing advisory board to discuss "the wide-ranging issues of 'affordable housing.'"[3] Several meetings later, longtime cityLAB fellow Jane Blumenfeld and I volunteered to draft an ADU policy with Bloom's legislative team. Based on Blumenfeld's track record as a forward-thinking LA planner and years of cityLAB's design testing, we knew that a by-right policy to incentivize secondary rental units had to include reduction or elimination of parking as well as setback requirements, unit size limits, the elimination of the passageway law, and limited local ability to change the standards. We began with the primary obstacle by eliminating required parking within a 500-foot radius of bus stops with frequent service, which captured about 85 percent of single-family homes in Los Angeles (not including hillside properties). Removing the parking requirement sparked a new design challenge,

FIGURE 2.3

The City of Los Angeles, shown in blue, is a mosaic of suburban lots ranging in size and configuration. Different neighborhoods, like the inserts on the map, can accommodate different arrangements of backyard homes (2007). Image by Per-Johan Dahl, courtesy of cityLAB.

and cityLAB in collaboration with Kevin Daly Architects worked alongside UCLA Architecture and Urban Design students to build a full-scale demonstration house. Called the BIHOME, it would occupy the same 400 square feet vacated by the two-car garage and achieve new carbon efficiencies as well as respect the backyard as a biome of flora and fauna.

By May of 2016, I learned informally that colleagues at UC Berkeley, led by Karen Chappel and Carol Galante at the Terner Center, were working with their own congressmember on an ADU bill. After several conversations, it became obvious that the housing conditions in Northern and Southern California were substantially different and that an effective statewide bill would require our collaboration. For example, some Bay Area suburbs were characterized by large houses from which an ADU might be carved, and parking issues were not as determining. We spent several hectic months aligning the two bills, negotiating with interest groups, and consulting with legal advisers. Bloom's legislative analyst would send emails with the marked-up, revised bill asking for immediate reads on "any red flags raised." Thousands of potential units, for example, were basically eliminated in lobbying by firefighting organizations that wanted hillside properties exempted. These consequential amendments required reexamining the entire bill over and over to make sure that we hadn't inadvertently created negative side effects in a design-policy testing process, fundamentally based on trust with our Northern California colleagues and the congressman. As any policy writer can attest, a single "may" versus "shall" can be consequential. By September of 2016, the dust had settled; the identical Assembly Bill 2299 (Bloom) and Senate Bill 1069 (Wieckowski) were passed by the state legislature and became law on January 1, 2017.

The Backyard Homes initiative began with an idea of creating affordable housing in Los Angeles and ended with a much larger impact on housing

FIGURE 2.4

A full-scale mock-up called the BIHOME was designed and built by UCLA architecture students under the guidance of Kevin Daly Architects and cityLAB. It demonstrated how accessory dwelling units could meet environmental objectives like backyard habitat management and a reduced carbon footprint (2015). Photo by Photekt, courtesy of cityLAB.

throughout California. There are almost 500,000 single-family properties in Los Angeles, but there are 8.1 million statewide. Several years have passed since the bill went into effect at the start of 2017, giving enough time to evaluate the initiative. Measures of success included whether it was easy for homeowners and planning departments to follow the ordinance, the numbers of building permits and certificates of occupancy issued, geography and rents for units constructed, effectiveness of local pushback, and the use of the bill as a model for other states. While data is available for some of these criteria, for others, anecdotal reports must suffice.

One goal was to increase the involvement of architects in the design of middle-class housing, particularly young designers for whom the small rental units might be well suited. But it is difficult to determine who is designing the new ADUs. Many young and established architects are designing and building backyard homes, and a number of others are involved with new business models that would design and build in quantity using web-based dashboards or new construction systems and delivery techniques.[4] The production possibilities are obvious to many, but few have found the means to unlock their potential. Tech start-ups have raced into this space, and I expect that despite the barriers of conventional construction practices and local codes, some will eventually succeed. Currently, the most prominent delivery models favor local general contractors and new service providers that blend web-based site assessment and cost estimation with analog building practices.

The emergent delivery models suggest that ADUs have become a specialized expertise. We wrote the legislation as plainly as possible, but all policy is arcane. A few months after the law was enacted, I called local planning desks as if I were a prospective ADU builder to ask questions they might have. Four calls later and I never received a correct answer to a range of fairly straightforward questions. In response, cityLAB, with support from the LA mayor's office, wrote and published "Building an ADU: Guidebook to Accessory Dwelling Units in the City of Los Angeles" as much for those planners as for homeowners and builders. The state distributes the guidebook for free, and it serves as a model for how websites, small builders, and other cities can explain the process in simple terms.

Four years after it became law, the ADU bill had increased production dramatically (measured by permits and certificates of occupancy/completion). In the three years before the bill's passage (2014–2016) a total of 248 ADU permits were issued by the City of Los Angeles; in the three years after passage (2017–2019), 13,168 permits were issued, a 530 percent increase. No other jurisdiction in California approaches Los Angeles's number of permits; there are indications that other jurisdictions were slow to start but are picking up the pace. More troubling is that the new ADUs are only slightly more affordable than other rentals. During the bill's development, I argued for a 600-square-foot maximum on the grounds that rents for small ADUs would be lower than for larger units. Although cityLAB developed models of well-designed small units, we lost that battle, and the maximum unit size was written as 1,200 square feet. In retrospect, the affordability problem has two roots. First, our architectural design demonstrations did not overcome the persistent bias for larger units. The second factor was more significant: ADUs became part of a historic, deepening housing crisis. Many homeowners are building rental units to lower their own mortgage bill and to increase their property values, pushing rents upward. Moreover, the systemic injustice intrinsic to homeownership is unaddressed by the ADU model. Monitoring the effects of the ADU policy has led cityLAB to undertake a number of new efforts, including an ongoing initiative on public school lands where affordability can be required, called Education Workforce Housing. Legislation and pilot projects with California School Board Association members are in the works. The Backyard Home project is the longest running initiative at cityLAB because each achievement also reveals new problems that produce new projects.

The final evaluative measure concerns whether the California law has opened the way for other, related housing policies and programs. Dozens of new ADU-related laws have been passed nationwide and locally since the one cityLAB coauthored. In 2021, Los Angeles initiated the Standard Plan Program in which architect-designed ADUs received preliminary planning approvals, saving homeowners time and money. Later that same year, the city's chief design officer, Christopher Hawthorne, organized a design competition called Low-Rise to explore "missing middle" housing solutions at even higher densities. The ADU law is clearly part of a large wave of housing policy, design, and planning that is

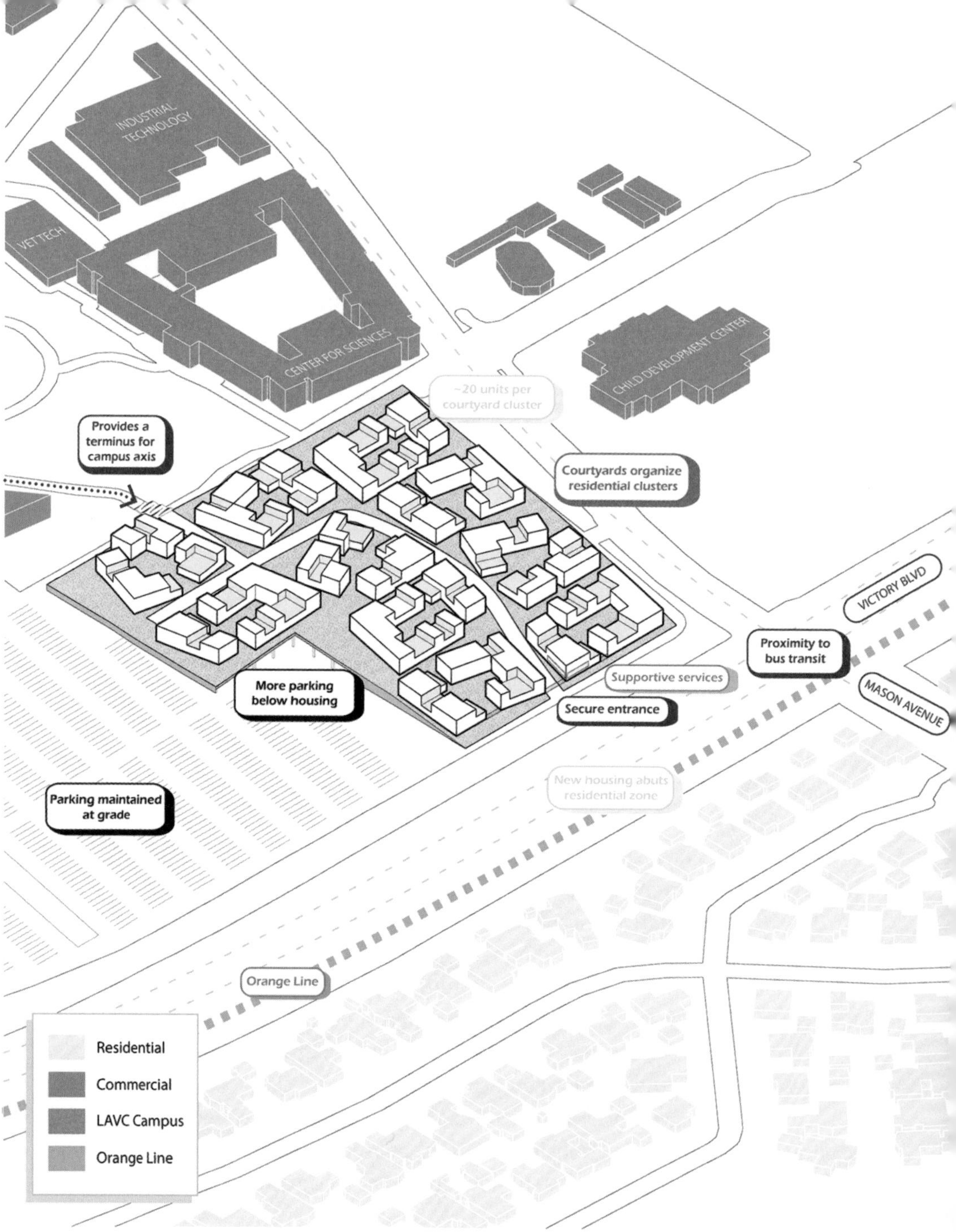
INDUSTRIAL TECHNOLOGY
VET TECH
CENTER FOR SCIENCES
CHILD DEVELOPMENT CENTER
~20 units per courtyard cluster
Provides a terminus for campus axis
Courtyards organize residential clusters
VICTORY BLVD
Proximity to bus transit
MASON AVENUE
Supportive services
More parking below housing
Secure entrance
New housing abuts residential zone
Parking maintained at grade
Orange Line
Residential
Commercial
LAVC Campus
Orange Line

FIGURE 2.5

Pierce Community College courtyard housing concept sited over surface parking lot (2019). Image by Rayne Laborde Ruiz, courtesy of cityLAB and SCANPH.

transforming the sprawling suburban landscape that characterized postwar urban growth. It is less important as a model than as part of a movement to densify the suburbs and eventually bring about an end to the inequities of single-family zoning. As for local pushback, cities across the state adopted the law with minor customization but little conflict. This has led us at cityLAB to the tentative conclusion that participatory processes for controversial social justice projects (for example, group homes or homeless shelters) may be best formulated as by-right state legislation that is shaped by broad engagement and data gathering, allowing limited local customization once the overarching law is enacted.

A prophetic aesthetic calls us to talk about what it means to raise generations of architects with a multicultural sensibility who will think about architecture not just as a profession but who will think about spaces that everyday people inhabit and about our accountability toward making those spaces wonderful and inhabitable space.
—bell hooks[5]

The connection between Backyard Homes (and affordable housing in general) and recent social justice movements is not an obvious one. The murder of George Floyd in spring 2020 following the brutal deaths of so many other Black lives at the hands of the police brought intense international attention to anti-Black racism. Architects along with others seek the role they can play in addressing systemic injustice. Black architects and urbanists continue their organizing to clarify and amplify their positions. Municipalities are scrutinizing their policies and procedures to weed out both tacit and explicit discrimination. Architecture schools are reassessing their curricula, climate, and recruitment. Statements of conviction abound, followed by efforts to practice those convictions through reform. However, structural problems necessarily require going beyond reform if structural change is to be achieved. At cityLAB, we believe widespread and fair access to decent housing and homeownership will be important parts of that change.

How can architects—and architecture more broadly—contribute to the movement for social justice? The agency of architects operates through design, meaning the act of opening previously unforeseen, possible, and hopeful futures, but it is not obvious how that agency translates into systemic transformation. What is the potentiality for architects to not only conceptualize equitable cities, buildings, and public spaces, but also advance them? The answers depend on how design can be leveraged for justice and against inequality. The opportunities to deploy design skills typically arise from the projects clients bring to architects, placing architects in the position of waiting for clients, seeking appropriate commissions, or persuading clients to extend their goals to include social justice. These circumstances are made more difficult by barriers fundamental to the architectural commission: the reliance on serial, finite, unrelated projects that are bound by budgets and fees.

To question the architectural commission (a client-initiated project with a budget and fee, tied to the architect's profit and sometimes also the client's) poses a significant challenge to the discipline. Compared to patronage or public projects, the private commission is more central to the profession, and it has become increasingly governed by neoliberal capital. Pushing architecture's potential within a spatial justice framework means determining to what extent architects can reverse their dependence on clients and their commissions to initiate and pursue work. In other words, *how can architects leverage their design agency for ethical purposes to undertake what are called here "spatial justice initiatives"?* Architects who lead spatial justice initiatives actively build connections between multiple projects, destabilize power relations, and rely on design to advance public, anti-racist placemaking. It is worth noting that architects can dedicate themselves to spatial justice in other ways, such as by founding service-oriented community design centers or holding public office. While these can provide platforms for advancing ethical agendas, they are alternative practices that sit outside the disciplinary core (discussed in other parts of this chapter). Instead, this book calls for both a theoretical and pragmatic inquiry to understand how architecture as discipline and practice can be transformed by the contemporary critique of its privilege.

Opening Possible Futures

The definition of design mentioned above—the act of opening previously unforeseen, possible, and hopeful futures—stands outside traditional notions of the architect's practice. It is an activist definition, distinct in its ethical imperative to imagine the world we want to live in, to speculate about alternative futures, to imagine what was previously unimagined and possibly unimaginable, and to open those speculations to others. This definition is fundamental to rethinking architecture in relation to spatial justice, and it builds on the work of two significant Black cultural critics who wrote about architecture: bell hooks and Cornell West. They uphold architecture as spatial politics and emphasize the importance of admitting lived spatial experience into architectural thought. In Black neighborhoods, in the ordinary spaces of home, porch, and yard, "poverty could not be viewed as a circumstance that suppresses creativity and possibility, for all around you were expressions of unique sensibility."[6] Like Hayden White, hooks and West argue for expanding historical understanding beyond disciplinary accounts in order to build *for all of us* a foundation with formerly repressed, polyvocal narratives. According to West, "the major challenge of a new architectural historiography is that its conception of the 'past' and 'present' be attuned to the complex role of difference–nature, primitive, ruled, Dionysian, female, black and so on. . . . This 'us' is a diverse and heterogeneous one—not just architects and their critics."[7] As a cultural practice, architecture can empower so long as we dignify spatial experiences that previously stood outside dominant models.

If the first step is to acknowledge a repressed past and present, the next step is to think the future. In her essays, hooks argues that documentary forms of art about the world as it is stand in contrast to the fundamental capacity of art "as a space of defamiliarization" with the potential for "reenvisioning black revolution in such a way that we create collective awareness of the radical place that art occupies within the freedom struggle and of the way in which experiencing art can enhance our understanding of what it means to live as free subjects in an unfree world."[8] Building on West's philosophy of prophetic pragmatism, in which something like critical hope opens the space for social and political transformation, hooks calls for a "prophetic aesthetics" in architecture. For design to open new futures, it defamiliarizes conventional assumptions about spatial experience and politics, about who architecture serves and who creates it. To imagine better worlds is the prophetic role of design, embracing its capacity for justice, truth telling, and transformation. To locate aesthetic practices in architecture for undermining canonized privilege and attuning to difference, we begin with a critical examination of professional conventions. The narrative below surveys a number of architectural examples in order to establish lateral connections where the Backyard Homes case delves deeply.

When cityLAB began the Backyard Homes initiative, it was unclear what was at stake for architecture, since granny flats, with their prevalence as do-it-yourself solutions in poor neighborhoods of color, were unlikely to become sites for professional design. Conventional, project-driven architectural firms did not see secondary units as a plausible market for services, in spite of the fact that highly regarded firms like Pritzker Prize-winning Morphosis Architects had designed and published secondary units over garages on alleyways. From the beginning, I argued a reverse set of stakes was at hand and that these stakes were significant. Architectural design could demonstrate how backyard homes would be sited, enhance sustainability, affect neighborhood character, and address a range of household narratives, thus opening paths to a postsuburban city. Design demonstrations could offer visions of small affordable rental units that both densified and stabilized neighborhoods. In turn, small residential projects would provide work, especially for young architects, and some of that work, like the Morphosis Alley Houses, would be noteworthy enough to advance the discipline. By shifting matters of project and fee from primary status to the end of the equation, design was leveraged toward collective good. The stakes for architecture became the stakes for the city—its density, sustainability, and affordability—but only with a change in the definition of the *project*. Rather than a sequence of finite, site- and budget-based efforts, the work is part of a spatial justice initiative that resembles what Horst Rittel calls a wicked problem with no end in sight, no intrinsic boundaries, and with real ethical implications.[9] More is said about leveraging design in wicked contexts in the chapter's conclusion.

Although Backyard Homes challenges standard practices, there are also conventional ways that firms pursue ethical goals, most often by seeking socially oriented commissions such as affordable housing, community centers, and public institutions. Not only is it difficult to gain such commissions, it is also difficult to do these projects well. Their budgets are limited, financing is complex, and decision-making processes are distributed among numerous stakeholders. The skills required to tackle these challenges are not taught in school nor tested in licensing exams, both because they have not been viewed as inherent to good design and because of their intricacy. As a result, it is no surprise that much affordable housing is unpleasant and uninspired. Good design affords dignity, attention to detail, and economies that do not undermine quality, all within restricted budgets and complex timelines. Practicing justly means providing an equal level of service to all clients, regardless of budget, which often requires doing more work for smaller fees. In the extreme, architects work pro bono on public projects or in under-resourced communities by borrowing time and money from more profitable work. In a 2021 *New York Times* feature, the architect Frank Gehry proclaimed, "I'm just free, now that I don't have to worry about fees," saying that at the age of ninety-two he had finally achieved enough financial success to focus on projects that promote social justice.[10] Hardly a model since most architects depend on commissions that prioritize private interests, Gehry's comment is another demonstration that social justice cannot wait for fame and financial independence to have the luxury to engage it. Reliance on private commissions is not just an individual constraint—it is also a structural hurdle.

The primary issue is where to most productively challenge architecture's conventions on behalf of spatial justice. Returning to an intractable problem like widespread homelessness in cities, for example, the design of permanent supportive housing is a conventional way to employ the architect's expertise. A nonprofit housing developer hires an architect, and by undertaking the commission the architect participates in a larger justice framework. Regulations and lending mechanisms like the Low Income Housing Tax Credit program create a gauntlet of requirements for design and planning. Developers who specialize in putting such projects together therefore have the most agency, along with the lenders. If the architect's agency is to be mobilized, she will need to become familiar with the arcane constraints in order to determine where design innovations might be possible. For example, if guidelines require an affordable housing development to have a community room, could that be a tenant-run café? How might a small unit incorporate an open plan with flexible room partitions if a bedroom count is required? Can part of the building be prefabricated and still meet construction and living wage requirements?[11] No project incorporates fees for such research. In an unconventional partnership, the architect Michael Maltzan collaborated with the nonprofit Skid Row Housing Trust to experiment with prefabricated

FIGURE 2.6

Star Apartments by Michael Maltzan and Skid Row Housing Trust for formerly unhoused residents with prefab construction in progress (2014). Courtesy of Michael Maltzan Architecture.

modules at Star Apartments and elsewhere with mass timber construction. The design innovations are risky ones that rely on architectural agency to develop benefits for subsequent construction projects.[12] But in the short run, the prefab experiment cost more than standard construction, and the architect surely overspent his fee. Counter to historical assignment of individual authorship, the architects' capacity for creativity (which is part of their agency) can be expanded by working in concert with others. The partnership between Maltzan and Skid Row Housing Trust has strengthened over a number of projects, such that the nonprofit developer has come to expect that their buildings' design will support goals of recovery, healing, and neighborhood improvement.[13]

In some instances, in addition to contractual clients and future occupants, there are sizable, unwieldy groups of other stakeholders. A key ethical question concerns who might be engaged and through what procedures since the voices of so many people have been silenced even in public projects. Although inclusivity and diversity define spatial justice theory, they must be continuously reformulated in practice. Architecture as a discipline offers neither guidelines nor techniques, even though there are often regulatory requirements for participation in the early phases of a project. For the Backyard Homes initiative, the value of listening was learned early on. In Pacoima, for example, a community focus group told us they wanted small-scale affordable housing for their grown children who found traditional design unappealing, thus opening opportunities for innovation. It was planners who explained that obvious legislative barriers were effectively maintained by ADU opponents. In such contexts, deliberative participation is a complicated ethical arena in its own right. cityLAB's agency was not constrained by limits incurred by project or fee, but the research did require intense, creative, and intelligent labor, which in turn required resources that cityLAB had to attract. The new conditions of deepening housing inequities and shortage of affordable units required unconventional approaches that cityLAB undertook and continues to explore.

Most architects considering how to undertake justice-based design find that old practices come up short. Some firms seek to "diversify their portfolios" with affordable housing projects but soon realize it is a competitive "market." Gaining new work, or "business development," has always been somewhat of a black box for architects, illuminated primarily by access to power and wealth. Although spatial justice work surely has different models, clumsy attempts demonstrate that these too are not always clear. For example, an architect who had been in practice for twenty years reached out to say she was determined to do work that was more socially oriented. Her four-person office currently undertook primarily private residences and small retail spaces. How could she break into affordable housing? Could we connect her with nonprofit developers? While probably well-intentioned, there lurks in the question the very privilege that architects take for granted: connections help make other connections for getting the work you want. There was already a plethora of firms more knowledgeable about lending requirements, nonprofit timelines, proforma expectations, and public processes, to name but a few specialized services. She would need to undertake the real labor of reeducating herself, gaining practical experience by working for or with another firm that had affordable housing work. It is difficult to break into affordable housing, and, unlike for other kinds of architectural projects, there is no "spatial justice market."

A long history of good intentions demonstrates the damage that powerful actors can bring to contexts where they lack understanding. Easy readjustments are effective cover ups, in fact, for avoiding systemic change, which does not come in project packages, and architects are not clear on what it takes to advocate for more inclusive housing, nontraditional collective housing alternatives, community land trusts to increase opportunities for ownership, greater density, or autoconstruction by future residents to build equity. Instead, existing structural conditions build in limitations that become the unquestioned status quo. For example, in public discourse around affordable housing, the high cost of construction has become one of its strongest detractors. However, instead of initial construction costs alone, we might assess costs in terms of quality of construction or years in service. When decent housing is tied to basic health, doctors will prescribe it; when viewed as a human right, governments will ensure its supply; when considered a public crisis, publicly held property will be deployed. When residential neighborhoods are defined not for a single-family but as a collection of households for each lot, as is the case in the Backyard Homes initiative, affordability increases independent of cost of construction.

The kind of labor needed to address the housing crisis in such nontraditional ways includes new kinds of architectural training, like spending time in existing affordable housing projects, talking to residents, reading community newspapers, or studying enabling legislation. Such knowledge follows from Hayden White's "practical past" discussed in the introduction. Memoirs documenting lived experience in housing projects, like Dickson Lam's or Janet McDonald's, are narrative archives.[14] My own education began when I moved to Texas to teach at Rice University and was introduced to the late Lenwood Johnson, resident of Allen Parkway Village public housing and president of its Resident Council. Houston was boarding up public housing units in Allen Parkway Village even though there were households on the waiting list, so I asked my students to instead imagine their rehabilitation. To learn more, I went to a community meeting, where Mr. Johnson recruited me into his small army fighting the regressive tactics of the Houston Housing Authority. Eventually, a court order stopped the housing authority from depopulating and demolishing its housing stock, but their neglect of security and maintenance had the same effect. This is what Ruth Wilson Gilmore calls "the anti-state state's organized abandonment and organized violence."[15] During the winter, Johnson heated his apartment with a fan behind lit burners on his range; during the summer, the same fan worked overtime between windows and doors that opened on both sides of his ground floor flat. For groceries, he walked to an overpriced corner market that carried no fresh food, and when his car was working and if he had a little extra cash or food stamps, he shopped at the Kroger. Len Junior, his young son, did homework at a coffee table stacked with Lenwood Senior's political and legal papers. At tenant meetings, the housing development's community hall filled with residents; half were Black and ran the resident organization, and the other half were recent immigrants from Vietnam for whom a teenager would translate. Younger children played as parents listened to speakers and gathered handouts that Lenwood and another officer produced on an ancient mimeograph machine. My education extended over years alongside him through his daily routines and political activism; my labor involved working with Lenwood to develop architectural visions or to add the institutional weight of Rice University to his efforts. He and his neighbors humanized the architectural history of modern housing as it appeared in Allen Parkway Village. In school, we learned about building form that provided light from two orientations and site plans that separated vehicular traffic from children's play. But time spent at Allen Parkway Village revealed the consequences of intentionally designing affordable housing so that it was not only discomforting but dangerous. Some public housing, for example, did not include cabinet doors or insulation around hot water pipes to discourage residents from staying longer than necessary. Although American public housing stands against systems of speculative real estate, it remains tethered to capitalist and segregationist injustices. Black Americans were more likely to be poor and in need of public assistance, and degraded public housing literally inscribed and reasserted the bias against them.

To break such cycles of discrimination necessitates major long-term changes under continual review. Despite claims to the contrary, an architectural education can make space for community engagement to open windows into worlds unknown to the students; practical training could require interns to conduct post-occupancy evaluations of their firms' buildings; licensure could involve humanistic study of urban segregation and housing discrimination; redesign of a public park might be based on extended observation of the existing space. Spatial justice will require prioritization, and precedents show such change is a continuous process. For example, codes that make building designers responsible for building safety go back to the Babylonian Code of Hammurabi (almost 2000 years BCE); professional licensure began in the United States after a construction worker's death was attributed to the architect in the late nineteenth century; and in 2014, architect Zaha Hadid was embroiled in legal and moral debates about construction worker deaths in Qatar, where she'd designed a soccer stadium. And the architect's responsibility for building safety continues to evolve. A more rapid transformation has taken place since LEED (Leadership in

Energy and Environmental Design) green building standards were initiated in 1993, and just two decades later, a Platinum rating—the highest awarded—has become the new standard.

Dismantling Conventions

Conventionally as architects we wait for the client who brings us a brief, a budget, and we execute. For us it has been essential to . . . reassemble and reorganize that business model to intervene in the process of the economic pro forma and political representation.
—Teddy Cruz, architect and principal, Estudio Teddy Cruz + Fonna Forman[16]

Along with restructuring architectural labor to include humanistic training, leveraging design for spatial justice means breaking the mold of other conventions, particularly the commission. Part of the research for *Architecture: The Story of Practice* led me to conclude that architectural practice was better described as a set of projects than as a firm.[17] Since then, I have come to see that the project structure reduces the architect's agency by consigning them to sites of privilege associated with fee-driven, client-governed work. Let me be clear: this is an argument in favor of finding forms of partnership and practice that enhance design for spatial justice causes, not for eliminating clients. Architects who seek spatial justice need the means to initiate and pursue work themselves or to resist the structure of projects. Is it possible that architects dependent on their clients' program and budget can enact their own agency through design itself? If so, the very expertise that focuses their training and distinction is the principal mechanism of architectural activism. To what extent can design be leveraged to uplift ethical goals that extend beyond program and budget?

In one example, the Tjibaou Cultural Centre in New Caledonia, the Renzo Piano Building Workshop has been characterized as an architectural firm using complex formal and technological agency on behalf of cultural authenticity. From an opposing perspective, the project "was commissioned by a colonial power in what remains a colonial context" as an instrument of postcolonial geopolitics awarded to a Western outsider who, in another layer of distanced othering, relied extensively on a French ethnographer.[18] Within these fraught origins, Piano resorted to neutralizing his design agency and expanded (rather than overcoming or resisting) the project's conditions. Piano sidestepped responsibility to politics by claiming his only desired agency was in the realm of construction. But such rhetorics mainly explain Piano's desire to limit critical review of his work. The project embodied a fundamental contradiction between addressing violent injustices wreaked against New Caledonia's Indigenous people and encouraging tourism. The Centre has been praised for its technological sophistication, deployed to reinterpret vernacular building patterns. The results of his efforts led to the widespread notoriety of the building, in turn increasing the visibility of the Indigenous Kanak people and their contested history. Whether the Tjibaou Cultural Centre in fact advances the Kanaks' political authority remains a speculative question relying primarily on the building's symbolism. Had the project actually granted power to the Kanaks in the center's decision-making and management, its program, form, and process would have been altered, and its architect would have had some grounds to resist the imperial foundations of the project to create a center that went beyond global symbolism to address local Kanak conditions. Convention argues such efforts are outside the architect's domain, but spatial justice goals insist that these conventions be challenged.

In contrast to Piano's deflection of spatial justice in a project that was explicitly grounded in justice concerns, it is valuable to examine a conventional project that grew more inclusive over time: SESC Pompéia in São Paolo by the Italian-Brazilian architect Lina Bo Bardi. This recreation and community center shaped within an old drum factory was completed in 1982, at the same time as the Pompidou Center in Paris. Though the latter became a touchstone within architectural discourse, Pompéia was a more radical, more agential work of architecture that has only recently received the disciplinary attention it deserves. For nine years, Bo Bardi and her team relocated, "working every day in the midst of the building site: monitoring the ongoing projects, the *in situ* experiments, the involvement of technicians, artists, and especially workers. This approach was a genuine revolution in the *modus operandi* of contemporary architectural practice," according to Marcus Ferraz, who was part of Bo Bardi's team.[19] Bo

FIGURE 2.7

Sunday at SESC Pompéia by architect Lina Bo Bardi in São Paolo, Brasil (1982).
Photo by Marcelo Ferraz.

Bardi invented program and strategy by linking the complex to the surrounding streets, creating vibrant open spaces, a public restaurant, and impromptu cultural accommodations—improvising along with the community-based arts already occurring on the site. "What we want is precisely to maintain and amplify what we've found here, nothing more."[20] Bo Bardi meant this not only in terms of the ongoing cultural practices, but also regarding the restoration of the pioneering reinforced concrete structures that she exposed and punctured with irregular openings. SESC Pompéia was a large enough project to contain multiple buildings and occupy the architect over several years, but Bo Bardi's manner of practicing from within the site alongside the workers and community residents allowed her a kind of agency within the project. She called it "a socialist experiment" because it was meant to elevate the collective lives of workers and São Paolo's residents.

Brazil's Serviço Social do Comércio, established in 1946, is a nonprofit organization dedicated to social transformation, so the commission was primed for her experiment, but Bo Bardi leveraged design in a wide range of on-site contexts that add up to what might be viewed as an urban oasis. Her achievement emanated from how she challenged standard practices in her close observation of ongoing activities, of the existing buildings' materiality, of the surrounding context, and of community possibility, as well as from her own office practices. She broke conventional approaches to design in order to directly invoke spatial justice, advancing the idea that Brazil's workers deserve dignified, elevated leisure and culture. Since spatial justice must be continually sought and reestablished, the dynamic nature of buildings cannot be ignored. As buildings are remodeled, rehabilitated, demolished, or expanded, an architecture that acknowledges such inherent evolution will be suited to seek spatial justice. SESC Pompéia is a demonstration that architecture's search for spatial justice is not outside either conventional practice or the discipline, even if it has been repressed. Given the enormity of the principle of spatial justice and the complex ways that architecture might be engaged, when architects initiate a series of projects it is imperative that design—architecture's primary tool for opening new futures—be an effective lever.

To expand the architect's agency beyond formal and technical capacities to include ethical goals means weakening traditional structures of power that govern the commission. Bo Bardi elevated the voices of workers and community members through nine years of everyday engagement on the site. Another way to resist a project's defining structures (its power dynamics, its economic determinants, its singularity) is to pursue public interest goals across multiple projects and with alternative financial means, essentially turning projects into initiatives. Opportunities to create initiatives are not as rare as might be imagined, but they do require unconventional approaches to a project's definition as scoped out in budgets, timelines, and fees. Michael Maltzan's construction experiments depend on long-term partnership with the Skid Row Housing Trust administrators and residents. Ethical goals, like creating spaces for community building within supportive housing, evolve over a series of linked projects, each learning from its predecessors. If shared gardening is designed into one development, it can be evaluated before being incorporated into the next. While learning like this is part of all architects' expertise, it is more effective and creative when projects are explicitly linked to initiatives.

Just Sites

To identify "sites" where spatial justice initiatives can be undertaken is antithetical to the fundamental idea that equity must be everywhere. Nevertheless, there are place-based and procedurally based conditions in which architecture can more effectively follow paths of equity rather than those of capital. Not all types of places or buildings are equally open to public interest design, so to illuminate the role that activism can play, I will focus on public spaces, including schools, memorials, and housing.

Public urban sites are places where collective engagement is definitional—that is, where access and public goods are expected. Moreover, they are rarely speculative undertakings and so the economics of these projects are not guided toward profit. The fee and budget problems of public projects tend to be insufficient funding, at least in the United States. Although such sites vary wildly, they

FIGURE 2.8

Aerial view of Memorial to Enslaved Laborers, showing its siting in relation to the University of Virginia Rotunda (2020). Photo by Alan Karchmer, courtesy of Höweler + Yoon.

hold manifest potential for justice in design thinking. They sponsor the terrain in which society is most invested, such as memorials, fire stations, schoolyards, government buildings, religious buildings, courthouses, and parks, as well as infrastructural functions like sidewalks, streets, alleys, reservoirs, or stormwater channels. Cities are identified not just by skylines, but also by the iconic public buildings and spaces where people congregate—from the Orquideorama in Medellín by Plan:b architects, to Roberto Burle Marx's Copacabana promenade in Rio de Janeiro, to the Hagia Sophia in Istanbul, to Kunlé Adeyemi's Makoko Floating School.

The projects that most directly inscribe racial justice are memorials designed for the purpose of recovering repressed histories and voices. For example, the placement of the Memorial to Enslaved Laborers at the University of Virginia (2020) was carefully selected to occupy a position originally meant to hide views of the Black forced laborers. The memorial's broken circle is a robust symbol of further anti-racist work to be done, openness to all, the ring shout rituals of plantation enslaved people, and shelter for their descendants. Creating this memorial broke with disciplinary convention in multiple ways, from interrogating the site itself to engaging historical and cultural research and sharing control over the project. Credit for the work is broadly assigned to architects Höweler + Yoon, designer and historian Dr. Mabel O. Wilson, landscape architect Gregg Bleam, artist Eto Otitigbe, and community facilitator Dr. Frank Dukes, as well as the students who raised awareness about the site's history a decade earlier.[21] This memorial is a reminder that architects can enact agency not on behalf of authorship but on behalf of more potent spatial justice design aims.

If a memorial to enslaved laborers explicitly calls for social justice thinking, there are other less apparent sites that can be recruited for public purpose. Housing is another type of project for which equity goals are particularly important and is the focus of the opening case study. Housing is significant for multiple reasons: It is the single most important space to an individual's well-being and quality of life, and, for many who can afford to own their homes, it is the largest investment they will make. Housing also enables cultural reproduction and provides the shelter needed for households to thrive. It is for these reasons that the United Nations considers adequate housing to be a basic human right.[22]

Access to housing and homeownership has been the site of deep-seated racism on the part of the state, cities, builders, landlords, and neighbors. As a result, housing is the most inequitably distributed form of built space, exacerbated by worldwide housing crises and their disproportionate impact on people of color. In global cities, there is an insufficient supply of affordable housing, and this is most disturbingly apparent in informal settlements ranging from favelas to encampments. Less visible are the ways in which households, particularly those of color, are burdened by rents, overcrowding, or substandard housing. For these reasons, every residential commission bears within it a question of justice and holds the potential for leveraging design toward that end.

Systemic racism around homeownership and the history of segregation have produced housing injustices, which have been intensified by the fact that housing is a speculative market as well as a basic human need. For-profit housing is a real estate development arena that creates commodities in the form of differentiated products such as live-work, multifamily, or micro-units. But the market analogy only goes so far since real property is fixed and does not circulate like other products. For producers, it involves a significant investment of finance and labor, which slows the market response to demand. In the short term, residents respond to a housing crisis by overcrowding, converting underutilized spaces (liked empty or abandoned buildings, garages, etc.), or living unsheltered; in the long term, builder-developers undertake construction once it is clear that a favorable market and financing are assured. Public or social housing is even slower to respond to housing crises for all the reasons above and due to the additional burden of working through legislative processes.

The inherent contradiction of meeting a basic human need through a racially prejudiced speculative market leads to multiple tragedies, from homelessness to communities blocking the construction of affordable housing to preserve their own property values (even though little evidence supports this link). It is this contradiction that pushes housing further forward as a task not only for more legislation and planning but also for architecture, with its capacity to imagine more just futures. Simple, conventional responses will not offer the transformational solutions needed.

The Backyard Homes initiative aspires to be transformative by exchanging norms of privacy for those of sharing. Rather than "a man's home is his castle," Backyard Homes says, "a home welcomes more neighbors." Property owners have the right to add an additional unit, or, put differently, residential land has a mandate to serve more than one household. Effectively, ADU legislation ends single-family zoning and takes a step closer to its actual abolition. Since property ownership has been and remains a tool of discrimination, particularly against Black and Indigenous households (but also all non-White people, people of Jewish descent, and women), breaking down forms of residential privilege, like single-family zoning, is one attack on the underlying problem. Leveraging design toward this end is no substitute for court decisions that can systematically chip away at residential racism, but the architect's responsibility to visualize the implications of going beyond basic needs to build a more just domestic sphere should not be understated.

Looking Back

Accommodating basic human needs has long been identified as part of architecture's responsibility, but leveraging design for social purpose is not the same as leveraging design for social change. Architecture's long history is tied to creating accommodating spaces (commodity, along with firmness and delight) that satisfy their purpose, and this has been positioned as the discipline's social agenda. Social purpose has been conflated with social change in ways that have benefited architects and enhanced their privilege. Vitruvius wrote in *De Architectura* in the first century BCE that commodity was as important as structure and aesthetics, but he did not intend for his words to elevate the status of building inhabitants, as is generally interpreted. In fact, his intent was to elevate the status of the architect. The ancient historian Diane Favro argues that as a practitioner, Vitruvius wrote to strengthen the architect's *autoritas* by bonding them to their prestigious clients.[23]

Thus, since as early as Vitruvius, architecture has *claimed* its association with privilege and distanced itself from the wider population. In the ancient world, vernacular building—or building without architects—constituted the majority of the built environment, but sites of wealth and power were granted the distinction of architectural design to put power on display. Such was the case at the Pyramids at Giza (ca. 2500 BCE) and the Tower of Jericho (ca. 8000 BCE). Many prehistoric and ancient artifacts comprise everyday buildings, yet the discipline's sanctioned history is overwhelmingly dominated by monumental sites rather than the vernacular architecture of settlements, even in the most recent historical surveys.[24] The emphasis on monumental building can—and should—contain a critique of power and injustice, but, at the same time, it upholds those relations of power when it represses narratives of the everyday. The material world complies, as "power gives access to the resources to build large and in ways that survive time."[25] To uncover an architect's agency to leverage design on behalf of social justice will require the discipline to admit the practical past—that is, the lived, everyday environment, including housing. As with other fields, the project of recuperating repressed historical narratives has become a central and contested task of decolonization.[26] This is the primary reason for working within the discipline rather than establishing an alternative to it, in order to shake up core assumptions that ground architecture in privilege. In turn, the beauty, dignity, and resilience of architecture becomes the norm for the wider built environment.

Modern Housing

It is remarkable that before the twentieth century, multifamily housing was not considered a fundamental site for architecture. Thoughtfully designed housing—that is, multiple units within a single building or apartment block—existed long before the twentieth century. Roman *insulae*, or terrace houses, remain standing at ancient sites like Ephesus from the first and second centuries CE and at Mesa Verde, where Ancestral Puebloans built cliff dwellings beginning in the twelfth century. Haussmann's housing blocks, which defined his better-known Parisian streetscapes, were built around the same time as the Pontalba Building's row-houses in New Orleans, designed by the architect James Gallier in 1849. While architectural history has long included the individual houses of the powerful and wealthy, housing became more of a disciplinary focus during the industrialization of the Global North and during its colonial exploits in the Global South. In the interwar years in Europe, modernism leveraged design to create housing for the masses, governed by an aesthetics of function that sought to create clean, efficient, and machinic spaces that were to be livable and beautiful. The very notion of "the masses" arose with industrialism and the Great Depression, and their needs became of interest to the state with the advent of world war.

Catherine Bauer, the noted American "houser," traveled to Europe with other architects to better understand the "modern housing" that was being built in places like Frankfurt, where Ernst May, both the city architect and city planner, constructed 10,000 units of housing between 1925 and 1930.[27] Attention to minimal, cost-effective housing in the Weimar Republic, whose 1919 constitution guaranteed decent housing for all Germans, represented a deep connection between architects and political power. Under May's broad control (he had jurisdiction over everything from city plans to tombstones), thousands of unhoused and ill-housed families were able to rent modern apartments in comprehensively planned new towns. Architects were engaged across Europe in the design of low-cost housing that emphasized livability in very small spaces, with little ornament and plenty of light and ventilation. Bauer and other housing activists and architects brought the lessons back to the United States to apply to the public housing being built as part of the New Deal through the Housing Division of the Public Works Administration and carried further by the Housing Act of 1937. Architects like Richard Neutra, Paul Revere Williams, William Lescaze, and others designed public housing in which the site plan and the building design worked much like their German counterparts. But unlike Ernst May, architects in the United States have rarely had public agency over more than their individual commissions.[28]

Richard Neutra's design for the public housing development called Elysian Park Heights in Los Angeles, was utopian, and a battle over its design (and fees) lasted for years. Ultimately, the development was not built, but Neutra used many forms of agency, from lobbying school principals to continuously revising his plans to address public criticism (including from Catherine Bauer). Was Neutra's agency directed toward seeking spatial justice, or did he mainly want to increase his own fame? Such questions must be asked by historians, and my own study of this project suggests that he had both goals in mind. Even so, his agency was both greater than and not the same as that of many public housing architects who followed their clients' directives to create livable if unimaginative developments. The broad critique of modern public housing towers—including those dramatically demolished at Pruitt-Igoe in St. Louis—demonstrates that architects' agency must be wielded with extreme care to avoid devastating consequences.

The German and American public housing programs, as well as the design of the developments themselves, are evidence of architects leveraging design in the public interest toward social goals without profit-fueled pressure. Housing for middle and low-income households was built by the private sector around the same time, notably by insurance companies. Metlife was particularly active, building Peter Cooper Village and Stuyvesant Town in New York as well as Parkmerced in San Francisco and Park La Brea in Los Angeles, among others. Some mixture of public finance, private capital, and civic influence—including some progressive activism—effectively laid out the seminal Garden City communities of Radburn in New Jersey; Sunnyside Gardens in Queens, New York; and Village Green in Los Angeles. The planner Henry Wright and architect Clarence Stein led large supporting casts of architects, landscape designers, and planners to test new models of middle-class housing that balanced outdoor parklands and separation from car traffic with thoughtful building design to demonstrate how health and housing quality rose when these three "specialties" were woven together. Such examples demonstrate that widely accessible, low-cost housing has occupied architects since the early twentieth century; some of them have worked to change the basic structure of residential design while others have leveraged building design on behalf of a larger complex's goals of better living.

The housing examples in this chapter illustrate the wide range of how and when architects can leverage design toward social goals. Theoretically, every project holds the potential to address spatial justice issues, whether a small ADU in Pacoima that allows an aging homeowner to reduce expenses and stay in the neighborhood where she has strong social ties or a large social housing project with hundreds of apartments—both have significant impacts that can be strengthened through thoughtful design.

If design has an inherent capacity to lead beyond project constraints, then design for spatial justice adds ethical pressure to identify non-project, differently structured platforms to reduce the exigencies of conventional practice. Alternative platforms exist, such as the relationship between cityLAB and UCLA, which provides infrastructure like office space and some administrative services that enables the lab to operate. It has academic and government-sponsored sister labs around the world. There are also a small but growing number of design firms that operate as nonprofit organizations, setting agendas for their work and finding funds to support it. The last formats raised here include building expositions and museum-based architectural exhibitions, both of which have historically provided models and provoked debates for public discourse.

Due to university support and its requirements for service and research, academic architects worldwide have created platforms to undertake work that goes beyond the standard expectations of commissions. Professors advance the field through research, train new generations of practitioners, and to varying degrees, address the interests of communities that have been historically "underserved." A service orientation, however, distorts spatial justice work which is more adequately framed as a partnership or cocreation. cityLAB is guided by research rather than service, since it seeks partners and instigates its own studies, each of which is expected to generalize to other contexts rather than solve some particular problem. At the University of California San Diego, political scientist Fonna Forman and architect Teddy Cruz are professors, directors of the Center on Global Justice, and principals of Estudio Teddy Cruz + Fonna Forman. Their nonprofit academic research unit blurs the boundaries of these entities. They are embedded in the border region, with long-term community partners creating political art actions, theory, and design provocations. When building permanent projects, they collaborate with architect partners who can shoulder the liability responsibilities (see figures 3.13 and 3.14). They have created a unique place where teaching, research, and interventions come together as a practice within the university, which recognizes the need to invest in its surrounding community.[29]

Different types of academic platforms exist worldwide, but nearly all consider their own urban contexts to be their primary responsibility and where opportunity lies. For example, Hong Kong University's varied HKUrbanLabs focus on conditions in Asian cities, and several of its constituent labs look at humanitarian issues. In the United States, well-known, university-based centers with social justice aims include Auburn University's off-campus Rural Studio, a design-build program grounded in community partnerships founded by Samuel Mockbee and later led by Andrew Freer. In Sweden, the cross-university program ResArc received federal funding to build a strong research environment in architecture education nationwide, most of which is oriented toward sociopolitical (rather than hands-on) agendas. In Ahmedabad, India, CEPT University hosts nine labs that deal with architecture and urbanism, several with implications for equity issues through sustainability, disaster relief, vernacular tradition, and quality of life concerns. At Waseda University, architecture faculty members run research enterprises like Keigo Kobayashi Lab, which confront conditions in Tokyo—such as its aging, shrinking population—that have spatial implications internationally. Other sites are data-coalescing clearinghouses, like Design Resources for Homelessness.[30] As wide-ranging as this sample of academic centers may be, they are all relatively well-resourced even if, like cityLAB, they receive little or no direct financial support from the university. Instead, they capitalize on the university's indirect support: their principals are paid faculty salaries, they have access to a collegial store of expertise, the university provides office space, courses offer a context to undertake research projects, and students supply skilled labor, both paid and unpaid, while they receive training. The university's infrastructure is another form of support for centers, which benefit from their institution's reputation, fundraising machinery, technical and media support, and administrative structure. Despite these advantages, each center is precarious; none is fully funded nor pays their directors to run their labs full-time. University-based design research centers are tenuous operations with lifespans dependent on department and center leadership.

In addition to academic platforms, nearly every major city or region has some kind of nonprofit urban research center, many of which deal with architectural concerns like housing. Two of the most respected examples of this genre are

SPUR, operating in the San Francisco Bay Area, and the Regional Plan Association in New York City's tri-state region (New York, Connecticut, and New Jersey), both of which are more than a century old. Their work centers around planning but involves architecture through housing, sustainability, and urban-rural built environments. The global entity that concerns itself with similar issues is UN Habitat, which has recently launched an initiative to reduce spatial inequality and poverty. Centers benefiting from public resources and public funding become models of research for social impact. One notable research center supported by a municipal government was Laboratorio Para la Ciudad in Mexico City, which had a five-year life span tied to Mayor Miguel Mancera's administration (2012–2018). At Laboratorio, all projects were theorized through "right to the city" forms of thinking and were evaluated in terms of their replicability in other settings. The notion of "legible policy" stems from its work, which we adopted at cityLAB after collaborating on the Peatoniños project in 2016 (described at length in the opening case of chapter 6).[31] Given the precarity of design centers, their lifespans and outputs vary. While Laboratorio surely would have had productive years ahead had the government support continued, other groups wax and wane in seemingly appropriate cycles. There is an inherent trade-off between the benefits of stability and the conservatism that grows with longevity, or, at the other end of the spectrum, between the benefits of agility and the impediments of precarity.

Along with design centers that situate themselves in academic, urban, or government settings in order to pursue spatial justice, there are a range of architecturally based organizations that to some extent resemble standard architecture firms but undertake social research. A relatively new format is the nonprofit architecture practice like the Institute for Public Architecture, which organizes a "residency" in which a group of architects concentrate on a public interest theme such as "Live/Work for the Workforce" (2016), or the Open Architecture Collaborative (formerly Architecture for Humanity, which declared bankruptcy in 2015). These groups survive or fail based on philanthropy rather than commissions.[32] Since nonprofit organizations are not permitted to be architects of record in some states, they focus on design-related work that does not involve architectural services or the concomitant liability (like Estudio Cruz + Forman, mentioned above). One of the longest-running nonprofits is Design

Corps, founded by Bryan Bell in 1991 to bring design and planning expertise to empower communities. While in the organization's early days, Bell sought to build social justice projects (primarily migrant farmworker housing), Design Corps no longer provides architectural services. It now seeks broader impacts by pursuing three initiatives: the Public Interest Design Institute, which offers regular trainings, the Social Economic Environmental Design (SEED) Network, which advocates that "all people can shape their world for the better through design," and the SEED Evaluator, which sets standards and offers certifications.[33] A younger organization with a related model is the group LA Más, a nonprofit community design and planning organization with a particular neighborhood focus on Northeast Los Angeles, though their work holds broader implications. They implement small projects, from storefront painting to pop-up parks in vacant lots, and operate in the policy arena, including some ADU initiatives. The practice is fueled primarily through publicly funded programs for which design is but one of several levers brought to bear to empower communities of color.[34]

Still other organizations take a hybrid form, in which a for-profit architecture office incorporates a research division. Rem Koolhaas' Office for Metropolitan Architecture launched AMO as a parallel, for-profit think tank in 1999 for the firm's non-building practices like research, media, education, and publishing. The mega-firm Gensler runs a kind of research operation that is unabashedly self-serving. For example, along with publishing data in its annual Design Forecast, Gensler Research Institute produces reports about its own office projects that are addressed to current and potential commercial clients. It labels trends that are identified by a mixture of its own clients and architects, as well as community and thought leaders. While the American Institute of Architects had traditionally led or vetted research about the profession, now it publishes Gensler's reports without critical review.[35]

Probably the most provocative and potentially groundbreaking spatial justice practice in the United States today is MASS Design Group, the architecture firm that designed the seminal National Memorial for Peace and Justice in Montgomery, Alabama (figure 2.13). MASS is organized as a nonprofit, 501(c)(3) organization and was founded in 2008 while the principals were still students working with global health partners to undertake pro bono work in Rwanda.[36]

The organization has grown dramatically to a staff of about 140 multidisciplinary professionals in 2020 and recently launched its own construction company in its quest to "hack the traditional business model of architectural practice," according to founding principal Alan Ricks.[37] Basically, Ricks and his partners recognize that standard business models lead to funding gaps in which the cost of design increases prohibitively especially when projects are not certain to happen. These gaps are damning for public interest architecture involving nonprofit clients and under-resourced community organizations that have limited capital and experience (often working on their first and only building project), and who thus would be unable to sustain the design effort required to bring their projects to fruition. Having given this systematic thought, MASS launched something

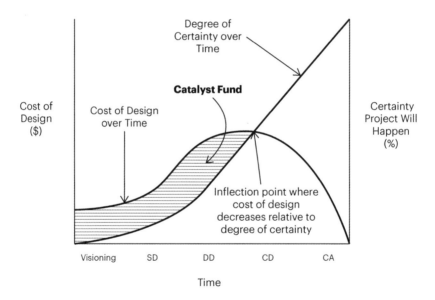

FIGURE 2.9

This graph shows the unconventional funding strategy of MASS Design Group. Since social justice commissions rarely have the money to initiate projects in their early phases when there is a great deal of uncertainty, the architects set up a catalyst fund for this purpose. SD: schematic design; DD: design development; CD: construction documents; and CA: construction administration (2020). Courtesy of Alan Ricks, MASS Design Group.

called the Catalyst Fund, raising "patient seed capital" through philanthropic means to undertake social justice work that would not otherwise happen. With the Catalyst Fund, MASS can contribute in-kind services to worthy projects while still creating a sustainable business model for practice, and supporting its staff who want to make a career of public interest design. At MASS, 80 percent of the revenue comes from fees and 20 percent comes from philanthropy. The latter allows mission-driven clients to start a project before they have the funds to build, after which point they should have the funds to pay the architect.

Other justice-based practices use a similar model of philanthropy to support pro bono work during early phases of the design process and rely on conventional commissions for more standard projects. The nonprofit firm Designing Justice + Designing Spaces (DJDS) in Oakland, for example, has created its Concept Development Fund, which is similar to the MASS Catalyst Fund. DJDS, comprised primarily of Black architects, takes justice to more systemic levels than perhaps any other design firm by asserting prison abolition as a necessary step for restorative justice, leading to investment in radically new typologies like peacemaking centers. As models of giving shift from charity or extractive practices to regenerative justice approaches, innovative architects with equity convictions like DJDS are finding it necessary to leverage their agency outside for-profit models.[38] Given increasing demands from young architects and from architects of color to undermine White privilege in design, we can expect models like DJDS and MASS Design Group to proliferate.

Exhibiting Concept and Form

Social and material transformation in the built environment may be the ultimate goal of spatial justice movements, but public displays that can envision transformed worlds play an important role in the process. No design exhibition can adequately address racism, the systemic inequities built into the material environment, or the brutality of policing on Black bodies. But exhibitions have explored "architectures of liberation" in transformed future worlds. Perhaps the most relevant form of such thinking is urban Afrofuturism. Examples include

Bodys Isek Kingelez's models (see figure 1.1) and Olalekan Jeyifous's photo-montages of imaginary, utopian African cities. We could also include Ta-Nehisi Coates's reconceptualization of the cities and settings in the Marvel Black Panther comic series. Another is June Jordan's 1965 Skyrise for Harlem project, executed with Buckminster Fuller and published in *Esquire Magazine*, which was a counterproposal to Harlem redevelopment and demolition plans at the time. Some of those redevelopment plans were commissioned by MoMA in New York in an exhibition entitled *The New City: Architecture and Urban Renewal* in 1967, in which no Harlem residents or Black urbanists were included, as architectural historian Rebecca Choi recounts.[39] Choi reads Jordan as resisting the real estate model of development that demolishes Black neighborhoods by instead creating residential towers with small footprints on infill sites. The debates and imaginaries that such conceptual designs raise remain in the public domain in the form of publications, exhibition catalogs, and archives.

The collective display of drawings and even buildings in design competitions, architectural exhibitions, and building expositions can leverage design for public interests. Such curated assemblies demonstrate a range of previously unimagined possibilities. When a few are selected, they elevate a particular approach, and a jury's choice of a winning scheme can put forward a solution for implementation.

The most resource-intensive form of exhibition is the construction of a collection of buildings. When an institution or government entity sponsors a building exposition, it makes that significant investment in response to a historic condition. New technology, a building boom, a natural disaster, and a housing crisis have spawned past building expositions that collected architectural examples at a critical moment in time to reshape the path forward. The long-term impacts of building expositions have been difficult to reliably evaluate. A common problem is that expositions are finite and do not incorporate a long-term commitment to match the systemic nature of the issues they try to address.

The most common form of building exposition focuses on housing and involves prototypes that could lead to new residential production. The Weissenhof Estate in 1927 in Stuttgart was a compendium of modern housing architecture by some of the most noted architects in Europe. In the 1940s and 1950s, the

FIGURE 2.10

Bird's-eye view of Skyrise for Harlem by June Jordan and Buckminster Fuller (1965). Courtesy of the Estate of R. Buckminster Fuller.

Case Study House program in Los Angeles aspired to reshape the postwar surge of suburban housing production. Although a hundred thousand people toured through the homes, their impacts were relatively minor. As Esther McCoy famously claimed, the primary change modern architecture provoked in conventional residential building was the removal of the wall between the kitchen and the dining room. After Hurricane Katrina, the Make It Right Foundation, led by actor Brad Pitt along with architect William McDonough and Graft Architects, set out to build 150 houses designed by a few dozen of the best contemporary architects to replace those destroyed in the historic Black Ninth Ward of New Orleans. While the failures of this program—from stylistic to safety and maintenance— have been widely publicized, the 109 homes were delivered as low-cost prototypes that would survive future flooding, and most are still standing. A lesser-known, limited competition to design and build new prototypes called From the Ground Up was undertaken in Syracuse, New York. An investigation of neighborhood infill housing, the three winning schemes were built as demonstrations of affordable sustainability. Each was intended to sell for $150,000 (the same price goal as for the Make It Right houses) but costs escalated to twice that amount.[40] More recently, in 2018, the severe housing crisis in Mexico launched the Architecture Laboratory, with thirty-two prototypical, very low-cost houses designed by architects from around the world, planned by the American architecture firm MOS, and built by Infonavit (the Institute of the National Fund for Workers' Housing). "The Apan Housing Laboratory shows how developers could build high-quality housing within the tight budgets of Infonavit credits," with which Mexican workers finance the purchase of their first home.[41] The architects who designed the houses in Apan operated with social and economic goals, but the real activists in this example are architects Carlos Zedillo and Julia Gómez Candela, who organized the exposition. Its impacts on housing production remain to be seen, but since Infonavit grants about 70 percent of all home mortgages in the country, they have an effective platform.[42] Building expositions like those sampled above lend exposure and authority to architects' designs, coalescing their individual projects into effective initiatives. When they are part of larger building industry systems or incorporate plans for further implementation, as at Apan, their agency is amplified, and their impacts are more likely.

FIGURE 2.11

Hilary Sample and Michael Meredith of MOS architects designed the nine-acre site plan and selected architects from around the world to create thirty-two affordable housing prototypes for the Mexican governmental agency Infonavit. Housing No. 8, Laboratorio de Vivienda, Apan, Mexico (2018). Photo by Jamie Navarro, courtesy of MOS.

Exhibitions of drawings and photographs are historically established—and far less resource-intensive—means by which design curators can assemble collections of architectural projects around social justice themes. In some cases, architects are invited to exhibit new work that explores ideas outside the project-and-fee structure. This affords architects the agency to step away from constraints, selectively determining the issues to address. The modern history of architecture is punctuated by significant exhibitions that have changed (or have tried to change) the way design is understood.[43] A subset of architectural exhibitions have focused on social and political issues, and these have been controversial. Henry-Russell Hitchcock, for example, wrote in 1938 to MoMA in New York (where, in a seminal exhibition in 1932, he along with Philip Johnson famously brought modern architecture to the United States in MoMA's first ever architectural exhibition) to voice his displeasure over a show including public housing. Modern architecture exhibitions, Hitchcock argued, should focus on aesthetics rather than sociological, economic, or political concerns.[44] Perhaps in delayed reaction to this White, privileged bias, MoMA also launched the most notable series of exhibitions about justice and inclusion (organized by Barry Bergdahl, Chief Curator of Architecture and Design from 2007–13), about sea level rise (*Rising Currents: Projects for New York's Waterfront*, 2010), and the housing crisis (*Foreclosed: Rehousing the American Dream*, 2012; with Reinhold Martin). MoMA has charted a persistent if slim activist course through its Architecture and Design Department, from early shows like *Houses and Housing* (1939), the one to which Hitchcock objected, to more recent shows like *Small Scale Big Change: New Architectures of Social Engagement* (2010–2011). Although MoMA's megaphone may be larger, the Cooper Hewitt's establishment of a curator of socially responsible design was a more pointed action in support of architecture as a progressive practice. Cynthia Smith, who has held the curator position since it was created in 2009, has organized multiple shows and published several catalogs about underrepresented architects, geographies, and architectures. *Design for the Other 90%*, her first show in 2007, boldly shifted architecture's political, social, and economic grounding. At the Cooper Hewitt, social impact is foregrounded; the shows travel to gain wider public audiences, and the museum uses varied engagement strategies—from social media to the interactive Process Lab—to establish itself as a home for public interest architecture. All these examples show that design expositions and exhibitions can embody a form of architectural activism with impacts on the discipline and the public.

Toward a Theory of Spatial Justice Practice

Spatial justice goals require leveraging design—architecture's core expertise—to lift up the collective with shared dignity. Within systemic structures of inequality, being a good designer is necessary, but without other skills and without applying that capacity in multiple contexts, it is not sufficient. Conviction, long-term commitment, and expertise related to community and justice are also necessary. One of the clearest examples is the work of Walter Hood, an architect and urban landscape designer who has a portfolio full of activist public spaces that address anti-racism head on. His projects, one of which opens chapter 4, form a family of responses to the question: How can public space be more anti-racist? His works place Black lives in the public sphere through remembrances of important figures, moments in history, heroism in the face of brutal discrimination, and also in the possibility of gathering together in spaces of joy and dignity, even in the context of disinvestment. Hood believes in the narrative power of design to tell the historical truths of a place and returns to what is here considered the very definition of design: "I've been impressed for years by the mantra from bell hooks that designers should have a prophetic aesthetic."[45] When Hood goes beyond the stated program to explore deeper issues of race and racialized histories, and when he explores those issues in project after project, his own agency is fundamental to the collaboration.

To conclude this discussion about leveraging design for spatial justice, I want to outline a preliminary theory for ethically based design practice. To do so, it is productive to return to the seminal work of Horst Rittel who, with Melvin Webber, laid out the context for design as "wicked problems" as well as a deliberative process for resolving problems. A particular form of wickedness underlies racist, discriminatory social practices, which grounds the present revision of Rittel's characteristics in terms of the specifically ethical implications of

FIGURE 2.12

Witness Walls in Nashville, Tennessee is one of many public spaces in which Walter Hood's design narrates civil rights histories (2017). Courtesy of Hood Design Studio.

architecture's wicked problems and the implications for architects' actions.[46] This outline builds on what Rittel called "dilemmas" in a general theory of planning to focus on leveraging design as a way to draw attention to possible futures, opening windows into worlds with more equity and less injustice. These are the principles that have emerged from practices like all those cited throughout this chapter.

Ethical projects in architecture are never complete. Linked together, they form initiatives that can be transformative. Rittel's thinking was framed within 1970s dominant theoretical frameworks of systems analysis and problem-solving that compared design problems to tame math problems. Fifty years later, the very formulation of design thinking as problem-solving is suspect. My own earlier work reformulates the problem as the project, and here projects are reformulated as initiatives; this refreshes the idea of wicked problems having "no stopping rule" but counters the idea that every design problem is unique. Design initiatives with ethical goals evolve indefinitely, only concluding when an external barrier (such as time, commitment, or necessary resources) cannot be overcome. Within design initiatives and the multiple projects that comprise them, the uniqueness of each problem is far less relevant than the connections that can be made among projects. Those connections need not be established on the basis of similarity-in-nature—projects may be related by any of a number of dimensions.

Leveraging design on behalf of social justice inherently means starting small, in ways that are likely to seem insignificant. A granny flat can be a spatial justice project at an intimate level but also, in combination with other granny flats, an effective strategy for addressing the housing crisis. This is not the same as "punching above your weight," which describes the small-change-large-impact approach. Significant in their specificity, architectural projects like disaster relief interventions or rural schools, particularly in the Global South, pepper the portfolios of practitioners in the Global North. Such projects become models without rules, in the words of theorist Francoise Choay, tending to stand alone rather than generate further work.[47] They transcend their particularity and increase their transformational effectiveness when linked into broader initiatives by the architect or by being part of expositions and exhibitions. To leverage design effectively toward spatial justice means demonstrating over a series of projects their principles, their means of becoming, and their transformative capacity. In the Backyard Homes initiative, individual projects grew more significant as they combined to form the larger effort. Even after the state policy was implemented, the work was not complete, since goals of affordability were not met. Another step of Backyard Homes, called Schoolyard Homes or Education Workforce Housing, is a more recent collaboration between cityLAB, Berkeley research centers, and the California School Board Association. This team has developed designs and state policy to open up public school land to dedicated, permanent affordable housing.

The designer occupies a position of power to be mediated and mitigated by knowledge, engagement, immersion, collaboration, and advocacy. For an architect, undertaking spatial justice initiatives requires ethical awareness of the asymmetries intrinsic to the work. Rittel called this the symmetry of ignorance, but insufficient knowledge is just one part of the problem; underlying all projects is a destructive imbalance of privilege and power among clients, architects, owners, funders, future occupants, and racialized others. While neither ignorance nor privilege can be fully overcome, both can be confronted via humanistic strategies that include meaningful engagement with other stakeholders, anti-racist approaches, active immersion in the project context, collaboration that distributes authority, and an openness to criticism about the process. In practical terms, architects seek long-term, public, and community-based partnerships as a means of building both trust and relevant cultural knowledge. In professional literature, architecture is defined by the services it delivers, but equitable architecture is never served up as a gift—it is coproduced through partnerships with others unlike the self. Over an extended period of time, with each interchange, collaboration, and undertaking, partnerships become stronger and the projects grow more insightful. Just as the call for anti-racism recognizes that being "not racist" has functioned as a kind of screen for explicit as well as implicit bias, being "inclusive" is insufficient. The architect must advocate against systemic racism and other forms of exclusion. A powerful model of cocreation occurred with the design of the National Memorial for Peace and Justice in Montgomery, Alabama by the Equal Justice Initiative and MASS Design Group mentioned earlier. Volunteers collected soil from eight hundred counties where lynchings occurred:

"In many ways, the sweat of enslaved people is buried in this soil. The blood of lynching victims is in this soil. The tears of people who were segregated and humiliated during the time of Jim Crow is in this soil."[48] Soil collection was one form of performative engagement in the early stages of the museum's design; the second powerful means is a form of reckoning: eight hundred monuments hang overhead that name the people lynched in each county. Duplicate monuments to those suspended lay outside the museum ready for each county to reclaim and bring home, to confront our violent past. These material practices engage those directly involved and all those who visit the memorial in a kind of ongoing cocreation, challenging established hierarchies of power.

To leverage design on behalf of spatial justice requires resources that are always insufficient. For many reasons, architects and other stakeholders of any justice initiative face inadequate means to accomplish their goals. Justice initiatives are never-ending spools of projects, which Rittel described as "symptoms of other problems." For example, in Backyard Homes, removing policy barriers to the construction of secondary units revealed significant barriers in the lending industry. In addition, some of the most egregious spatial injustices occur in underresourced communities, like among the unhoused population, but secondary units did not target this group. Further efforts are necessary, and these efforts reveal the next level of barriers to overcome.

To offer the same level of design services in a justice initiative that would be rendered in a conventional commission requires amassing necessary skills, time, and funding through unconventional tactics like building constituencies, donating time and money, and redistributing resources. Principles of restorative justice apply to the built environment in the sense that those harmed by discrimination must be healed and those who inflicted the harm, directly or indirectly, must engage in the healing. Within the architectural office, the city planning department, or the developer's firm, restorative justice obligates investment of resources to achieve greater equity. In practice, projects and programs with more resources redistribute them in order to undertake inadequately funded projects for harmed communities.

Justice initiatives carry a burden of legibility and must be made public so that they can be built on by others. Because they continue to grow, justice initiatives

FIGURE 2.13

Monuments in the foreground are duplicates of those suspended in the background, and are intended for counties to retrieve and account for their local history of lynching. National Memorial for Peace and Justice, Equal Justice Initiative and MASS Design Group, Montgomery, Alabama (2018). Courtesy of Alan Ricks, MASS Design Group.

have the potential to increase equity and access beyond their own lifespan. This is possible when they are made publicly legible in some way, inviting the proliferation of further iterations, revisions, and applications. This opens their transformative capacity, expanding the range of people they touch. Although Rittel emphasizes the uniqueness of each problem, spatial justice asks architects to find and display the links between them. Since all works of architecture hold some public component or can make some contribution to the commons, they can also create something equivalent to legible policy in planning. For example, the Backyard Homes initiative was made legible in a number of ways, from a publicly distributed do-it-yourself handbook to a full-scale prototype (figure 2.4). A profound and powerful model of legibility is embedded in the building itself at the National Memorial for Peace and Justice. There, the voices of enslaved, terrorized Black people are uplifted and memorialized, inscribed on the walls and made visceral by the suspended steel monuments that display the names of the people who were lynched. The didactic goals are to make clear the ongoing violent legacy of racism and to educate visitors about racist policing, incarceration, and other forms of human rights injustice. The open-endedness of the memorial leads visitors, architects, and others to extend its teachings.

Spatial justice initiatives are built by constituencies, rather than by individual clients or architects. In the ten dilemmas identifying wicked problems, the client and other stakeholders are not part of Rittel's formulation. The problem itself, disembodied, has the greatest agency by its wicked nature, but such disembodiment obscures who is defining and resolving the problem and to whom it matters. By making these explicit, wicked problems are reinscribed with power, privilege, and inclusivity, and the role of client and architect can be critically evaluated. The four characteristics of spatial justice undertakings outlined above lead to the fifth: that the conventional role of a project's architect, client, or owner is subsumed by the necessity for a constituency or advocacy group. In the case of the National Memorial for Peace and Justice, the activist lawyer Bryan Stevenson founded the human rights organization Equal Justice Initiative, which has advocated against systemic racism in many ways, including the memorial. Stevenson is an instrumental leader, but not the sole author. Initiatives can have architect partners, but they can also be launched by architects. This means that even if there is no client for a project, designers can still pursue it. To do so, however, will require cultivating support for the work and building the constituencies through which committed partnerships are created. Such constituencies are necessarily a mosaic of advocates that fluctuates over time and who range in terms of their commitment, contribution, and ability to advance the effort.

These five principles derive from the theory of wicked problems overlaid with the wide-ranging examples cited in this chapter, including cityLAB's Backyard Homes. The next chapter dives deeper into the final principal to better understand the nature of spatial justice initiatives in which clients, communities, and architects are mobilized by present and future collectives, shaping radically public architectures.

3

RADICALLY PUBLIC ARCHITECTURE

REBUILDING COMMUNITY AFTER THE GREAT EAST JAPAN EARTHQUAKE, ARCHIAID AND TOYO ITO AND ASSOCIATES, EAST JAPAN

Contemporary architecture has become a tool to visualize capital in a global economy.
—Toyo Ito[1]

The triple disaster triggered on March 11, 2011, by the Great East Japan Earthquake killed more than twenty thousand people and wiped away miles of coastal infrastructure and inhabitation. The earthquake, tsunami, and subsequent nuclear meltdown partially or entirely destroyed more than one million buildings, resulting in some $2 billion in damage and leaving the Tohoku region shattered. These estimates—including the number of homes destroyed (approximately 390,000)—have been contested; some 120,000 survivors were displaced into prefabricated temporary housing, half of whom were still there five years later.[2] The most heavily damaged area encompassed three prefectures, thirty municipalities, and more than two hundred villages primarily occupied by small groups of elderly residents who depended on local fishing for their livelihood, according to the architectural planner Yasuaki Onoda who was central to the recovery efforts.[3] Immediately following the disaster, reconstruction initiatives were mobilized at all levels of government. The central government set budgets and laws, the prefectures undertook hazard mitigation planning, and the municipalities took on local planning and reconstruction. This gave the latter the greatest decision-making authority and led to a range of strategies and degrees of success. Within this structure, however, there was no formal role for architects or architecture.

Planning for future earthquake-tsunami risk was the first step of reconstruction, and, as a result, the focus turned to seawalls, inundation levels, elevated grounds, and other civil engineering works. Alongside long-term engineering solutions, 48,700 temporary emergency shelters were deployed in the Tohoku region. A powerful lesson about social isolation had been learned after the 1995 Kobe earthquake, when a similarly vast number of temporary shelters were deployed. That disaster broke community networks and displaced people experienced isolation in their small replacement dwellings. Suicides increased as a result, as did *kodokushi* cases, or lonely deaths, when people die without the care of another person and their bodies are found days or months later. Post-Kobe, guidelines were developed for Temporary Housing Areas that encouraged the provision of mental health services and the support of social well-being by relocating communities together near their former homes.[4] Nonetheless, after the Great East Japan Earthquake, Temporary Housing Areas provided no communal spaces, and, more importantly, the engineering approach to long-term reconstruction plans was not concerned with how communities might want to rebuild. This significant shortcoming became the rallying cause of Japanese architects who sought to contribute to the recovery efforts.

Without architects' involvement in the reconstruction planning, little connection was made to the specific social and cultural circumstances of the many small towns along the coast. Top-down, large-scale solutions like sea walls were implemented, which play an important disaster prevention role but are fixed landscape elements with little ability to evolve or respond to particular local needs. Such infrastructural works are inherently rational in demeanor, representing cost-effective, secure solutions. Residents and community organizations, scattered and displaced, sought something beyond walls and breakwaters to reflect their mourning, their collective solidarity, and their resilience. Such cultural, humanistic visions of the future were not considered by government projects or in the Temporary Housing Areas. The civil engineering emphasis in the recovery period made little room for resident participation or concerns, and moreover, some villages remained temporary for many years because they required significant relocation to safer terrain and permanent "public" housing. Threats of social isolation loomed large.

FIGURE 3.1

Temporary housing area in Date city for 3.11 evacuees from Iitate village, comprised of small individual shelters with little opportunity for social life or connection. Photo by Kosuke Okahara, courtesy of National Public Radio.

FIGURE 3.2

Temporary housing in Kamaishi City, with rows of individual units and the infrastructural, industrial atmosphere of an emergency settlement after 3.11. Courtesy of Japan Times.

It was in this context that Japanese architects located their role in the disaster recovery. Despite being "outsiders" to the multi-layered government response, two overlapping groups—ArchiAid and Home for All (*Minna No Ie*)—organized collaborative volunteer efforts primarily at the local level by taking rebuilding projects into their own hands alongside residents.[5] The initiatives demonstrate distinct ways that architecture and architects can adopt an extreme public orientation in a situation that demands nothing less, outside the conventional economic relations between owners, designers, occupants, and regulators.[6] Architects formed collectives to enhance and go beyond the basic emergency shelter provided by the government. These efforts were intended to empower the communities directly impacted by the disaster so that they might have fresh visions of possible futures and a stronger voice in rebuilding at a time when most people were suspicious of the government.

ArchiAid was founded by architect Hitoshi Abe, coordinated by architectural planner Yasuaki Onoda, and based at Tohoku University in Sendai. The organization took a leading role in long-term recovery visioning, sponsoring design competitions for permanent housing and working directly with residents to reimagine their communities in order to "build back to future advantage."[7] With more than three hundred members, ArchiAid operated from 2011 to 2016 as a clearinghouse and advocacy group, dispatching pro bono design service providers, workshop leaders, and connections to academic platforms. The group collaborated with numerous municipalities and villages using a range of strategies. Abe recalls that "the local residents were frustrated because, even though they explained what they wanted, the civil engineers didn't really respect what they had been told. ArchiAid put together counterproposals, and our professional drawings gave residents a stronger voice in the process."[8] In his study of engagement strategies after 3.11, Onoda found that the most effective were early and ongoing sharing of specific information to survivors, information sharing across segmented municipal groups, the rebuilding of new housing developments within existing residential areas, a "community friendly" orientation in all new housing, and involvement of highly capable architects and contractors.[9]

Shared open spaces are specifically designed into the larger public housing complexes. Breaking with traditional floor plans, the apartments open onto

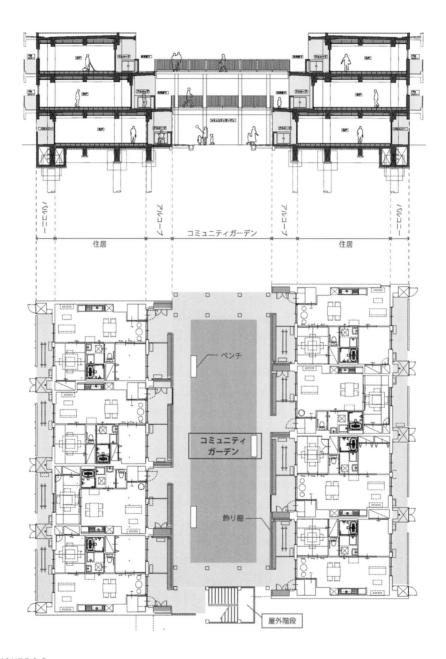

FIGURE 3.3

Public recovery housing that emphasizes community, by Atelier Hitoshi Abe. Courtesy of Atelier Hitoshi Abe.

these shared spaces with a social orientation intended to facilitate community building among relocated residents. The collaborative spawned by ArchiAid continues to work on architectural contributions to disaster planning on the Pacific Rim. The public nature of ArchiAid's work is grounded in a fresh and unconventional notion of architecture's role. ArchiAid seeks nothing short of long-term, systemic change in which both architects and local representatives play a significant role in building back communities for the future. One of the most exemplary efforts by ArchiAid was in Kamaishi City, where town planning took place for the city center, public housing, and a school. Dense housing by architect Manabu Chiba (with Daiwa construction) stands out as an example of the effectiveness of highly capable architects. The high-density housing is planned for community socializing, and new buildings are tactically scattered throughout the post-recovery city. The ArchiAid strategy was to avoid massive redevelopment by infilling with clusters of houses and buildings placed tactically throughout the fragmented, post-tsunami towns.

FIGURE 3.4

Publicly funded housing in downtown Kamaishi City, designed by Manabu Chiba with the Daiwa House Group (2016). Courtesy of Yasuaki Onoda.

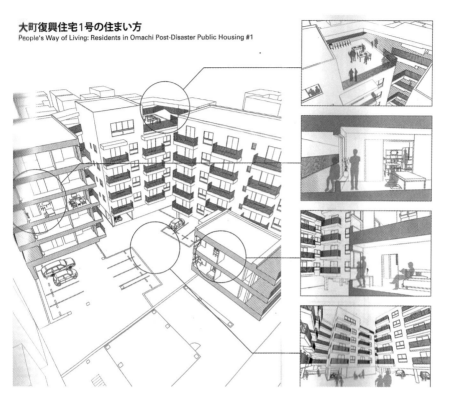

大町復興住宅1号の住まい方
People's Way of Living: Residents in Omachi Post-Disaster Public Housing #1

集会所と屋上テラス
住宅の集会所は6階に設けられている。当初は2階に設けられることも検討されたが、必要な住戸数を確保しつつ、斜線規制等に対応するために、最終的に最上階に設けられた。釜石市街を一望することができ、屋上テラスと一体的に利用することで様々な活動が展開できる空間となっている。

隣近所との交流の接点──共用廊下に接したパブリックリビング
不透明ガラスの玄関部を開けると、フラットフロアで玄関、椅子戸を介してリビングに繋がっている。このリビングにはキッチンが設置されていて、ダイニング的な使用が想定されている。隣接する和室と連結させて使用することも可能で、日常生活の中心の場であり、隣近所との接点となることが期待されている。

全住戸の緩やかな繋がり──中庭に接したプライベートリビング
パブリックリビングとくびれながら繋がるように中庭側にはプライベートリビングが設けられている。よりプライバシーが高い使い方もできるが、全住戸が囲む中庭を介して、違う住棟の居住者とも声かけが可能で、住宅全体を繋ぎ、緩やかな関係性を形成する空間としての役割も期待される。

住民と地域が出会う中庭空間
1階には駐車場と中庭（通り庭）が設けられている。この中庭は住民だけでなく、地域の人の通り抜けや、地域諸活動での利用も想定されており、住宅内だけでなく、既存の町内や尾立の新し

FIGURE 3.5

This drawing shows how Chiba's housing in Kamaishi was designed to encourage community, which was a significant emphasis in cities damaged during the Great East Japan Earthquake. Courtesy of Yasuaki Onoda.

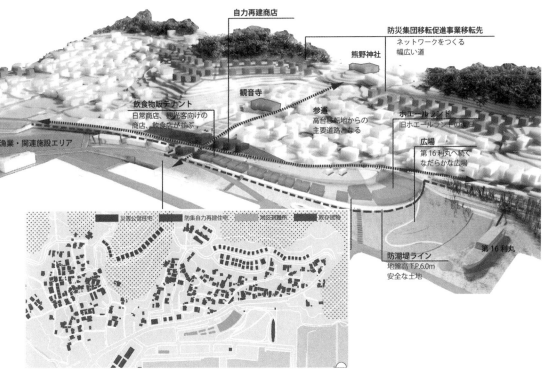

Ayukawaminami Post-Disaster Public Housing

石巻市営鮎川南復興住宅

漁業・観光・商業・居住が一体となった拠点整備

自力再建商店

防災集団移転促進事業移転先
ネットワークをつくる
幅広い道

熊野神社

飲食物販テナント
日常商店、観光客向けの
商店、飲食店が並ぶ。

観音寺

参道
高台移転地からの
主要道路となる

ホエールランド
旧ホエールランドの旧

漁業・関連施設エリア

広場
第16利丸へ続く
なだらかな広場

防潮堤ライン
地盤高 T.P.6.0m
安全な土地

第16利丸

災害公営住宅 防集自力再建住宅 地区活動所 既存建物

FIGURE 3.6

ArchiAid planned clusters of infill housing in villages like this one to replicate former housing patterns more closely than would large housing developments. Courtesy of Yasuaki Onoda.

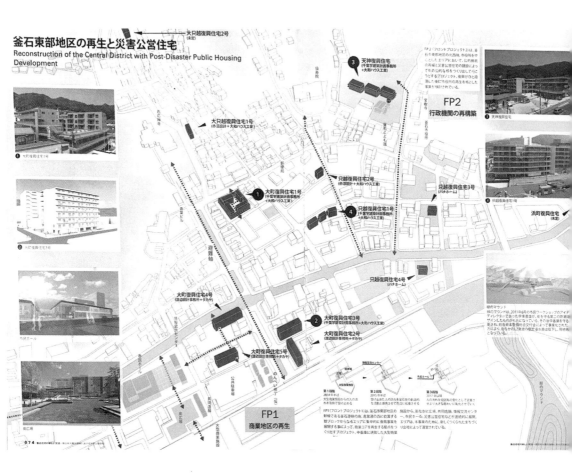

FIGURE 3.7

This plan shows how housing and other new buildings comprised an infill strategy for rebuilding the city of Kamaishi. Courtesy of Yasuaki Onoda.

Distinct from ArchiAid's multifaceted, long-term architecture and planning approach, Home for All built sixteen small demonstration projects in the decade following 3.11. Led by architect Toyo Ito with Riken Yamamoto, Hiroshi Naito, Kengo Kuma, and Kazuyo Sejima, the team inserted delightful, unconventional buildings into the desolate fields of emergency shelters and into the wreckage of former villages.[10] These small community centers provide collective spaces in a sea of small, tightly spaced isolated shelters. The group of five architects described their intentions in a letter written soon after the tsunami: "We have been engaging in various supportive activities for the affected people by the earthquake that struck Japan on March 11. One of them is a project named 'Picturing "Home-for-All."'" . . . Currently a number of people in the disaster areas have lost their homes and have been forced to live in temporary housings. We have been working on making a space called the 'Home-for-All' which is sized approximately 30 square meters and acts as a small living room for the people affected."[11]

The letter announced that the first Home for All would be realized in Sendai City in the Miyagi Prefecture (see figure 3.8), and it was so loved that it was moved to a permanent location when the emergency shelters gave way to public recovery housing. The "living room" or intimate shared space was intended to house community rather than individuals and constitutes a radically public form of architecture. The concept was formulated in direct response to the disaster housing made available in the region, which consisted of small, private, isolated spaces with nowhere for meeting neighbors. Each one is unique because of the connection to a locality, its residents, and their needs. Some are for children, some are multipurpose gathering spaces, and all are relatively simple, open community buildings that create a welcoming gesture to the residents in the area. Design services were donated and construction was publicly or philanthropically funded, so there were no proprietary interests. All this laid the groundwork for highly public shared spaces. In built form, these structures pay tribute to shared public life and to the resilience of the people who survived the Great East Japan Earthquake. As such, they also serve as public memorials to those lost.

The recovery efforts after the Great East Japan Earthquake demonstrate a radically public role for architecture. A decade after the catastrophe, few people remain in temporary shelter, some of the Home for All spaces are shuttered or

FIGURE 3.8

The first Home for All in Miyagino, Sendai, a timber structure of forty square meters, demonstrated the value of these small gathering spaces for people to reconstruct community after the 3.11 devastation (2011). This photo was taken at the third anniversary celebration. Designed by Toyo Ito with support from the Kumamoto Prefecture. Photo by Ito Toru, courtesy of Toyo Ito & Associates, Architects.

FIGURE 3.9

The Home For All in Iwanuma is a popular community hub built in the tradition of Japanese farmhouses. It hosts a café and market area for local produce, both organized by community members. Designed by Toyo Ito with support from the Kumamoto Prefecture (2013). Photo by Infocom, courtesy of Toyo Ito & Associates, Architects.

FIGURE 3.10

Home For All in Iwanuma on a farmers market day, which has helped local agriculture recover after the tsunami. Photo by Infocom, courtesy of Toyo Ito & Associates, Architects.

FIGURE 3.11

Home For All in Rikuzentakata. In the early post-earthquake period, residents scattered by the disaster came back together at these community centers. This one was built with local cedar damaged by the tsunami salt water (2011; now disassembled). Photo by Naoya Hatakeyama, courtesy of Toyo Ito & Associates, Architects.

FIGURE 3.12

Because there were no shared spaces in the Temporary Housing Areas, the Homes For All architects built these three small structures for displaced children to play within the settlements, which became active community centers for families. Higashi Matsushima Children's House, Toyo Ito Architects and Maki Onishi / o + h (2012). Courtesy of Toyo Ito & Associates, Architects.

demolished, and permanent housing has largely been completed. With architectural relief and social gathering provided in the short term, and with long-term guidance from ArchiAid, the rebuilding of communities—rather than merely housing—has lent greater autonomy to displaced residents, has integrated smaller, publicly constructed housing developments with private homes rather than setting them apart, and has specifically given voice to community members to counter top-down government and engineering solutions. The ArchiAid organization was established with a five-year plan, which provided a useful deadline for all of those involved. Former members now continue working on projects in the region following more conventional, pre-3.11 practices.

While acknowledging the fundamental importance of post-disaster shelter, emergency relief organizations do not prioritize public or shared spaces, even though crucial social networks depend on them. Despite the fact that the government's official plan did not include architects, activist architects formed effective groups for short-term demonstration projects as well as long-term plans. These groups intervened early, during the emergency phase—a period characterized by researchers as the time when rubble is cleared and temporary shelters are constructed—and stayed throughout the restoration and reconstruction phases (figure 7.12). According to National Science Foundation researchers, emergency conditions prevail for the first month after an event, with populations in temporary shelters reaching their peak about six months after a disaster. In Japan, the physical devastation was so extensive that these phases extended over years. *Minna no Ie* is variously translated, but stands here for radically public architecture that opposes architecture as a symbol of capital, as Ito put it: "In contemporary society, I think that 99 percent of architecture has become the instrument for economical activities, and I am very sorry for that, because I think that architecture is supposed to be something that links people to other people. Architecture has to become a sort of form of cooperation . . . so it should not be something that is going to be controlled by economy but it should be something that creates a relationship of trust among people. And this is what architects are supposed to do when they create architecture."[12]

The previous chapter outlined a theory of design for spatial justice. Its five principles can be summarized as follows: initiatives rather than projects, immersed engagement, insufficient resources, legibility and access, and constituencies rather than clients. Beneath the five principles that outline a theory of design for spatial justice lies a fundamental question about who that design is for. The principles about immersed engagement, legibility, and constituencies contain an enigmatic presence—just who are those engaged constituents who must find the design legible? History cautions that such ghosts readily reproduce existing power structures and embed implicit, as well as explicit, biases, so these people—with their bodies, genders, ages, races, identities, histories, geographies, economies, and cultures—have the potential to be better off if they are revealed. All together, they constitute our publics.

To create a built environment that dignifies, invites, and delights those publics means to configure a radically public architecture that is equitable, adaptive, and fresh. Along with the East Japan recovery initiatives, this chapter describes a number of examples from around the world, ranging from Colombian urban architecture to universal design proposals of disability activists. Together, the examples raise the fundamental issue that architecture must determine who is meant by "the public." A clear position is staked out: the publics that a building or open space will serve is a political determination that is often used as an exclusionary tactic for social control that furthers systemic discrimination and maintains the status quo. Moreover, the "politics of the public" holds implications for *how* architects might come to know the variegated publics their project will welcome or exclude. The architect holds an outsider status because of asymmetries of knowledge (architects know about building, residents know about community programs, etc.) that is exacerbated by the widely held perception that architects work in service of power and privilege. For architects to establish the constituency for a radically public architecture, they will need to build trust through sustained engagement and demonstrations. ArchiAid and Home for All are strong examples of how this could be accomplished under violent conditions. In the pages that follow, more fortunate conditions set up other projects where spatial justice is advanced by architects who expand their definition of the public.

Removing the primacy of owner and client—along with notions of any sin-gular authority the architect may have held—creates a fortuitous vacancy that opens space for a critical rereading of who inhabits the city. In the literature, there are multiple names for this real yet unidentified public: the collective, the commons, constituencies, stakeholders, users, occupants, the community. In turn these characterizations heighten awareness of the existence of publics, counterpublics, and undercommons as explained in the coming pages. Given the shortcomings of past constructs of the public in practice, and thus the com-plicit discrimination that architecture displays against people of color, women, and those of differing abilities (to name a few), this chapter begins by developing an alternative construction of publics to take up residence in a notably open, hospitable, compassionate architecture. This chapter is not an examination of design process or participatory planning—these are considered in chapter 4—but instead focuses on the physical spaces of our collective lives.

Rebuilding Japanese coastal towns after the 3.11 devastation is an extreme case in which the design of both housing and shared public space was consid-ered essential to emergency settlements by the architects who volunteered in the recovery process. Even though much of the rebuilding was publicly subsidized, architects added a significant humanistic dimension to otherwise engineered solutions to create a more robust design process and a form of public building. We can also imagine such spaces outside of catastrophes. Think about the mul-tiple public projects in Medellín, Colombia, which began under the leadership of Mayor Sergio Fajardo: a beautiful library and park in the favela above the city, the Orquideorama canopy in the city's botanical gardens, innovative infrastructure like the Metrocable, a gondola that serves the steep, densely populated hillsides, and the extensive Atanasio Girardot Sports Complex with renovated facilities.[13] Medellín's array of public architecture, including ten "library parks" built be-tween 2008 and 2011, exhibits the model that architectural initiatives are made up of a sequence of varied projects that gather political strength as they advance toward implementation (described in chapter 2). The architectural initiative in Medellín was instigated by the public sector for the public sector, investing pub-lic funds to counter the extreme violence in the city during the 1990s, especially in its underserved neighborhoods, and dignifying the effort with thoughtful

FIGURE 3.13

Biblioteca de España in Medellín, by Giancarlo Mazzanti (2007). Photo by Carlos Tobon, courtesy of Giancarlo Mazzanti.

architectural design. In government-led initiatives like Medellín's, public funds are marshaled for decades over multiple administrations. As a result, the built environment's insurgent potential is unveiled.

After decades of violence and decline, Medellín literally rebuilt its relationship to its citizenry through investment. Beginning in 2007, the Fajardo administration demonstrated using material intervention that the city's own people, in their everyday lives, deserve the kind of spaces typically reserved for the wealthy and powerful. A forceful rebuke to the idea of exclusivity, the spaces contain a dose of populist surprise. Each of the Medellín sites reveals exciting architectural spaces and invisible norms about who deserves municipal investment. We can distinguish these civic acts from those in other places, like Bilbao's spate of projects beginning with the Guggenheim, because the Medellín projects are first and foremost for residents rather than a means of attracting global capital and tourism.[14]

Radically public architecture destabilizes the status quo often as the result of resistance, social movements, explicit spatial interventions, agonism, or friction. Architecture can play a role in such resistance by actively advancing new public imaginaries in built form. Architecture's discomfort with explicit political agendas is countered by radically public architecture like that of both Medellín and East Japan. In these examples, the architecture is characterized by several distinctive qualities. We will look briefly at the historical and theoretical roots of each quality as well as a work of design that embodies the idea. First, radically public architecture aspires to be equitable and dignifying. It actively rejects discriminatory practices that disadvantage people, for example on the basis of age, gender, race, wealth, or property. It is anti-racist, explicit both in its rejection of White supremacy and its inclusivity, with the goal of shaping a humane commons. Second, it aspires to be open-ended, inviting its own evolution and adaptation and taking into consideration future generations. Third, it aspires to be *fresh*, meaning that it does not fall into conventional patterns but instead asks its occupants to be present and engaged in the space. Together, these qualities describe a built environment that upholds the well-being of all its human and non-human populations. Just because this may be difficult to imagine does not mean we should not work toward both the imaginary and its realization.

Although spatial justice is a fundamental ethical principle within architectural practice, in reference to radically public architecture it must be called out again as the proactive foundation that means different things in different contexts. For example, in Japan after the earthquake, it meant assuring that the voices of the displaced were heard, that victims were foregrounded, and that the elderly, who made up most of the devastated towns, were engaged as well as cared for. Although racism plays a role in Japan's imperial history as well as in its contemporary cities (as foreign or non-Japanese, Korean, and mixed-race people will attest), other forms of discrimination formed the post-3.11 struggle for spatial justice as they sought to empower repressed voices. In the rebuilding, architects encouraged the contributions of women and youth in particular, knowing that the participants would otherwise consist mostly of older men. As Japanese recovery initiatives demonstrate, a perfect spatial justice is never achieved but is constituted as ongoing, agonistic contestation.

In much of the world, violence centered on ethnic, religious, and national difference is commonplace—consider immigrant refugees in Europe, sectarian conflict in the Middle East, or ethnic divisions in Africa. There is no equitable, shared public space when authoritarian control or the status quo goes unchallenged. In imperial as well as postcolonial states, injustice is deeply tied to structural racism. In the United States, to be anti-racist is to acknowledge the role that race has played throughout American history, including far beyond its national borders. The American landscape was shaped by the historically specific and violent exploitation of Indigenous peoples and enslaved Africans. To recognize the harm exacted on Black and Indigenous peoples, and on all people of color in the United States, is to begin to repair the larger social and cultural fabric of everyday life as well as the spaces in which it is lived.

The most explicit demonstrations of anti-racist public space are the memorials to Black lives and history, like those mentioned in the previous chapter and in the opening case of chapter 4. But we could also examine the Living Rooms at the Border project in the Latinx San Ysidro community of San Diego, less than a mile from the Mexican border, by Estudio Teddy Cruz + Fonna Forman. The

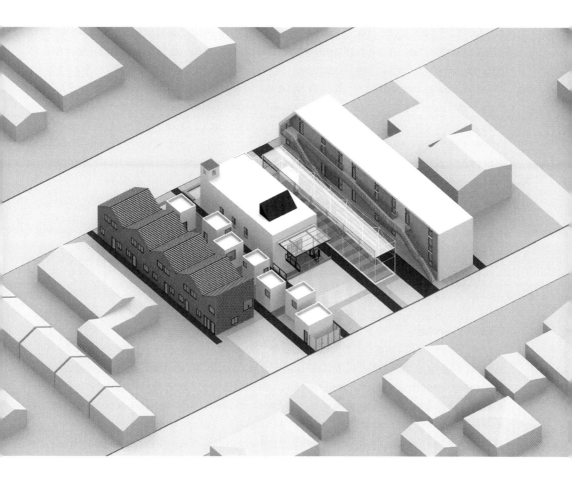

FIGURE 3.14

Living Rooms at the Border in San Diego, California, is a complex of different community functions in new and adaptive reuse structures. Designed by Estudio Cruz + Forman (2020). Courtesy of Estudio Cruz + Forman.

project is a prototype that includes ten units of affordable housing, a restored church converted into a multipurpose theater, space for the expansion of immigration services and a youth training program, and a University of California San Diego Community Station. Rather than the conventional border wall mentality in which movement from Mexico to the United States is regulated through restriction, security, and ultimately violence, the series of Community Stations will create a network of civic classrooms, or "public spaces that educate," located on underutilized land in disadvantaged communities on both sides of the border.[15] At the San Ysidro site, the unexpected public spaces of the theater, an open-air pavilion, and social service offices all strengthen the local community. The public facilities are linked to the public university so that it is more accessible to the Latinx neighborhood youth. The UCSD Community Stations acknowledge the importance of crossing borders within the families they divide and within the communities that exist continuously on either side.

Adaptive Futures

Spaces that are inclusive of a wide public also exhibit qualities of being polyvocal, open-ended, and adaptable rather than totalizing, final, and highly scripted. Such places invite their own evolution, both in terms of rejecting authoritarian control and by respecting the potential input of future generations. Adaptive projects invite multiple voices to engage and express. They embrace transformation and make it legible. The architect is less like an author than a conductor or director who recognizes that a creative work depends on the resources, inspiration, and collective enterprise in a dynamic performance.

This concept can be difficult for architects to turn into practice because buildings are legally formulated as independent projects that require completion. An inherent finality is associated with architecture that posits buildings like a static work of art rather than like a performance or living organism. To overcome its own finality, architecture has generated theoretical directions, such as landscape urbanism and ecological urbanism, that explore continuity and fluidity in principle and in form. Since at least the mid-twentieth century,

FIGURE 3.15

The decades-long collaboration between architects and community resulted in Living Rooms at the Border (2020). Courtesy of Estudio Cruz + Forman.

architecture has been explored as an adaptive infrastructural system through conceptual design, as in Constant's New Babylon and the Japanese Metabolist movement. In the 1960s, the collaborative practice Archigram developed conceptual projects with massive fixed infrastructure that accepted plug-in, inhabitable components. What such schools of thought have in common is the notion that an architectural project should evolve, fundamentally operating more like a piece of the city than an individual building. Cruz and Forman's Community Stations are an example of this same thinking, conceived as a network capable of expansion, and although each station operates within a local community, their larger impacts result from the network's extent.

Adaptive futures combined with equitable spaces make for powerful public architecture. In such initiatives, like the Congo Street Initiative in Jubilee Park in East Dallas, justice principles motivate the evolution of an environment. In Jubilee Park, long-term residents turned around plans for demolition and redevelopment of their neighborhood. In 2008, they received a sizable community revitalization donation to build a community center for after-school education, healthy meals, computer labs, and other services. That same year, the design firm buildingcommunityWORKSHOP (or [bc]) and students at the University of Texas at Arlington began their partnership with the neighborhood. Together, they rehabilitated five deteriorated houses on Congo Street and built a sixth from scratch as a "holding house" so that residents would not be displaced while their homes were being rehabilitated.[16] Several years later, [bc] partnered with the community again to build another six sustainable homes on the other side of the street with new homeowners. The Jubilee Park effort is ongoing and is far more than a conventional project. Residents and trusted design collaborators are building social justice, environmental and social sustainability, neighborhood stability, and community development without displacement in a long-term initiative that is open-ended.

Both the Congo Street Initiative and the Japanese post-3.11 collectives have already demonstrated their capacity to build for adaptive futures. They share qualities of long-term initiatives, community participation, and multi-use programs. They also evolve across sites, which allows them to be guided by issues other than property ownership while setting their budgets and not to be tethered to a single client. These are some of the ways to generate architecture for adaptive futures.

Fresh Engagement

The third quality of radically public architecture—fresh engagement—describes projects that provoke surprise because they lack known scripts for use or interpretation, prompting people to actively engage with the built environment. Here, the term *fresh* is employed in contrast to the term *innovative*; the former implies

FIGURE 3.16

Congo Street Initiative created this holding house so that existing residents could remain in the neighborhood while their own houses were being rehabbed. Design by buildingcommunityWORKSHOP, University of Texas at Arlington students, and Jubilee Park community members (2013).

a humanistic relationship, whereas the latter implies a novelty that resides in the thing. A building or space that engenders fresh engagement depends on its connection to its occupants. Among possible origins, that engagement can be borne of resistance, translated into space that does not conform to repressive power but instead opens liberatory futures.

When Paul Virilio and Claude Parent developed the theory of the oblique function in the 1960s, they based it on a specific idea about freshness, arguing against conformist, orthogonal Euclidean space. Instead, an inclined floor plane would invite people to participate in the architecture through the flow of their movement and deepen their relationships to one another and to the world around them.[17] An inclined plane is incorporated within SANAA's Rolex Learning Center in Switzerland (2010), which sparks the kind of response Virilio and Parent imagined: "The experience of meandering through the space is magical, and one that challenges traditional notions of movement through man-made constructions as strictly vertical or horizontal."[18]

The construct of fresh public architecture has two related implications concerning breaking conventions and controversy. On one hand, for architecture to be surprising it must hold something unexpected or nonconforming. Conventions surround many aspects of architecture, from orthogonal construction to localized norms, such as the consistent walls of five-story buildings shaping the Haussmannian streets of Paris. A break in those conventions is at least slightly destabilizing, though with the construct of freshness, the break is also to some extent positive, pleasurable, or "magical." But since publics are not homogeneous, part of what it means for a building or public space to be fresh is that it will also be cause for controversy. For example, the Eiffel Tower, with its steel skeleton looming above the consistent height of buildings in the city, was highly controversial when it was first built in Paris in 1889. Only decades later did it become part of a beloved skyline (and as Roland Barthes writes, not everyone agrees even now). Radically public architecture, then, is tied to both contestation and delight, which is consistent with agonism, rather than consensus, as a model of public discourse. The pleasures of debate, instability, and surprise constitute a legitimate form of engagement. And even those who appreciate the Eiffel Tower might doubt whether recently built skyscrapers add anything pleasantly surprising to the Paris skyline or streetscape.

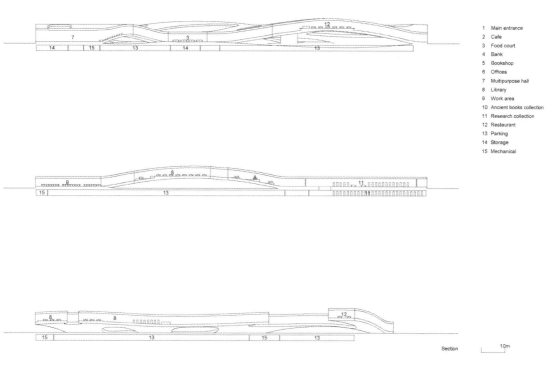

1 Main entrance
2 Cafe
3 Food court
4 Bank
5 Bookshop
6 Offices
7 Multipurpose hall
8 Library
9 Work area
10 Ancient books collection
11 Research collection
12 Restaurant
13 Parking
14 Storage
15 Mechanical

Section |_____| 10m

FIGURE 3.17

Undulating interior of SANAA's Rolex Center in Lausanne, Switzerland (2010). Courtesy of SANAA.

Perhaps the clearest spatial acknowledgment of the rule that fresh spaces will be contested spaces are the temporary, playful installations that occur in contemporary cities. Whether a dumpster turned into a public swimming pool for hot summer days, a street painted with giant polka dots and closed to vehicular traffic, or an environmental art installation like the Floating Piers in Italy's Lake Iseo (2016) or The Gates in Central Park (2005), temporary projects can create radically public spaces by virtue of their nonconformity. It is indeed the temporary nature of these interventions that add to their surprise and tend to quiet their detractors, even if such event-based public spaces presage more permanent transformation.

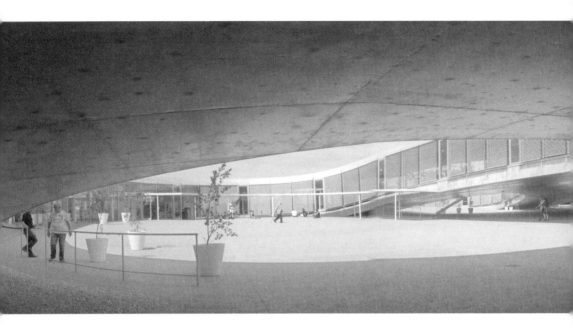

FIGURE 3.18

Moving beneath the Rolex Center, a visitor experiences the rolling floor planes overhead. SANAA, Lausanne, Switzerland (2010). Courtesy of SANAA.

Historical Overview

It is valuable to rehearse a brief history of the concept of the public, particularly in relation to its geography, to build a foundation for architecture's potential to transform collective everyday life toward a more just society. When we think of public space, we are likely to think of urban spaces: civic buildings, sidewalks, parks, plazas, religious spaces, transit stations, courtrooms, shopping streets. When Habermas, the father of the public sphere, introduced his seminal work in 1962, he defined the public sphere in terms of the rise of bourgeois urban life of eighteenth-century Europe, specifically France, England, and Germany.[19] Cafés and print journalism bred the social construction of political discourse through universalized argumentation in public forums. The very public sphere, then, was a space for the male, White, European, owner class as it contested the absolutist state of monarchs. The birth of modernity is tied to the creation of a public sphere by a privileged group of private citizens, but, since Habermas, *public sphere* has been too often used as a fixed term rather than one that has historical specificity not only in its internal references, but also in Habermas's own time when the book was first published and then thirty-seven years later, when it appeared in English. For the English-speaking audience, this time warp dehistoricized Habermas and contributed to the universalizing of his concept.

Since that time, multiple critiques of the construct of the public sphere have arisen to show that presumptions of its homogeneity reveal implicit biases. What Habermas viewed as public life, others saw as the inescapable contradictions of modern life, the tools of segregation as thin as a café window separating the bourgeoisie from the lower classes. Public architecture and public life, as Marshall Berman observes, displaced the private lives of rich and poor onto the streets so that they became visible, inescapable, and more readily policed.[20] From the perspective of queer cultural theory, Michael Warner argues that modern life is a struggle among publics which in turn contributes to the formation of counterpublics. His counterpublics follow from Nancy Fraser, who upholds Habermas's public sphere on account of its distinct characterization that "political participation is enacted thorough the medium of talk." But she argues that the public sphere is darker than Habermas would admit, since there were always multiple publics, or counterpublics, competing with his bourgeois public, which was (and is) the prime site of cultural hegemony. She defines *counterpublics* as "parallel discursive arenas where members of subordinated social groups invent and circulate counterdiscourses, which in turn permit them to formulate oppositional interpretations of their identities, interest, and needs."[21] The public sphere then is intrinsically a space of conflict, exclusion, and domination that requires analytically expanding the concept to include counterpublics. Feminists demonstrate that the very notions of public and private form a gendered binary that enhances the threats against women in public spaces and furthers their restriction to the private, domestic realm.

If Fraser's critique is largely based on gender and class, the sociologist Elijah Anderson explicitly calls out the racialized nature of public space, suggesting that there are distinct White and Black spaces in everyday lives, along with what he calls racially cosmopolitan mixed spaces.[22] Harney and Moten's undercommons is the most revolutionary construct that stands against a universal public sphere. The undercommons is a zone where marginalized subjects, most particularly Black persons, take back their labor and capital rather than be exploited by dominant institutions like the university or spaces like the shopping mall. The undercommons is a space of Black futures and optimism, according to media theorist Chip Linscott's reading of Moten, even when Black Lives Matter protesters meet armed police at the Mall of America's locked doors, "there is room for struggle every day; there is an inside to anti-blackness' outside."[23]

Inequalities have shaped counterpublics among similarly situated groups who are unable or unwilling to bracket their identities in order to participate in the "public" of the Habermasian bourgeoisie. These critiques lead to questions of identity with the implication that the city's balkanization into, for instance, ethnic and immigrant enclaves is a natural or necessary result. The public sphere then is fragmented among homogenous components, yielding at least two problems: first, denying the enclaves their own heterogeneity, and second, retaining the subaltern relationship of the enclave to the city. Identity, then, is bound to geographies of power, and, to expand on Fraser, "actually existing *spaces of* democracy." To talk, participate, or enjoy open access is historically a matter of proximity as well as what can be called land claims.[24] The expansion of digital publics notwithstanding, the material spaces of public spheres are our concern, and these exist in cities in patterns that are inequitable. As such, radically public architecture's aspirations to be equitable and open-ended support the restitution of rights to the public sphere as well as the expanded notion that Fraser advocates, of a multiplicity of public spheres, of its conflictual nature, and of its incorporation of private interests.

What if Habermas, and those who critique his work from a social justice perspective, were asked to create a public sphere not as a form of utopia (for the ideal polity), but at a particular point in space and cultural history? Such a call to action is, at some level, what an architect faces with each project.

If one dimension of a radically public architecture concerns the definition of public space and public sphere, the second dimension builds from social practice in the arts. Social practice is socially engaged art, where the interaction or participation constitutes the work to at least some degree. Architecture has only occasionally been viewed as part of social practice because buildings are such a peculiar, costly, top-down form of art. By contrast, social practices in the arts favor engagement, informality, impermanence, and coproduction. While architecture is and has always been social, this chapter identifies a smaller realm of design practice in which the public nature of buildings and spaces is advanced as the aesthetic and political focus. The relevant conditions for social practice in architecture concern who produces and invests in the work as well as who benefits from it and in what ways. While there are many who would suggest that social practice in architecture must push architects themselves into a new, sublimated role, this work argues instead that the architect's creative agency is a necessary ingredient to radically public architecture.

If the relatively recent upswing in attention to social practice in the arts builds on what was called "creative placemaking," the latter has come under fire because of its promotional essentialism—the making of "great places," "animating" the built environment through the arts, or "rejuvenating streetscapes."[25] Placemaking apparently succeeds without contestation and resistance and presumes that it is possible to create a naively "happy urban design" outcome for all. The placemaking movement acknowledges its role in gentrification but cannot integrate the agonism that is fundamental to every part of the city. In a way, the flaws of creative placemaking go back to the limitation of a "project" orientation to urban and architectural work; problems can be solved, a community's identity can be located, projects can be isolated from one another, and outcomes can be successful. This reductive, chamber-of-commerce narrative glosses over the power dynamics that allow such narratives to persist. Now, in response, a "placekeeping" narrative is growing to explicitly uphold the protection of current residents and the preservation of existing businesses and affordable housing.

The Case for Universal Design

The public sphere and public space are theoretically, if not practically, linked by *universal access*, which embodies Derridean hospitality by welcoming and granting entry to all. Typically, urban spaces are considered public if they are open, free, accessible, publicly-owned, and tied to democratic life, but this ideal has been challenged throughout urban history. Along with fences and gates, all public spaces are governed by regulations as well as by norms of behavior. Of all the public space critiques, disability advocacy has been one of the most potent. Indeed, it is a civil rights movement with direct implications for architecture, and it has generated broad constituencies like universal design and human-centered design movements. For these reasons, I describe universal design in some depth.

The field of disability studies distinguishes a "medical model of disability, which locates physical and mental impairments in individual bodies, from the social model, which understands the world as disabling people." In the latter, both architecture and social norms construct disablement.[26] Rather than understand people of differing abilities in their complex and heterogeneous humanity, architects and lawmakers turned them into singular, ergonomic data points—numbers of individuals with some measurable range of motion or sensory capacity. As a result, a single seat is removed so someone using a wheelchair can attend the theater, a conspicuous sling lifts a swimmer into the pool, a parent pushing a stroller must enter at the back of the bus, a young child cannot see the screen at the movies. This ableist world disables people—a formulation of the built environment that leaves many people out much of the time because we fail to keep them in mind. Blind spots and the inability to keep people in mind are forms of implicit bias, that is, a spontaneous stereotype-confirming attitude that has real and negative implications when the concomitant discriminatory behavior goes unattended. Such discrimination fed disability rights activism, which led to some of the most transformative legislation ever enacted related to public space and architecture: the Americans with Disabilities Act (ADA) of 1990.

Four great citizenship debates have occurred in America over the last two centuries. They centered around Black emancipation and civil rights, women's right to vote, immigration restrictions, and the disability movement. The last pinpoints architecture's complicity and responsiveness more than any other social movement. Disability activism reveals to architecture that the public is not fixed or homogeneous, and that the built environment plays a role in equity and inclusion. Might this translate into a broader discourse about civil rights, inclusion, and equity, not only about physical and mental ability but also about racism? If so, we might find that an architecture of racial equity bears an analogic relation to universal design. In architecture, universal access is first considered through spatial mechanisms like turnstiles, gateways, or doors. If a public space is open, like a park or a plaza, then it is imagined to be accessible. The seminal work of historian Douglas Baynton lays out these connections to civil rights and how othering of nonnormative bodies and groups has justified inequality in American history. Immigrants in the early twentieth century were subjected to medical examinations where anything from flat feet or poor eyesight to hysteria was grounds for exclusion. Similar disability arguments, as Baynton calls them, gave alibis to White slaveowners resisting Black freedom. Likewise, disability arguments about women's frailty, intellectual limits, and unstable temperament were used to resist women's right to vote. Disability advocacy points out that abolitionists and feminists themselves excluded differently abled persons from rights to citizenship. "Instead of challenging the notion that disability justified political inequality, like antislavery writers[,] feminists maintained that women did not have the disabilities attributed to them and therefore deserved the rights of citizenship."[27]

If attributions of defects have long served as effective tools of oppression and inequality and hold in common the assignment of disability, we can illuminate the broader discriminatory practices in architecture by examining the disability movement. That is, how did architects and architecture respond to the disability movement's direct call for transformation of the physical environment? Leading up to the ADA was a long struggle of legislation, argument, and social movement. Beginning with the Architectural Barriers Act of 1968, disability laws were established that changed architects' awareness of accessibility. Suddenly, the city was alive with barriers that confronted some 20 percent of Americans with different kinds of disability. In 1973, Section 504 of the Rehabilitation Act (based on the Civil Rights Act of 1964) stated that no disabled person "shall, solely by reason of his handicap, be excluded from participation in, be denied the benefits of, or be subjected to discrimination under any program or activity receiving federal financial assistance." This clause was written without much discussion about how it would be implemented, but it became central to advocacy efforts as well as to the institutions recalcitrant about all the facilities they would need to upgrade. Buildings and transit systems would have to remodel stairways, elevators, doorways, parking spaces, ramps, aisle widths, signage, curb cuts, and restrooms. Colleges and governmental agencies argued that such wholesale remodeling would be prohibitively expensive, and that instead they could meet specific needs when requested. It was self-fulfilling, as activist Fred Fay noted, to say, "Well, we don't need to make things accessible. People with disabilities never come in here."[28] The historian Bess Williamson, in her recent book on disability and design, shows that the backlash against inclusion was framed by all sides of the debate as an overwhelming design challenge, citing the *New York Times*'s editorial about "extravagant and utopian" transit adaptations.[29] In public transit, a separate-but-equal form of policy wed to privatized services led those agencies that resisted acquiring special equipment, like kneeling buses, to support dial-a-ride options for riders who registered as disabled. The argument should sound familiar, between an inclusive and transformative option that would in fact have advantages for many riders (elderly, injured, babies in strollers, and wheelchair users) versus a marginalizing option that keeps the "problem" out of sight, maintains the status quo, and requires little investment. Whether the other is stigmatized by disability, race, gender identity, immigration status, or religion, the debates focus on metrics and trade-offs, at least at the outset, between how wide a doorway needed to be, how many people in wheelchairs would use it, and what it would cost. Williamson points out that this carried over conservative views that associate design with luxury and "access as excess." More comprehensive narratives of rights and inclusion were drowned out by the arguments about the cost and illogic of government regulation. No surprise then that arguments about reparations to formerly enslaved and Indigenous people follow this pattern.

The advantage of universal design over separate-but-equal fictions is a focus for legal historian and economist Heather McGhee, who traces the active destruction of public amenities and infrastructure by White civic leaders when desegregation was required. Significant collective spaces, like public universities, were lost or replaced by privatized, inequitable stand-ins. In her 2021 book, *The Sum of Us*, she analyzes the ways that racist responses to integration disadvantaged the whole population, even if the effects were most inequitably experienced by the Black citizens targeted.[30] Her most vivid example is the draining rather than integration of public pools in the mid-1950s when desegregation laws began to be enforced. Amenities like public pools were lost to everyone rather than becoming a collective resource for all people's enjoyment. McGhee shows that this same racialized zero-sum attitude led to the defunding of public libraries, public universities, public parks, and other pieces of our shared infrastructure. Basic forms of discrimination blind privileged defenders of the status quo to the possibility that inclusivity benefits the whole of society.

In architecture, the blind spot around disabilities is reinforced by a discipline implicitly guided toward able-bodied, White, middle-class publics, as most renderings suggest. Practitioners implicitly segregate differently abled, non-White, non-middle-class populations from their design thinking. In other words, most architects should not leave the public to their imagination. The absence of real publics, clients, or occupants creates the very blind spots that lead to inequitable collective spaces. The ADA made such exclusions impossible, particularly when it came to historic public buildings like courthouses, train stations, libraries, and municipal government buildings and their awkward renovations. These were the very same monuments that were elevated in architectural and cultural histories and that would be made accessible by the addition of ad hoc lifts or by directing people with disabilities to rear entries and loading docks, providing separate but certainly not equal access. Spaces that were supposed to be open to everyone were brought into compliance through stigmatizing means, discriminating against the individuals using the adaptation and working against the spirit of the ADA regulations. The Law Courts at Robson Square in Vancouver British Columbia (Arthur Erickson, 1973) was one of the first buildings to formally wed the ramp and the stair as a monumental gesture.[31] But most architects struggled with ADA regulations, and few found ways like Robson Square to celebrate accessibility. Instead, ADA regulations were absorbed into requirements of conventional architectural practice, growing more codified with more "compliance experts" added to the staff of facilities departments. The most significant

FIGURE 3.19

The stairway-with-ramp at Vancouver's Law Courts in Robson Square, by architect Arthur Erickson (1980). Courtesy of Michael Elkan Photography.

advances in universal design emanate from Scandinavia, where since the late 1990s, Design for All has become a source of innovation, social responsibility, and business development.[32] Elsewhere, to resist implicit othering, architects can assemble diverse partners willing to offer perspective and knowledge about possible future publics in all their heterogeneity. Since radically public architecture is actually a sequence of projects, varied in nature, that gathers political strength as those projects advance toward implementation, the partnerships will have lasting value. Partnerships, collaboration, and participation are the focus of the next chapter.

Why "Radically"?

Civil rights and equitable access are fundamental to universal design, which holds an ethical dimension that can be made more explicit. Together, goals to create space that is equitable, adaptive, and fresh are at the root of radically public space, which is itself an ethical project. The adverb *radically* is appended to public architecture to call attention to an active relationship to the public, one that is indebted to Jacques Derrida's notion of hospitality. According to Derrida, whose work *Of Hospitality* zeros in on formulations of the Other, the stranger, and particularly refugees or foreigners, "hospitality is culture itself and not simply one ethic among others."[33] In architecture, this directs us to pay particular attention not only to public space or to the commons, but also to the thresholds that mark its precinct. At a building's threshold, a doorway is open or closed, the perimeter surveilled or welcoming, a window shuttered or ajar. At political borders, the stranger might be welcomed or imprisoned upon crossing. In the built environment, thresholds carry powerful meanings, give definition to identities, and shape experience.

In the most extreme and fundamental form of hospitality, Derrida argues that host is bound to welcome guest into a shared commons without concern for imposition. Thus, the hospitable park, library, school, and plaza would welcome housed and unhoused neighbors alike, citizens and refugees, people of varying abilities, children and seniors, and so on. For radically public architecture, this includes an imperative to search for excluded occupants and occupations and dignify and destigmatize their interests. In post-3.11 Japan, for example, the design of collective spaces sought to embrace the elderly and socially isolated people of all ages. By turning apartments toward shared space, the architects privileged the commons over privacy, offering welcome to those who might be alone.

But perhaps a radically public imperative is too significant a burden for the architect. How can she welcome all strangers, redress harms of the past, seek out those who may not be present, encourage engagement that has yet to be tried, and ensure that future generations will have the same access? Like other moral imperatives, it compels action unconditionally and out of rational necessity rather than on the basis of likely success. For the moral philosopher, such an imperative defines our agency as actors in the world. For architects, this suggests not only the need to articulate such ethical goals but also to evaluate whether our actions lead in that direction. There is no test that can be applied to each work to see how well it achieves those goals, but the three qualities above are offered as evaluative structures; to what extent is the space designed to be equitable, adaptive, and fresh?

To suggest that architecture should express these qualities is also to recognize the inevitable, and even desirable, friction or agonism that radically public architecture entails. When spaces welcome difference without hierarchy or othering, negotiation, debate, and contestation will arise. When urban planner Janette Sadik-Khan talks about "street fights" that occurred during the transformation of New York City's traffic-laden roadways into new public spaces, she acknowledges the conflicts inherent in a city's evolution.[34] A humane public architecture is not the result of consensus, which is why we must be especially thoughtful about power and control in its shaping.

Radically public architecture is design that goes beyond conventional practices to advance the collective nature of building for publics and by publics and beyond individual clients and architects. This was the explicit intention of Archi-Aid, and we can test the notion against another set of projects by the Berlin-based practice Raumlabor that emerge not from disaster but from everyday circumstances. One well-known installation is Spacebuster, an inflatable, translucent room trucked to various sites to create a spectacle for an event, making inconsequential public space (a parking lot, the underside of a bridge, a vacant lot) into something temporarily special. Raumlabor's space activations bring with them a decidedly engaged quality that encourages people to interact with others and with the space itself. Often this involves food, inviting people to sit down to break bread together as part of community discussion sessions. A social practice leader, Raumlabor is one of many arts and design instigators who build fresh publics and public spaces. As evident in the illustrations, their artwork ranges from relatively refined to completely ad hoc but always has a clearly legible community-based intention. Spacebuster is fresh and open-ended, but to be a form of radically public architecture it should also aim for equity. How might that be evaluated? One measure would be whether it was or could be launched in a diverse range of communities. Another measure would be the metaphorical and literal accessibility of its threshold, or whether it makes entry and hospitality easy. A final measure is whether it laid out anti-racist intentions. On all these scales, Spacebuster comes up short. There is nothing inherently racist about the Spacebuster, and yet it does not go far toward including those who have been historically excluded from the commons. According to its makers, it aims to be inclusive in two ways: its ability to travel to unconventional sites and the ability of its semi-permeable membrane to dissolve the distinction between inside and outside. But when it travels to those spaces, it operates as an incursion of something totally foreign—that is, in fact, its power. Its redesign would attend to the threshold and boundary to signal an openness and welcoming to strangers and those outside. The stoop, porch, or patio offer models for a transformation of the Spacebuster so that its hospitality is both enhanced and made legible to a broader public.

FIGURE 3.20

Spacebuster inflated in a New York parking lot, Raumlabor and Storefront for Art and Architecture (2009). Photo by Christof Franz, courtesy of raumlaborberlin.

FIGURE 3.21

Inside Spacebuster. Like many of its gatherings, this one in the New York parking lot centered around a shared meal (2009). Courtesy of raumlaborberlin.

FIGURE 3.22

Raumlabor's installations seek myriad ways to engage the public, like this mobile radio station called Boulevard Broadcast in Milton Keynes (2019). Courtesy of raumlaborberlin.

FIGURE 3.23

Junipark was an elaborate temporary space in Berlin for a month-long youth, art, and culture festival and civic discussions (2014). Photo by Carli Matteo, courtesy of raumlaborberlin.

If we try to characterize the public that Raumlabor imagines will interact with its interventions, its members are playful, curious, and open to engagement. It may also be a public that is privileged enough to have no qualms stepping through an unknown truck to enter an enclosed, inflated room. All designers carry a public in our minds, a collective homunculus that guides our design thinking.[35] Is the public litigious, clumsy, and frail? Or is the public dangerous, impatient, and strong? Rightfully wary, rebellious, or rule bound? Seeking adventure or comfort? How is the public racialized and gendered? Designing for tacit, absent others has plagued architecture from its earliest days yet without due attention. Variously described in seemingly neutral terms as some kind of "users," the people who will inhabit the future building for an hour or a lifetime are rarely more than vague imaginaries. The accompanying normative assumptions about bodies, economies, racial identities, gender, and activity erode the distinctive differences that bring vitality to design solutions. Instead, the public becomes a white-washed and biased imposition that is spread by the physical environment onto the specific individuals who experience it.

Struggles over public space have occurred throughout the history of capitalism, with legal determinations about appropriate and inappropriate uses. In cultural geographer Don Mitchell's writing about rights to public space, he argues that contestation and resistance are intrinsic to the formation of a more inclusive public: "The solution to the perceived ills of urban public spaces over the past generation has been a combination of environmental change, behavior modifications, and stringent policing. The putative reason is to assure that public spaces remain 'public' rather than hijacked by undesirable users."[36] The built environment enacts its own form of policing through fortress-like architecture, indestructible materials, and the removal of places to sit. Such defensive tactics are, as historian Dianne Harris reveals, explicitly repressive norms of Whiteness that shape the built environment. She identifies the "ordinary" house as one built to uphold White supremacy.[37] Harris pays particular attention to rendered images of suburban life, and those same imagined people who occupy the houses she studies are populating the public spaces that are planned in most cities. No wonder, then, that scholars find parks operating as "White spaces."[38] White, well-behaved, nuclear families, particularly able-bodied young adults with young children, form a thin stripe of the general population considered the "ordinary" folk in the public sphere. It is important to recognize that the so-called ordinary is neither a demographic average nor uncodified cultural practice; such built form relentlessly imposes a narrow norm.

Ordinary houses, ordinary neighborhoods, ordinary parks, ordinary coffee shops—all are revealed as systems of social control in which a normative ordinary population modeled on White privilege is constructed. The perpetual deployment in public spaces of these repressive, racialized norms has been made clear in a spate of violence, like the rash of attacks against people of Asian descent since the start of the pandemic, as well as in viral videos showing White women officiously calling the police on Black men who are birdwatching, napping, jogging, or drinking coffee in public space. To counter and create new public perceptions, the city of Oakland hosted two Barbecuing While Black parties to affirm the rights of Black people to the city's parks. This was a public retort to a woman, known as #BBQBetty, who called the police in 2018 because a group of Black residents was picnicking and barbecuing in the park. The city campaign intended to reclaim Oakland's public sphere for Black residents.

People of color, with differing abilities, or who are not cisgender all experience unequal rights to the city. French social theorist Henri Lefebvre omitted any explicit analysis of such discriminatory geographies when he constructed the notion of an everyday "right to the city." Yet the social construction of urban and architectural space, who has a right to public space, and what they are allowed to do there are fundamental to the construction of culture and its authoritarian control. Walking on the sidewalk is policed as loitering for some and enticed as window shopping for others. Urban scholars note that street vending is contested in cities worldwide and has become a lens for wider public space debates: "One's race, class, and legal status significantly determine the range of activities and liberties that one seeks and can practice in public space."[39]

One of the most complex and contested public space concerns in global cities, especially in the United States, is the growing population living unsheltered in streets, on sidewalks, and in parks. In my city of Los Angeles, at the time of this writing about seventy thousand people are experiencing homelessness. This literal occupation of public space, particularly streets and sidewalks, is a humanitarian crisis, and is the result of both "the enduring impact of systemic racism, an inadequate housing supply, and income inequality"[40] and the prison industrial complex. But as the cultural geographer Don Mitchell shows, there is a long history of struggles over public space intertwined with homelessness that comprise the landscape of capitalism: "Struggles over the relationship between homelessness and public space within capitalism are decisive for what public space is and how it is regulated and policed for society as a whole, the majority of which is housed."[41] Although Mitchell does not focus on racialized contestation of public space and homelessness, it is clearly a prime driver of spatial regulation and violence.

It is not surprising that it takes a public movement to overcome the discrimination that occurs in public space against marginalized people. These are struggles of and for hospitality and a right to the city. For example, a group of housing-insecure mothers led by Black women activists formed an organization in Northern California: "Moms For Housing is a collective of homeless and marginally housed mothers. Before we found each other, we felt alone in this struggle. But there are thousands of others like us here in Oakland and all across the Bay Area. We are coming together with the ultimate goal of reclaiming housing for the community from speculators and profiteers. We are mothers, we are workers, we are human beings, and we deserve housing. Our children deserve housing. Housing is a human right."[42]

Moms For Housing inspired a group of women of color in Southern California to organize under the banner Reclaiming Our Homes. They occupied thirteen state owned vacant houses as a restorative justice undertaking to reclaim publicly held land for housing-insecure families. The mothers called themselves reclaimers rather than squatters, arguing that their taxes had been paying for the vacant houses: "There are families waiting in shelters for three years for housing. We can't wait for years. That is ludicrous when there are vacant homes everywhere. It is immoral to have these houses vacant." said an activist, former social worker, and mother who moved into one of the houses in March 2020.[43] She and fellow reclaimers were subsequently evicted by police in riot gear in the middle of the night, and later that year they were reinstated as legal, if temporary, residents.

We can see the catalysts for change in the housing reclamation movements in California where women of color—typically mothers operating outside conventional structures of property ownership—organize against the intersectional repression of their lives. Direct action is needed because social norms like those surrounding property claims are not benign. Such norms are established on the violent enforcement of segregation, which constructs a socially recognized public to welcome and another group to whom access will be denied. Redlining was the most explicit and definitively recorded version of urban segregation, a surface structure that mapped multiple discriminatory practices in the built environment. The long-term goal of some right-to-housing movements is to retain ownership by transferring properties into community land trusts. Los Angeles, Oakland, and Philadelphia are just a few of the US cities where reclamation movements are happening.[44] Collective land ownership is a long-standing alternative that decommodifies the housing market and builds community empowerment. It also redresses historic inequities, particularly those experienced by Indigenous and Black residents but also those experienced by women and people of color more broadly. The community land trust movement is growing. For example, the Los Angeles area witnessed an expansion from two to five formal community land trusts in 2020 with five more organized in 2021.[45] Architects can be involved all along this continuum if they so choose, but it requires expanding professional skills to address public, ownership, tenant, and economic concerns so that the design embodies the collective, reflects new forms of shared ownership, and helps resist displacement. The rebuilding after the Great East Japan Earthquake is an example of how national, state, and local interests can be mobilized in concert with architectural activism to build back communities.

4

PARTNERSHIPS OF DIFFERENCE

DOUBLE SIGHTS, HOOD DESIGN STUDIO, PRINCETON UNIVERSITY, NEW JERSEY

Rarely is difference validated, unless it is economically profitable.
—Walter Hood and Grace Mitchell Tada[1]

On November 18, 2015, as part of nationwide protests against racial injustice, some two hundred Black Justice League students occupied Princeton University President Christopher Eisgruber's office. High on their list of demands was the removal of Woodrow Wilson's name from the public policy school and other campus buildings. Black Justice League public actions had exposed Wilson's White supremacist views and racist proclamations. On November 19, Eisgruber reached an agreement with the protesters that included a "commitment to working toward greater ethnic diversity of memorialized artwork on campus."[2] Four years later, the university dedicated a public "marker" featuring Wilson along with his vociferous contemporaneous critics. And on June 26, 2020, five years after the sit-in, the university finally agreed to remove Wilson's name from what are now called the Princeton School of Public and International Affairs and First College.

During this five-year period, the university administration inadequately—from the perspective of activist students—and bureaucratically moved toward redressing Princeton's legacy of anti-Black racism. It formed committees (there was a committee on Wilson's legacy and another on principles to govern renaming),

FIGURE 4.1

Posters circulated on Princeton University campus by the Black Justice League in October 2015. Courtesy of University Press Club and Destiny Crockett.

deliberated, sought input, conducted surveys, held exhibitions, and convened listening sessions. Eventually, there was a decision to create a new historical marker (there was also a Woodrow Wilson marker committee) in Scudder Plaza, in front of the public policy building. A design competition would be held to literally build some critical perspective on campus about Wilson's legacy, and in 2017, Walter Hood's competition submission was selected. Walter Hood is an architect, artist, landscape architect, and winner of a 2019 MacArthur Fellowship. Hood's copious body of work resists singular readings, but it often lifts up Black lives and history in the making of the public sphere. His Princeton installation, Double Sights, was dedicated on October 5, 2019, in a cacophony of public speeches and protests by students and alumni.

Hood faced a difficult charge, one that he describes as probably the most onerous of his career. Woodrow Wilson, the twenty-eighth president of the United States, was an alumnus, faculty member, and, in 1902, president of Princeton University. His name is deeply associated with the university through this history and its memorialization, with Wilson's name included in the name of a college, a professorship, awards, fellowships, and, most notably, in the name of the Woodrow Wilson School of Public and International Affairs. A high profile committee appointed by the University in November of 2015 recommended against changing the name of the Wilson School, but made two recommendations, among others, that gave birth to Double Sights: "We encourage the [Wilson] School to install a permanent marker on-site that educates the campus community and others about both the positive and negative dimensions of Wilson's legacy." And in the next section: "We encourage the administration to make a concerted effort to diversify campus art and iconography, and to consider the possibility of commissioning artwork that honors those who helped to make Princeton a more diverse and inclusive place."[3]

Hood thought about the project as a means to open up Wilson and undertook something like a pros and cons analysis of his legacy based on a long list of themes. For example: "Education at Princeton. Positive: Increased academic rigor, defense of liberal arts, education's role in civil society. Negative: Rejection of African American students."[4] Hood originally entitled his prospective installation Double Consciousness, based on W. E. B. Du Bois's *The Souls of Black Folk* (1903). Du Bois identified an inescapable "two-ness" for Black Americans: "An American, a Negro; two souls, two thoughts, two unreconciled strivings," a concept to which Hood often returns when he talks about Black landscapes. He eventually renamed the project Double Sights (Wilson, as a White man, did not have that same two-ness), which embeds a number of binaries or doublings. The work is based on a two-part formal move: a white column leans into a black column. The two are clad in different colored stone but made from the same square extrusion cut on the diagonal to form triangular prisms. Standing thirty-nine feet high, the white column presses down on and at the same time is upheld by the vertical black column. For Hood, this would have been enough, but the university expected the work to be didactic. On the two exterior faces of each column, etched in the stone, are quotations from Wilson that represent his historical contributions as well as his regressive racist and sexist views. The wider interior planes of the columns illuminate the words and faces of his contemporary Black critics, including Ida B. Wells, W. E. B. Du Bois, and Monroe Trotter. At night, the interior faces of the stellae and the critics are illuminated, while Wilson's words go silent. The quotations inscribed on the columns are described by Hood as well as by the university as both the positive and the negative, where Hood later says a reader will find information "of interest and of disdain."[5] The dualities of black and white, good and bad, positive and negative, are made somewhat ambiguous by the reflective surfaces and the changing light over the course of a day.

"Through the support of one column on the other, the piece offers a dialectical, rather than polemical, conversation," Hood says.[6] But the oppositional stances there at the beginning with the Black Justice League, lived on through opening day through protesters who proclaimed that a complex history did not mean Princeton could absolve itself from answering the essential question: On what side of history does it stand? Alumni who had occupied Eisgruber's office in 2015 challenged Princeton's delayed response as well as the premise of Double Sights. They pointed out the flawed thinking behind a monument dedicated to a White supremacist serving as a gathering space for student protest. Hood viewed Double Sights not as a monument but an anti-monument, and as a space that would provoke difficult conversations. He recalls that the opening of Double Sights was unique in his experience; the university scheduled it on African Americans' Homecoming Day at Princeton, setting the stage for protests that in Hood's words were "righteous, loud, intense."[7] Now that Wilson's name is removed from the school that forms the installation's origins and context, Hood wonders if Double Sights is permanent or temporary: "For me, it had its moment, the name is down, and how it will read in the future is up to us, how we actually transform as a culture."

Hood suggests this project is the best embodiment of what he calls partnerships of difference. The partners would not resolve their differences but instead bring their opposing perspectives to the work. The university administration wanted the installation to be "pedagogical" in its critique of Wilson's legacy. The administrative partners controlled the official narrative, the selection of the

FIGURE 4.2

At Princeton University, Double Sights stands in front of the building previously named for Woodrow Wilson (2019). Courtesy of Hood Design Studio.

FIGURE 4.3

Inside the prism-shaped columns, the words of Wilson's cotemporaneous critics are inscribed along with their portraits (2019). Courtesy of Hood Design Studio.

artist-designer, the resources, and the timeline. The students and their Black Justice League activist predecessors constituted another partner, forcing the University to give them a seat at the table and broadcasting views in opposition to the slow, steady, mostly White hand of Princeton. Their resistance to the controlled narrative effectively wedged open the space for Double Sights and for the removal of Wilson's name from the campus, which they sought as an important step in redressing racism at Princeton. Another partner was Hood himself, who wanted to create a new public space through art that asked viewers to "do the work" of

FIGURE 4.4

At night, the reflective black stone on the marker's interior illuminates critical Black voices while silencing Wilson's words inscribed on the exterior white stone (2019). Courtesy of Hood Design Studio.

understanding Wilson. Hood's goal was to create a landscape in such a way that it "might imbue those memories of diverse perspectives, as well as force us to stop trying to narrow things down to a single, clean set of identities."[8] His difference was born of his own biography, hybrid training, and his interest in the way common space (a street, a square) is a palimpsest of experiences and meanings that layer up over time into a hybrid. Such hybridity incorporates many views at once, so that differences can be recognized and can be shared. Double Sights aspires to such hybridity, a space in which differences rather than diversity are present.

FIGURE 4.5

A loud and angry crowd of protesters made their views known at the opening of Double Sights on October 5, 2019, at Princeton University. Courtesy of Hood Design Studio.

FIGURE 4.6

Designer Walter Hood stands inside Double Sights (2019). Courtesy of Hood Design Studio.

The prior chapter makes a fundamental claim that architecture actively determines who is meant by "the public." This chapter considers how architecture becomes radically public. Part of the answer to the question of who will be accommodated by a design can be found in a project's evolution, particularly within the partners who conceptualize and develop the design thinking. What we mean by partnering, designing thinking, or accommodating is taken up in the chapter's opening case Double Sights. We can see that there was no definable, formal path by which the installation—a radically public work of architecture—was created. Instead, strands of resistance, institutional processes, artistic practices, and larger political contexts were woven together over time. The commission itself was a by-product of a larger social justice agenda. Under such circumstances, to plan or design a sculpture and public space requires maintaining an agile, responsive notion of the goal as contributors navigate the process. It remains the challenge of the artist-designer to shape an aesthetic and material record of that navigation.

Given the public nature of architectural artifacts, designers are caught in a contradiction that must be resolved in every project. On one side, architects are trained and licensed to responsibly bring their expertise to the making of the built environment, with skills acquired through long-term training. But when architects "bring" expertise to unfamiliar socio-spatial contexts, their actions represent a form of professional imperialism. James Midgley coined this phrase in reference to international social work, arguing that the imposition of technical expertise has a historical, political foundation that needs to be explicitly challenged in each particular cultural context.[9] The historical and situational power of architectural expertise, communicated through building designs and city plans, is external to the project at hand, which simultaneously renders the architect a spectator to its reception. On the other side, local actors embody lived experience and accumulated histories of a place that are thick with another kind of expertise significant to the design of buildings and cities. Local, lived knowledge, if it becomes part of the design process, adds dimensionality and polyvocality. In the Double Sights project, Walter Hood centered himself at the intersection of local, political, and professional expertise, which was an uncomfortable position at times, such as at the sculpture's unveiling when university administrators and protesters jockeyed for the public stage. This is what Hood calls a partnership of difference. Among partners with relevant contributions to make to an architectural project, inevitable contentions expose different forms and relationships of power. Within this contested space lies the means to advance social justice, which is a fundamental task of a public architecture.

The everyday public sphere of sidewalks, streets, schools, parks, and plazas is ground zero for catalyzing cities that value spatial justice. If systemic racism and structural inequities have a material form, they will be visible in these likewise systemic, urban infrastructures. The public sphere has been the focus of Hood Design Studio, which undertakes projects where partnerships of difference play an unmistakably important role. Throughout his work, Hood seeks communities' disparate voices, explicitly lifting up difference over diversity. For him, diversity has become an empty script to fulfill predetermined narratives. By contrast, difference provides an opportunity to raise contested issues in which all public spaces are grounded.[10] In his formulation, difference is to be identified and engaged while partnerships are to be actively constructed. Hood's partnerships of difference add dimensionality to some of the ideas I developed in my first book, *Architecture: The Story of Practice*, where I peeled back conventional wisdom around design decision-making by closely observing how architects and clients negotiated their projects. Partnerships of difference, as a concept, deflects the focus first from decisions to the *relationships* between partners, and second from architects and clients to the wider array of parties with valuable insights or insistent stakes in a project.

Well-rehearsed myths of the architect's idealized, creative independence meeting the public's harmonious reception disserve both the designer and the public. There is a lot at stake if architecture is to reframe design in relation to productive difference. Architects and artists may struggle creatively, but not with partners in the contested contexts of difference. Caricatures of the isolated, individual originator of a work of art operate as myths that fuel theory and simplify historical interpretation, and they also provide counterproductive models for architects. When community groups contest development, for example, architects who feel defensive, resistant, impatient, or resigned are unlikely to undertake the difficult work of inviting those groups to become contributing partners. Professional imperial practices would more likely lead to their suppression or marginalization. However, there are other difficult constraints, like building safety regulations or planning codes, that architects accept and take at face value as part of the process. Some architects find ways to turn codes and regulations into creative opportunities, but no one imagines they can be ignored. To ignore the wide range of participants with a say in the architectural project is to imperil the work and forgo opportunity.

The model of the singular design genius remains stubbornly dominant despite evidence to the contrary and sociopolitical pressure. A forceful testimony to the sole architect-author myth is the Pritzker Prize, arguably the most prestigious award in the field. Beginning in 1979, the Pritzker was bestowed on one architect each year. Even for husband-and-wife design team Venturi, Scott Brown and Associates, the 1991 prize was awarded only to Robert Venturi. Despite petitions to retroactively honor Denise Scott Brown alongside him, the Pritzker jury in 2013 refused to reconsider.[11] While protest about Scott Brown's exclusion has been justifiably framed in terms of gender discrimination, it is also a denigration of artistic collaboration. Not for another decade, until 2001, was the partnership of Herzog and deMeuron—two men—recognized with a Pritzker. Then, in 2010, SANAA's Kazuyo Sejima and Ryue Nishizawa won, and this recognition of the legitimacy of creative partnerships informed four subsequent juries. Of the forty-four prizes awarded by 2021, thirty-nine went to single individuals (Zaha Hadid being the only sole woman recipient) and only five went to designer teams. It is worth noting that, in addition to SANAA, three of the other premiated partnerships included women: Rafael Aranda, Carme Pigem, and Ramón Vilalta in 2017, Yvonne Farrell and Shelley McNamara in 2020, and Anne Lacaton and Jean-Philippe Vassal in 2021. Gendered stereotypes of collaboration are surely at play, but rather than corroborate the idea that women are more collaborative, the record of Pritzker Prizes confirms that architecture has historically been restricted to those women practicing alongside male partners.[12] The other thirty-nine Pritzker winners were also practicing in male-dominated collectives that went unrecognized in pursuit of the sole artistic creator. Though the Pritzker is just one measure, the four recent anomalous prizes to design teams point to the profession's acknowledgment of engagement and collaboration. Perhaps the recognition of designers' collaboration will accelerate the recognition of non-designers' contributions, which are intrinsic to partnerships of difference. Such recognition opens doors to not only more accurate but also more just theories of participation in the field and shines a light on narratives of creative collectives.

Those doorways are defended at the core of the architecture discipline, with its well-developed resistance to shared decision-making. Even the clients who are essential to conventional practice figure as supporting actors in architectural history and theory, when they are noted at all. The architect working at the heart of a large cast of characters is portrayed as a business manager in a large firm or a solo artist in a cutting-edge design firm. Unlike fields that recognize an individual's artistic leadership of a collective, like a film's director or the conductor in music, architecture is stuck in an outmoded and simplified business-art dichotomy. In practice, some architects credit specific partnerships as fundamental to their creative output, such as Louis Kahn and his engineer August Komendant, or Eric Owen Moss and his patrons the Samitaur Smiths. But acknowledgment of a project as an aesthetic cocreation remains newsworthy. The structural engineer Cecil Balmond cultivates his reputation as a cocreator rather than a consultant. According to the artist Anish Kapoor, "the traditional role of the engineer is to perform, so to speak, the ideas of the architect, or of the artist, or whatever. Cecil and I decided, quite clearly, that we were going to put that aside and invent together."[13] To share invention within the architect's cast is transformative, particularly when members of the cast represent divergent views. Shared, inventive collaboration requires further elaboration, resting on the history and theories of participatory creation.

PARTICIPATION, PARTNERSHIP, AND CONFLICT

In the 1960s, an expanding literature about participatory planning and democracy originated in America and other places around the world, based on the principle that individuals, especially residents or citizens, should directly participate in decisions that impact their daily lives. This fundamental challenge to representative democracy is a recognition that many individuals are not adequately represented through conventional political processes, particularly because of systemic racial bias, or at the micro-spatial level where local planning impacts are significant. This is not a disciplinary notion of planning, but a pragmatic question that applies to architecture as well: What forms of participation ensure inclusive, equitable planning for the future, whether for a building or for a policy? The embrace of difference and partnership launches a response to the question about forms of inclusive, equitable participation. Numerous corollary questions spill out from this starting point: Are there anti-racist, nondiscriminatory forms of participation? Are there forms of participation that are better suited for creative outcomes? Where is the boundary between participatory decision-making and professional responsibility? Over time, can a building retain its integrity while remaining open to participation-based change? As mentioned earlier, at its margins, architecture has sporadically admitted experiments in cocreation or shared authorship, but for the most part, those experiments have not colored the disciplinary core, largely because they downplayed formal aesthetic concerns. Given the extensive ideologies of participation within the planning field as well as in the arts and other professions (for example, in medicine, progressive thinking revolves around community and patient engagement), architecture is long overdue for a similar reckoning. That reckoning will be grounded in the work of contemporary architectural theorists like Ammon Beyerle and Jeremy Till, along with those who underscore architecture's repressed global and racialized narratives of participation, like Anooradha Iyer Siddiqi, Teddy Cruz, and Fonna Forman, and the work of public space artists like Theaster Gates and Pope.L.

Before moving forward, we should examine the relationship between participation and partnerships of difference. Participatory planning often privileges consensus and, by doing so, represses fundamental disagreements people hold about their cities, which in turn reinforces the status quo. Partnerships are a particular form of participation or collaboration that imply coproduction of knowledge and actions. Again, a relevant framework comes from the design and planning theorist Horst Rittel who argues that decision-making around design depends on a "symmetry of ignorance." Since no individual or profession holds sufficient knowledge, Rittel proffers mutual dependence among stakeholders in the planning process.[14] The notion of partnerships of difference is an argument on the flip side, to acknowledge a symmetry of expertise. Architects necessarily bring their own proficiency to the table, alongside the intelligence of local communities, civic representatives, and, when possible to identify, future occupants. The potential for innovative, unconventional solutions resides not only in an awareness of distributed expertise and ignorance, but also in the trust among partners who disagree, which in turn stems from respect built through long-term engagement.[15]

Architecture will also benefit from a critical examination of the existing models of participatory planning and community engagement processes that stand as ideological pillars in the field of planning. An indication that a contemporary discussion of participation, as well as partnerships, is dire is the fact that nearly all scholarship on city-making participation starts with Sherry Arnstein's eight-rung "ladder of citizen participation," published more than a half century ago in 1969. She built her typology to clarify the Office of Economic Opportunity's requirement for "maximum feasible participation" in the Model Cities Program, which was created during Lyndon Johnson's presidency in reaction to the violent, repressive urban programs that demolished communities of color across the country, as a response to the August 1965 Watts rebellion, and as part of Johnson's War on Poverty initiatives.[16] Key to Arnstein's analysis of participation is a distinction she makes between tokenism and citizen control—the latter "focused on citizen participation as a means of redistributing power and resources to low-income communities."[17] Arnstein's ladder, a clear diagram of urban political agency, captures the contestation about who is in charge of community destiny and suggests that the primary actors include neighborhood residents or citizen groups (who are to eventually be in control), local government (which was generally viewed as an opposing force that would need to be transformed), and the federal government (which would moderate between the two as needed). Federal funding was the mechanism leveraged to wrest control—that is, power—from "local governments naturally disinclined to share that power." While Arnstein's ladder is seminal, it is also historically tied to an era when the federal government was not widely recognized for its own culpability, especially its role in systemic anti-Black racism. Nor does it acknowledge the roles of nongovernmental organizations, activism, or resistance, even though resistance was cotemporaneous. Writing at the same time in the *National Black Law Journal*, Kline and LeGates argued that in the Model Cities Program, "the contemporary consciousness of black communities will settle for no less than the right to engineer their own development."[18]

Arnstein's ladder acknowledges the importance of community self-determination but directs its recommendations to those with formal authority over the development process. Nonetheless, she situated three "degrees of citizen power" above tokenism: partnership, delegated power, and citizen control. Arnstein came to her conclusions based on humanist social science; she went to Model Cities sites to observe firsthand how citizen participation was working and conducted interviews with program directors. Her analysis is grounds for this formulation of partnerships of difference, since she saw and documented the structural issues that still pertain if cities, and thus the architecture within them, are to be shaped with and by residents. In concluding her exegesis on participation, Arnstein offers a checklist for action that is organized around questions addressed to what she calls the "executive group" who will initiate the establishment of citizen participation as a decision structure. To create a representative "all-neighborhood group" there must be accountability back to the community, a policy about financial assistance to participants, and an affirmative answer to a key question: "Will the process for selecting neighborhood representatives deal with the need to hear the voice of youth, the aged and those who are different from the majority residing in the model neighborhood area?"[19] The inclusion of minority views, Arnstein imagined, following an ideal of pluralism, was fundamental to the making of model neighborhoods.

As we saw in the opening example at Princeton University, executive groups have their own vested interests that "all-neighborhood groups" may need to resist. Likewise, while inclusion and equity are related, the former does not ensure the latter, especially when consensus is the goal. Instead, dissensus and resistance must be considered, and with them fundamental differences in power. Critics argue that participatory planning tethered to political pluralism privileges consensus and thus represses significant disagreements people hold about

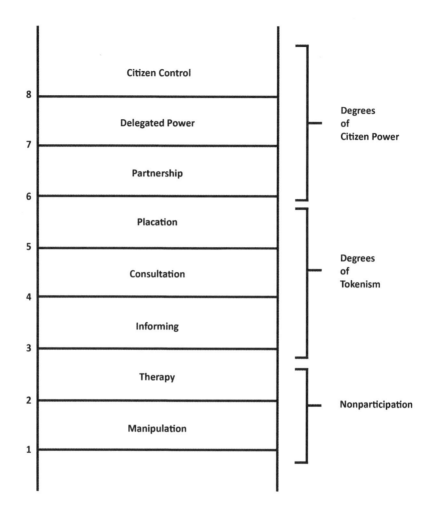

Eight Rungs on a Ladder of Citizen Participation

FIGURE 4.7

Arnstein's ladder. Redrawn by Miranda Hirujo-Rincon.

their cities, which in turn reinforces the status quo. If in the 1980s, participation was theorized as a form of consensus building and empowerment, more recently a number of scholars, especially scholar-practitioners like Miessen and Beyerle, argue that participation's bias toward amicable consensus masks underlying contention and power imbalances.[20] As a result, democratic processes are themselves unjust in one way or another unless intrinsic conflict and contention are acknowledged. In a series of critical analyses, Markus Miessen decries the "tyranny" of participation, and in conversations with political philosopher Chantal Mouffe argues that the implied agreements and smooth interactions beneath participatory processes would be more productive if Mouffe's agonism were the model. They discuss the ways that democratic processes, or even more problematic consensus-building processes, are abuses of power. For Mouffe, this is not a matter of agreeing to disagree, but recognizing that incompatible views are inevitable. She builds a theory of "agonistic pluralism" that explicates the intrinsic conflict built into all politics and the value of tension in democratic processes. In architecture, both Miessen and Beyerle adapt her ideas about agonistic practices as a model for participatory design.[21] But processes built on contention and disagreement have proven difficult to convert from theory into normative practice, particularly in the arts. And yet when the production of a single outcome based on agreement is emphasized, the inherent multiplicity of contentious, divided political voices is repressed. In partnerships of difference, sustained engagement rather than closure is the foundation on which agonistic democracy rests.[22] Similarly, Hood's design partnerships of difference imply irreconcilable tensions that are viewed with respect by political actors who continue to engage one another as partners. For Hood, this agonism continued to swirl during and after the opening of Double Sights, as well as within the debates it records between Wilson and his critics.

Architecture, like other professions, frames its relationship to the public as an ethical duty and the relationship to client as a contractual one. But since architecture is never produced single-handedly, we should instead focus on collective characterizations of the design process variously called participation, negotiation, teamwork, or collaboration. When the idea of partnership is invoked, the legal or managerial organization of firms comes to mind. Business models deploy partnerships for two purposes: to manage people fairly and to extend moral responsibility beyond profit.[23] Such purposes are relevant to more procedural partnerships of difference, whereas contractual partners can share ownership, management, and responsibility—that is, control. Partnerships of difference imply that control over public design works is distributed among parties with interest in the project. A partnership model gives agency to publics and clients who, in the most extreme formulation, become cocreators with the architect. Architectural history rarely admits such discourse, keeping exemplars—like Walter Segal's self-build housing in England, Dutch architect N. John Habraken's supports and infills system, and Christopher Alexander's Pattern Language—at the margins. Even among these cases, none is characterized as agonistic or as having an ethico-political foundation like social justice. Instead, these models of participation are ascribed economic, symbolic, and practical motivations.

Partnership is the term used here rather than *participation* for two reasons: first, participation has been so overused that it operates as virtue signaling by those in power, and second, partnership embeds the idea of distributing power, decision-making authority, and control. In theory, partners have some equal footing in their undertakings, standing on a relatively even playing field. Expounding on Walter Hood's partnerships of difference, the partners deliberate, negotiate, argue, or participate in a continuous balancing of power that reflects their valuable, independent knowledge. For example, a neighborhood organization's knowledge of its own history and conflicts offers an important ingredient to any plans for its transformation, as does the local government representatives' knowledge of policy avenues. Partnerships of difference aim not toward consensus but toward persistent engagement and debate.

ARCHITECTURAL SITES OF LOCAL KNOWLEDGE

There remains a question about which partners will engage or contribute, and, in architecture, this question has a geography. It is political action that determines the appropriate partners, who has relevant experience and knowledge, or whose justice will be taken into account. When we are dealing with spatial justice, locale plays a central role because the communities with lived, local experience are themselves key. Municipal regulations reflect this fact. When a new civic project is being planned, the voices to be included are governed by notification requirements that mandate inviting comments from neighbors within some geographic radius of the project site. Alternatively, public hearings are an open forum where all concerned residents can air their views, although they are limited to a few minutes each at the microphone. Such administrative constraints are arbitrary means to define—or, more accurately, *limit*—participation as well as conflict.

By contrast, partnerships of difference demand decidedly more engagement. In design, the approaches to encouraging respectful conflict, attending to symmetries of expertise and ignorance, and identifying who constitutes "the community" revolve around the site to be architecturally transformed. Site analysis typically involves an exploration of material conditions (like wind patterns, topography, or design context), but it should also involve social, political, and historical conditions as well. Although the cultural conditions surrounding an architectural site are rarely studied, such practices are analogous to anthropological fieldwork. Architects undertaking such fieldwork would immerse themselves over time in the everyday life settings of their partners. There are well-known examples of architects living on-site, immersed with the current and future occupants of their buildings. Lina Bo Bardi set up her architectural office, where she operated for years, within the former factory that she ultimately converted into the SESC Pompéia cultural center for São Paolo (as described in chapter 2; see figure 2.7). In Newcastle's Byker neighborhood, architect Ralph Erskine set up his office as a drop-in center to develop a pilot project with about fifty families who would be rehoused in his design for the new Byker Wall's 1,800 households.

Such experiments are noteworthy in part because they are so rare. In architecture, fieldwork is generally limited to the practice called the "site visit." It was Venturi and Scott Brown, in their "learning from . . ." format, that extended the site visit into something more akin to fieldwork. Still, what is gleaned from *Learning from Las Vegas* is the view from the outside of the outside by outsiders. It does not involve speaking with insiders, or anyone else for that matter, or reading historical accounts. While fieldwork in anthropology has been roundly theorized, recounted in memoirs, and codified in required coursework, the discipline is primarily interested in human interaction and ethnographic accounts, with the physical environment serving as a backdrop or prop. Architecture, on the other hand, measures, maps, and photographs the physical environment with no expectation that a site visit should include conversations with the people there.

When designers step into the field, they mean the "world itself," rather than the workplace or home—for practitioners, the field begins where the office ends; for students and faculty, the field is everywhere except the school. Basically, the field is where social theorist Pierre Bourdieu says we turn on the scholarly habitus of observation and turn off the practical habitus of doing. In the field, we listen rather than hear, interpret rather than think. Parallel to Hayden White's critique of historical scholarship, for architecture, fieldwork is part of the professional world rather than the life-world. But life occurs in the field, and sites are by definition in the field.[24]

For architects, field geographies are important because sites have legal, spatio-political boundaries. But the "world itself" of the field is not limited to geography; it includes culture, bodies, languages, histories, desires, and actions. In this sense, the field can include all that is determined to be part of a relevant context. In architecture, context studies are historically dependent—today, we look at solar shading, heat gain, traffic patterns, topography, and land use. At the Beaux Arts, students looked at classical precedent, potential ornament, proportion. In the 1970s, when the functional program rose in importance, the fieldwork or site investigation included user behavior. The inclusion of humane subjects, characterized more fully beyond behavior to include imaginations, histories, and narratives, has yet to become a conventional practice. If architects are to engage partnerships of difference, the humanity of those partners will be intrinsic to those interactions. Such humanistic qualities are a wellspring for both art practices and justice practices. The repressed spatial histories of displaced, disenfranchised people, particularly Black and Indigenous groups, have led to some form of reparations from Evanston, Illinois to Bruce's Beach in Southern California. These stories are only partially visible on their sites, adding an important dimension to necessary fieldwork.

Architecture's conventional project structures, with set fees and services, seem unable to make room for humanistic partnerships and long-term engagement. But one project that demonstrates how a decidedly different approach can operate within a conventional structure is the Tour Bois-le-Prêtre. The tower of ninety-six affordable apartments built in the 1960s at the Paris periphery was slated for demolition but was instead remodeled for its residents (2006–2011). Architects Lacaton, Vassal, and Druot undertook extensive research, considering the tower's neighborhood, France's history of marginalizing immigrants, the underfunding of social housing, other housing towers in the architectural canon, the climatic conditions, as well as occupants who live there now and those who might come in the future. Their expanded sense of site analysis and fieldwork put them in touch with the lived experience of tower residents. The project was featured in a MoMA exhibition at the end of 2010 entitled *Small Scale Big Change*, in which curator Andres Lepik explains:

The architecture was blamed for social problems in the [massive social housing built on the] outskirts of Paris. And the research which [Anne] Lacaton, Jean-Phillip Vassal, and Frédéric Druot started, was 'Why should we tear these houses down and are they really, let's say, guilty for what the social problems are?' It started not on the desk of the architects but really with interviews with tenants in their houses, and what came out is they don't want to move out, they want to get a little bit more light, maybe a balcony, they want to get more space. So the basic idea is to keep the structure as it is but to build a new façade like a shell that comes around of glass and a structural frame so people will get a sort of winter garden or balcony to the outside of their apartments; they will get more light, more floor space, and at the same time this glass facade creates also a thermal buffer for the old building. . . . These architects reversed the idea of the architecture being the cause for the social problems, but they say you can also change the future of these houses in just giving them a better shape and restructuring them.[25]

Lacaton, Vassal, and Druot interviewed all ninety-six tenants to develop a solution that let them remain in their apartments through most of the construction, since staying in place was a high priority. The building was refurbished to be more energy efficient by adding a thickened exterior glazing, one-room wide, that functioned as a new sunroom for each apartment so that residents could live more spaciously and comfortably. The architects' thoroughness lent trust to the

FIGURE 4.8

Stages of remodeling the Tour Bois-le-Prêtre in Paris's seventeenth arrondissement, showing the gradual transformation of the exterior as it is thickened with a cladding of glazed rooms (2011). Courtesy of Druot, Lacaton & Vassal.

design process, as did their listening to residents' priorities. The greenhouse addition was not definitively programmed to become a garden or living room or office; its purpose was to "emphasize freedom as well as function—leaving spaces undefined, which allows the tenants to be inventive." The architects maintained an aesthetic direction not as a formal end in itself but as an intrinsic part of the programmatic and ethical goals set with the residents.

From the architects' perspective, Bois-le-Prêtre was not an isolated commission but a model for a common problem: how to remodel the extensive corpus of housing towers failing in terms of social, structural, and energy criteria. Lacaton and Vassal's design and design process in partnership with tenants constituted a generative demonstration, as the next chapter will explain. While the five-year

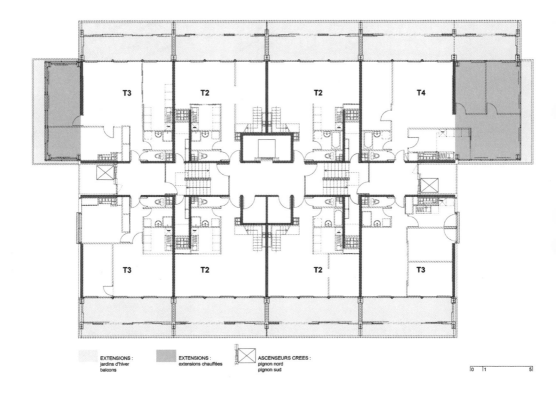

T3   T2   T2   T4

T3   T2   T2   T3

EXTENSIONS :
jardins d'hiver
balcons

EXTENSIONS :
extensions chauffées

ASCENSEURS CREES :
pignon nord
pignon sud

0   1   5

FIGURE 4.9

Plan showing a typical floor in the Tour Bois-le-Prêtre. The blue and green areas add square footage to the existing apartments. Courtesy of Druot, Lacaton & Vassal.

time frame was long, it was not significantly longer than that of similar projects. The remodel and expansion of the tower cost half the estimated cost of demolition and rebuilding. In addition, Bois-le-Prêtre generated more work for the architects, and the project contributed to their winning the Pritzker Prize in 2021.[26] In other words, what was good for the apartment residents was also good for the owner-clients and the architects. It is also a model for breaking normative expectations about feasible levels of engagement, and perhaps more significantly,

FIGURE 4.10

Interior of one inhabitant's apartment that shows the open connection beyond the former exterior wall to a greenhouse-like room for flexible uses. Courtesy of Druot, Lacaton & Vassal.

for making the design compromises such engagement requires. The architects had sufficient skills and perseverance to listen closely to tenants and to negotiate a solution that addressed energy, function, aesthetics, and economy. To evaluate social justice implications more specifically, post-occupancy conversations included tenants who were not satisfied with their apartments. The architects returned to listen again to residents because they had established genuine, long-term engagement that would also inform subsequent design projects.

Resident dissatisfaction falls within Mouffe's characterization of difference as antagonistic, contingent, and conflictual. Rather than coexisting, diverse identities, difference requires the construction of us and them, not as enemies but as respectful adversaries. Mouffe seeks the means to turn antagonism into agonism. Hood's partnerships of difference suggest such antagonisms are turned agonistic through partnerships. In the case of Bois-le-Prêtre, discussion and debate about resident dissatisfaction was a form of agonism that acknowledged solutions are imperfect and will continue to be revised.

WHAT PARTNERSHIPS IN ARCHITECTURE COULD BE

If architecture is to address the suspect constructions of participation, consensus, stakeholders, community, and expertise, it can do so by reformulating its notion of design thinking in terms of difference, conflict, partnership, and even site. At the level of architectural practice, the task would begin just as Hood or Lacaton and Vassal did, by stepping directly into the uninterrogated notions of the project at hand. On a disciplinary level, the academy is a natural place for such reformulation, but architectural training has barely scratched this surface. Historical accounts sideline questions of power and conflict to foreground the architect's biography and the building's formal qualities. The discipline's professional past, in Hayden White's terms, has drowned out its practical past, along with the narratives that might inform present-day architects. In school, there are effective and expedient ways to build knowledge of others and their conflicting identities. Some instructors develop a project's program with firsthand input from relevant partners or by bringing partners into the academy to meet with students. They might record listening sessions with community members answering questions about their neighborhood, site, and interests.

It is reasonable to ask how architects and architecture students can ethically and aesthetically engage with communities to which they do not belong, or with whom they have no lasting relationships. When architects study some situated group in order to understand their interests more fully through interviews, observations, mapping, listening sessions, or focus groups, they reproduce a form of professional imperialism that needs critical acknowledgment. The power imbalance involves knowledge extraction, not unlike other hegemonic colonial practices in which the dominant force gathers for its own advantage the resources of a weaker entity. Partnerships of difference admit that power is always out of balance, and that designers must practice their art within extended relations of tension and conflict. Like other practices emanating from a spatial justice framework rather than economic or efficiency models, this initially seems impractical, but the examples within this chapter prove otherwise.

In architectural training and practice, the most basic question is the same: *Why* might some spectrum of the public or community be meaningfully engaged in architectural creation? By now the answer should be apparent: to cultivate the full potential of architecture, particularly for its public partners. The preceding pages explain *how* to engage architecture's politics through inherent difference and conflict; expand understanding, knowledge, and experience; create radically public architecture that is open, inclusive, and fresh; and advance architecture's integration into the social fabric of everyday life. Architects hold instrumental goals of avoiding future resistance, but partnerships of difference provide a better map of the inevitable contestation, or agonism. Without the meaningful engagement of partners who may range from civic leaders to unhoused residents, architectural and urban works cannot become robust public places. Given such value, it is surprising that participatory processes have become so perfunctory. It was for these reasons that cityLAB launched its off-campus, satellite design research center in 2019. Located in the historically underserved Los Angeles neighborhood of Westlake/MacArthur Park, cityLAB-Westlake deepens our community design practices. Amid a diverse range of community partners, we set up shop in a youth after-school program called Heart of Los Angeles, or HOLA. Early in the partnership, cityLAB-Westlake's team, led by Dr. Gustavo Leclerc with research associates Rayne Laborde and Nallely Almaguer-Rodriguez, collaborated with HOLA art teachers to create thick maps of the public spaces in the neighborhood, learning that the best results came when we "experienced" the maps by walking as we thickened (annotating, telling stories, etc.). Based on these "fieldwalks," students showed us their sidewalks, which offered too little shade, too much policing, friendly street vendors, evangelists, and unhoused residents. Leclerc entitled the initiative Banqueteando or "sidewalk-as-a-verb." At the off-campus site, we hope to perpetually build understandings of the neighborhood with the residents over years, experiencing its spaces together, building trust. With those gains, our continued engagement in the community would be more likely to shape a path forward with and for the residents. There is no end state to cityLAB-Westlake as a partnership of difference; instead, there is an unfolding series of projects that build on the trust and engagement of all the preceding engagements.

Along with the qualities of being fresh and equitable, radically public architecture is open-ended in two additional ways elaborated by this unpacking of partnerships of difference. First, the object itself can remain unfinished or open to subsequent engagement, transformation, and evolution. Second, its interpretation remains open to new narratives and new performances. While some argue that leaving an object open to continuous renewal or transformation is not feasible,[27] one need only look at buildings or collections of buildings where individual interests or owners, over time, reshape their circumstances. When taken together, a campus, a neighborhood, or a group of buildings along a street is transformed by collective, incremental renovation. Business owners form an improvement district, for example, partnering to coordinate their actions when it comes to design, infrastructure, events, and services. Such transformation occurs because of certain conditions: there is sufficient participation among actors, they agree to some form of shared governance, and they persist in the face of difference and conflict. What architecture can contribute to the intrinsic dissensus that characterizes partnerships of difference—and participation more broadly—is the material culture or visions of alternative futures around which conflict constellates. In the prior chapter, Japanese architects worked with residents of devastated communities to literally render their future so that they could be more effective in negotiations with the national government. In Princeton's deliberations about memorializing the conflicting sides of Woodrow Wilson, Walter Hood's Double Sights represents perpetual antagonisms. The new greenhouse spaces wrapping Bois-le-Prêtre offered open-ended possibilities for inhabitation, but residents persist in their desire to remake their apartments differently. Architectural design, as drawings or built form, give shape to conflict, and, in the best situations, convert antagonism into agonism.

Westlake - MacArthur Park Neighborhood

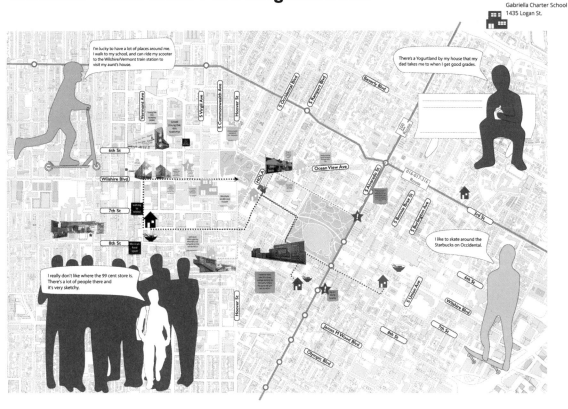

FIGURE 4.11

This "thick map" aggregates sidewalk stories from numerous children in the Westlake community to show how they experience their neighborhood and its parks. Image by Gibson Bastar, courtesy of cityLAB.

FIGURE 4.12

MacArthur Park is the subject of a "thick mapping" exercise in which local students add their impressions of the existing park and what might improve it. Courtesy of cityLAB.

GENERATIVE DEMONSTRATIONS

HALF-HOUSES AT QUINTA MONROY, ELEMENTAL, SANTIAGO, CHILE

Architect Alejandro Aravena, principal of the studio Elemental, designed the Quinta Monroy housing in Iquique, Chile in 2003. He describes the housing as "porous and incremental," but neither term fully captures the distinctive quality of the ninety-three affordable units; each construct one portion of a residence while leaving another portion open for completion by the occupant at a later date. What is notable about Quinta Monroy is that the formal porousness—so imageable in the photographs—is just one of many interrelated facets that create a generative demonstration of innovation in more equitable housing provision. The most comprehensive, influential facet is the design itself, but the project gains further authority in terms of investment, anti-displacement, construction, and wealth building. By putting these varied aspects of building together, Aravena created a prototype, which I will call simply a "half-house," that is fundamentally a new type of accommodation. The model depends on leveraging design to make the new type legible. It is no wonder that photographs of Quinta Monroy's initial construction prior to inhabitation are so widely circulated. The project, with further study, also demonstrates how such open-endedness transfers agency over time from the architect and governmental sponsors to the occupants, with unexpected and sometimes unwanted results. Because Quinta Monroy is relatively well-known, this is less a description of the project than an analysis of the prototype's distinctive qualities and their implications for its proliferation.

FIGURE 5.1

Four half-house developments in Mexico and Chile for which plans were released as public-use, open-source documents: Monterrey Housing, Monterrey, Mexico (upper left; 2010); Quinta Monroy, Santiago, Chile (upper right; 2005); Villa Verde, Constitución, Chile (lower left; 2010 post-tsunami); and Lo Barnechea, Santiago, Chile (lower right, 2008–2014). Courtesy of Alejandro Aravena, Elemental.

FIGURE 5.2

An interior courtyard at Quinta Monroy.shows how half-houses have been infilled by the occupants.
Courtesy of Alejandro Aravena, Elemental.

The half-house first is a strategy to utilize available funds for residential construction in an unconventional way. The state housing authority uses its limited funds to construct a well-built but partial house rather than an entire house that is poorly built, which leaves the unbuilt portion to be completed by the residents when they are able to assemble the resources. Circumstances at Quinta Monroy set the terms of this strategy once the architects began work with the existing on-site community to be rehoused. After the Pinochet dictatorship ended in 1990, over a quarter of Chile's population was living in poverty and informal settlements. In the city of Iquique, the Quinta Monroy project involved plans to demolish and relocate a community that had occupied the site in the center of the city for three decades and was made up of primarily single-parent, female-headed households. The standard practice of relocation to the outskirts saved on land costs, allowing tight public housing budgets to be extended. In early meetings with the residents, Elemental learned why living in the center of the city was important, why being displaced would be so detrimental, particularly in terms of jobs, and why maintaining existing social networks mattered.

Since the state ministry of housing's debt-free affordable housing program capped expenditures at $10,000 per unit, by rehousing residents on the current site, a full quarter of that amount would pay for land costs at Quinta Monroy. With the remaining $7,500, Aravena decided to build only a portion of each dwelling, with the rest to be completed over time by the occupants following the informal practices of the existing settlement. Elemental was strategic about the portion provided and the portion for self-building: the most expensive, difficult-to-build, and technical parts of the house would be constructed by the housing agency, leaving the simplest, safest, and least expensive portions—as determined in participatory design processes—for the occupants. After calculating construction costs for the basic structure, stairs, and service cores, Elemental determined that 40 percent of each house could be provided while 60 percent would be infilled.[1] Elemental designed a supporting framework for improvisation that included not only the half-houses, but also a handbook for residents about building out the rest. On a nine-by-nine-meter parcel, both the ground floor patio house and the two-story unit stacked above could be expanded by about thirty-six square meters. Guidelines negotiated with the residents would regulate their construction of the infilled sleeping and living spaces. Beyond the individual units, the site plan of Quinta Monroy underscored what Elemental learned from listening to the community. The housing was laid out to form a defined border for the whole development, with four interior courtyards to demarcate different communities therein.

The assumption behind Quinta Monroy is logical if radical: when a site and budget offer real and extreme constraints, extreme design solutions need to be considered in order to ultimately serve the interests of the occupants. The project assumes that residents themselves are part of the housing provision equation by designing units that reflect their requirements and encourage their future interventions.

In material form, the housing *demonstrates* how it should grow and change. That first level of generativity is compounded by a second level, since Quinta Monroy explicitly displays how its design-build strategy can be applied elsewhere. Elemental deployed versions of the prototype in subsequent housing developments like Villa Verde in Constitución, Chile (completed 2010), Monterrey Housing in Monterrey, Mexico (2010), and Lo Barnechea, a suburb of Santiago (completed 2014; see figure 5.1).

Although the contexts of each development differed, common issues included the economics of affordable housing and displacement. For example, when residents in Constitución learned they might be relocated, they threatened a hunger strike and were eventually rehoused on-site in Villa Verde. As at Quinta Monroy, residents resisted displacement in order to maintain their social ties as well as their in-town proximity to sites of employment. The new developments' success can be measured by whether the residents received better housing and potential ownership and by whether their existing socioeconomic networks were maintained. Via Verde offers evidence that the half-house model is a means of building wealth through ownership, investment, and labor (figure 5.1). According to *New York Times* architecture critic Michael Kimmelman, the Chilean government subsidized Villa Verde's construction at about $22,300 per unit (in 2016 dollars), and residents paid $700 to own the unit, completing the construction of the second half over time by investing their labor and an estimated $2,000–$3,000. Equivalent market-rate houses in the area sell for about $100,000, which

FIGURE 5.3

In Lo Barnechea, a basic interior for occupants to complete. Courtesy of Alejandro
Aravena, Elemental.

means that residents can build wealth against the structural conditions of poverty in a way that informal settlements preclude.

Elemental's four half-house projects demonstrate the strategy—not only the form, but also the overall approach that depends on form—to other developers as well as ways to build out the vacant portion of each house to the residents. In 2016, Aravena went one step further by making the drawings of these four incremental housing developments open-source and accessible for free. This final step is an explicit invitation to others to borrow the prototype so that it will proliferate. In terms of this analysis, the drawings are central to the model, but it would be equally useful to give open access to the financing structure, development agreements, and architectural services contracts.

Now that Quinta Monroy is more than fifteen years old, post-occupancy evaluations can compare the original goals in light of ongoing self-building. For the journal *Architectural Review*, Sandra Carrasco and David O'Brien considered the project's success in terms of how easy it was for residents to expand their homes, and, in turn, whether their quality of life improved when compared to the informal housing they had previously occupied. Quinta Monroy received a mixed score. Of the ninety-three original houses, all but one have been expanded, but 64 percent of the homes were extended beyond the framework defined by Elemental. Some cantilever over the building line, some infringe on the shared courtyards, and some rise an additional floor, to four levels. All this is very much in the tradition of informal housing, leading the authors to conclude:

> Elemental initiated a process that, over a 15-year period, reconfigured Quinta Monroy from an informal settlement through a formalizing process only for it to return to a state of informality. . . . Elemental's design strategy, however has inadvertently created household spaces that in many instance replicate the 'slum-like' conditions they attempted to address. At the same time, they have set the scene for a range of ongoing and contested community interactions that might have been avoided with a more nuanced understanding of the community relationships and a more nuanced urban design strategy.[2]

The writers' biases are captured in the "slum" pejorative, as if informal settlements are without positive conditions. However, it is important to recognize the unsafe conditions and community disaffection that the authors identify. But rather than avoid the ongoing agonism among residents, Quinta Monroy set a stage that allowed it to be part of community relations.

Is it too much to ask that architects stay on the job, monitoring how people use, build, and socialize in their community? Perhaps. But since Elemental left residents with a "habitability manual," they clearly accepted some responsibility in helping guide future building expansion. The manual was apparently not followed at Quinta Monroy, yet in Elemental's subsequent half-house projects, habitability manuals were more effective. Thus, as the model proliferated, improvements were made both to the manual, and to the design of the half-houses. In particular, at both Monterrey and Via Verde, the housing is "capped" with a roof to limit the number of stories residents can infill, preventing unsafe expansion to a fourth floor.

section AA

site plan of original self-built settlement

site plan as built, 2005

site plan, 2017

FIGURE 5.4

These site plans show the original settlement at Quinta Monroy (left), the site plans by Elemental when residents moved in in 2005 (middle), and the same plan indicating how residents extended their units beyond the intended footprint (right). Courtesy of Alejandro Aravena, Elemental.

The post-occupancy evaluation by Carrasco and O'Brien concludes, wrongly in my view, that more nuanced knowledge of the community might have prevented unexpected outcomes like overbuilding, dangerous building, and encroachment. These are likely due to the limits of the conventional architectural project. Imagine if, rather than ending on the move-in date, the architects' services included ongoing community engagement. Elemental provided continuing services insofar as the porous housing model proliferated and the architects continued their engagement with a series of similar communities. But through sustained engagement with the same residents, architects would gain valuable insight into how to improve the demonstration model and could partner with the community when site and building conflicts arose. In addition, community members in partnership with the state sponsor could create a more agile, robust community governance structure. Architects should also participate, since governance constraints may lead to new design opportunities or guidelines. More

FIGURE 5.5

This aerial photo, taken in 2020, shows Quinta Monroy's transformation from the regular saw-toothed half-houses into an active, self-built community. Courtesy of Alejandro Aravena, Elemental.

fundamentally, the housing prototype, with its ability to be owned and appropriated, served as a starting point for social transformation. For the neighborhood to thrive according to more formal standards, the project could have also involved an economic program, social services, and community organizing. Here again, if architects want their housing to be a key part of long-term social justice goals, they will need to break through professional conventions to engage their projects and their occupants more holistically.

In the half-house projects, Alejandro Aravena has upended disciplinary conventions, most pointedly in relinquishing claims on the finished building and, by implication, on the final creative outcome. The ties between architecture and unique artistic production are so strong that critics were surprised that he was awarded the Pritzker in 2016. Aravena makes clear why generative demonstrations are laudable architectural outcomes: they have greater impact than singular solutions. "Architects like to build things that are unique. But if something is unique it can't be repeated, so in terms of it serving many people in many places, the value is close to zero."[3]

In academic discourse, much has been made of architecture's "autonomous" capacity. Theorist Mark Foster Gage, for example, argues that design is the creation of "unique and ineffable things"—that is, autonomous objects that exist independently from other things and cannot be understood in relation to context. To underscore the point, he goes on to say that design is not "abject relational problem-solving."[4] Singular outcomes may be particular to a designer, site, client, program, or historical moment, but they are definitively discrete, autonomous objects, in contrast to objects-in-relation. Versions of this duality, including the denigration of architecture that addresses real-world concerns, have dominated disciplinary debate, but it poses a provocative question: What does it mean for objects or buildings to aim not for unique ineffability but instead hold ambitions of proliferation? The closest conversation in the field revolves around architectural precedents or models. Identifying a project's precedents is a reliable practice among architecture students as well as professionals. But when taken literally—when one architect copies another—it is grounds for disdain or even legal action. For example, when Philip Johnson recreated Claude-Nicolas Ledoux's eighteenth-century House of Education for the University of Houston (completed 1985), he was thumbing his nose at the architectural establishment, which predictably accused him of plagiarism.[5]

There are many ways in which architecture acknowledges that buildings are tied to historical precedents or might even become one; examples include Le Corbusier's "streets in the air" and the sectional innovation at the Unité in Marseille. Precedent, type, diagram, and model are all terms that describe formal iterations of buildings. But another set of terms—catalyst, rules, and prototyping—describe procedural practices in design versioning. While there is an abundance of conceptual thinking about an original work of art, or about difference and repetition, the questions raised here concern whether architecture can strategically intervene in the larger system of building production to produce fresh outcomes designed to serve social justice goals and to proliferate—in other words, to produce generative demonstrations. A focus on the system requires attention to the objects, networks, and procedures encompassed by architectural production in order to arrive at a unique object that serves as a demonstration. The opening examination of Elemental's Quinta Monroy offers a multifaceted object for our analysis, especially when its systemic innovations are revealed.

In post-Pinochet Chile, Aravena recognized that the destabilized conditions afforded and required new systemic strategies for producing affordable housing. The architectural instantiation of that strategy was a set of buildings or objects that made legible the idea of starter houses for owners to complete. The idea is embedded in the site plan and section and visible in the photographs. The questions raised by these documents—Why are these buildings only half-finished? How did they get that way?—lead us to another part of the strategy that is explained in the site plan's evolution, in the subsequent iterations at other housing sites, and by the narrative around finance. This is because Aravena's principal innovations contravened the established housing production *system*.

Over the last thirty years, the privileging of architecture's autonomy has been steadily eroded by both theory and practice. When Stan Allen shifted the architect's gaze in 1996 from the building-object to the city-field, there were ripple effects not only from building to city, but also from vertical to horizontal, containment to extension, and architecture to infrastructure. At the same time and in parallel, arguments against criticality and formal theory turned instead to embrace market forces of branding, identity, atmosphere, and consumerism in architecture. The post-critical project slipped easily into the logics of "free market urban order," particularly in the hands of Patrik Schumacher and Michael Speaks.[6] With this, architecture found itself theoretically in the grips of neoliberalism, which underpinned the market logics that had taken hold within the context of an ever-weakening public sector in late capitalism. The rhetorically flamboyant Schumacher makes an easy target. He has been reviled for his widely circulated 2016 statements that London's housing crisis would be solved by liberalizing and deregulating the real estate market and that tenants in central London's subsidized social housing should be displaced to give the subsidizers a turn: "Housing for everyone can only be provided by freely self-regulating and self-motivating market process." He went on to welcome foreign investors buying second homes: "Even if they're only here for a few weeks and throw some key parties, these are amazing multiplying events."[7] Notwithstanding the shock effect that Schumacher seeks, feminist, anti-racist, and income-equality movements (such as Occupy or living wage) resist such glib statements and reveal their prejudices. By now, there is abundant evidence that free markets are not free but manipulated by those in power to extend the dominance of White, male privilege. To be blunt: greater accessibility to housing and urban space requires an anti-free market approach.

My own work stands entirely in opposition to Schumacher's, but, perhaps surprisingly, on the same continuum. Architecture's building-objects that have urban or field implications arise from the building system. By that I mean so long as we look to transform architecture solely within the autonomous disciplinary boundaries of the built form, both architecture and urbanism will remain marginalized instruments in the hyper-political economy of real estate development. This is not a new observation; many architects have recognized the need to contribute to larger thinking about intractable problems.[8] For the most part, those architects step outside the profession to assume new roles, bring new knowledge to the table, or be more effective collaborators. I support this perspective along with the architects who move outside the profession into urban planning, public service, elected positions, or general contracting. But here I am advocating an intrinsic approach that does not depart from the profession but augments it from within. The idea of the generative demonstration relies on our disciplinary capacity to leverage design to effect change as discussed in chapter 2. And not just any kind of change (since Schumacher is also interested in leveraging transformative design) but change that produces greater equity and reduces disparities due to race, income, disability, sexual orientation, and gender. Let me be clear that this does not instrumentalize architecture any more so than suggesting architecture operates as a primitive hut.

DEFINING A GENERATIVE DEMONSTRATION

The generative demonstration respects the collaborative model for engaging the system within which architecture operates but goes beyond process-oriented solutions to return to the building's performative capacity (a notion fleshed out in chapter 6 about legible policy). Built form can materially demonstrate systemic intervention. As such, it literally stands as a model for reiteration, critique, and the suspension of disbelief. Aravena's half-houses are just such a demonstration. They emphatically depend on creating prototypes that intervene beyond form, modeling ways that design innovation unleashes new strategies for sites, regulations, lending, ownership, construction practices, and occupancy.

Unlike an architectural catalyst that accelerates subsequent actions toward a desired goal in an if-then relationship, generative demonstrations seek out the generic and generalizable to set up now-next relations. At cityLAB, for example, underutilized suburban backyards and vast community college parking lots are two generic conditions that provoked prototypical site designs, design-inflected policy, and built and rendered design demonstrations—all meant to be "plagiarized" (see figures 2.4 and 2.5). Other demonstrations may not be so generic but still call on their typological or generalizable qualities. A public aquarium that is more research center than tourist spectacle, like Esherick Homsey Dodge and Davis's Monterey Bay Aquarium, serves as a model for Mazatlán's Sea of Cortez Aquarium by Tatiana Bilbao. An architect advocating the use of contemporary architecture and the arts for economic revitalization of a small town or village can reference Naoshima, Japan or Columbus, Indiana. The success of a prototype is measured by its mutations, the extent of its replication, or the precedent it establishes; the success of a generative demonstration goes two steps beyond the prototype. First, generative demonstrations are designed to proliferate, and second, they *inscribe their potential proliferation* in some manner: in form, documentation, or process. In this sense, such demonstrations depend on baking propagation into the project and on the legibility of the model. Another way of putting this: generative demonstrations rely more on lending than on borrowing. Unlike precedents borrowed by others to ground a future project, a generative demonstration is offered by the maker for sampling. Finally, to proliferate, the model is a cocktail of design-led ingredients that can include financing, siting, contractual agreements, allyships, or political tactics. The recipe is never exactly the same, and the variants depend on the model put forward not as an original but as a template. Elemental's half-houses were inarguably generative demonstrations, especially when the firm gave open access to the documents and plans.

With these distinctions clarified, there are many examples that blur the boundaries. Sometimes what appear to be unique solutions hold demonstrative potential. And while prototypes are sometimes at the core of demonstrations, they are not the same. A prototype is generally considered an early design of a thing that serves as a standard for further iterations. The prototype's primary function is as a model. In industrial design, prototypes like the clay model for a new car design stand in for a more complete future version and help identify potential problems. Technological inventions rely on prototypes for proof of concept. Prototypes serve a parallel role in architecture in the case of prefabricated building, when a module, component, or process is tested prior to full implementation. For example, Frank Lloyd Wright tested the structural capacity of the Johnson Wax columns by loading a full-scale mock-up. In generative demonstrations, by contrast, the "prototype" is fully functional and serves as an early iteration, plus it guides its subsequent iterations toward further development and refinement.

In architecture, we tend to speak of precedents rather than demonstrations or prototypes. To elucidate the commonly upheld principle of architectural precedents and distinguish them from prototypes, we can look to the Guggenheim Museum in Bilbao by Frank Gehry, a precedent sometimes mistakenly characterized as a prototype or demonstration. Frank Gehry, Guggenheim Museum administrators, and civic leaders in the exhausted industrial city of Bilbao partnered to build an ambitious museum. It might be said that they were preparing for a "miracle," an urban economic recovery now called "the Bilbao effect."[9] The museum's exuberant design helped catalyze a family of subsequent projects around the city, and together they appeared to lay out a strategy for other cities seeking economic redevelopment through global tourism. But the Bilbao Guggenheim was never intended as a generative demonstration, and cities have struggled to discover the recipe's ingredients: some tried hiring Gehry to make an even more exotic building (Panama City's Biomuseo), others amplified the recipe with a cornucopia of architectural wonders (Saadiyat Island in Abu Dhabi), and still others built their own Guggenheims (the one in Las Vegas closed after seven years). In fact, according to some critics, the Guggenheim was only the most imageable piece of a comprehensive and strategic Bilbao Effect in which

FIGURE 5.6

Designer Jack Chen working on a large-scale clay model, prototyping a car at
Pasadena Art Center (2002). Photo P110.9949.5 by Vahe Alaverdian, courtesy
of ArtCenter College of Design.

FIGURE 5.7

Palm Pilot wooden model by Jeff Hawkins (ca. 1995). Photo by Mark Richards, courtesy
of Computer History Museum.

FIGURE 5.8

Frank Lloyd Wright watches a full-scale mock-up of a Johnson Wax column as it is structurally loaded with sand. Courtesy of the Wisconsin Historical Society.

many other pieces of the city's rejuvenation were undertaken by civic leaders and other institutions. This wider model intervened in the building system by planning architectural increments and infrastructural interventions in concert. As analyzed in this chapter, the generative capacity of the prototype is not a hoped-for miracle but a planned-for conceptual model that demonstrates its intentions to propagate and uses design to make those intentions legible.

Key to the transformative nature of generative demonstrations is how they intervene in the economic production of architecture. At present, architecture exists in two overlapping economies: that of custom building relatively unique solutions for private or public clients, and that of the development industry, both for- and not-for-profit, which builds redundantly and speculatively insofar as future profits or occupants are unknown. Real estate development proceeds via reproductions, in which a model is repeated in order to reduce financial risk and uncertainty. Generative demonstrations are a third option, borrowing from both the development model and custom building to establish a distinct means—a systems-based prototyping—of producing the benefits that architecture can bestow. The economies of development are combined with the responsiveness of custom building to establish a means for architecture to solve problems in new ways. While architectural practices are organized around singular design commissions, they gain those commissions in part because of their portfolio—that is, on a family of custom solutions that point to the direction the architect will take in forthcoming projects. But what if instead of centering on the architect, proliferation was centered on the object? This would set up the prototype as an early model for reproduction. Beyond that, if proliferation is centered around neither the author nor the object, but instead around what I am calling the system of production, then space opens up for generative demonstrations.

DEMONSTRATIONS AND SPATIAL JUSTICE

If the architectural commission—with its established practices of customized building, architectural fees, and timelines—intrinsically privileges privilege—that is, those with sufficient resources in terms of time, money, expertise, and access to resources to undertake the project—then the generative demonstration is an important contrasting alternative. It overcomes several fundamental and systemic barriers to undertaking architectural work and generally reduces uncertainty. At the same time, it affords architects the means to turn a conventional commission into a model. Qualities of demonstrations that serve the interests of a spatially just architecture include their plausibility, iterability, and open-source nature. Each of these characteristics reduces risk and increases certainty in the design process. They are interventions in the building production system, not in the architectural object.

First, an observable pilot project of an original or unexpected model helps overcome disbelief and increases plausibility. To paraphrase a popular maxim: If you build it, they will believe it. Given the conservative nature of building production systems, especially in the development and lending industries, a demonstration goes a long way toward convincing stakeholders that they should support the next project. It took numerous attempts, for example, to make lending on the construction of backyard homes plausible for low-income households. Community-based lenders and investors came up with new financing strategies to show the way, as did full-service, nonprofit architect-developers. A conceptual prototype may not be as powerful as one that is built, but one of architecture's real contributions is rendering plausible futures that do not yet exist. Design competitions formalize this role, generating multiple demonstrations and paving the way for subsequent built experimentation. Likewise, some prototypes are temporary or event based, demonstrating the plausibility of more permanent instantiations.

Second, it is important that architectural demonstrations involve recursive cycles of evaluation, feedback, and redesign. Subsequent versions learn from their predecessors, affording opportunities to enhance and improve on the project. Where possible, privileged communities should be the testing grounds for marginalized communities and absorb the risks of innovation rather than vice versa. But when architecture is formulated as a unique, singular solution and autonomy is prioritized, there are no means to learn from past examples.

Finally, generative demonstrations are open source and nonproprietary. They exist to be repurposed so that exclusivity and ownership are effectively denied. This constructively transforms the economies of architecture and its dependence on property, with all its historic and potential inequities. When architects and other stakeholders willingly share the documents of their labor, the project's recipe is made public and the ideas can proliferate. This must be the will of not only the architects but also their collaborators, since client-owners often withhold information about their projects and community participants are due rights of ownership as well. It is common for generative demonstrations to have public or mission-driven clients. The City of Medellín, for example, offers itself as an example for other cities wishing to leverage architectural design in poor communities for both local benefit and that of the larger urban context. Contrast this open-access and public orientation with the proprietary logics of corporations. For example, Google requires nondisclosure agreements of its design collaborators. Architects who have designed Google's offices, housing prototypes, or workstations cannot publish their projects or even include them in their portfolios because they are proprietary, just like the company's search algorithms.

ORIGINS OF FIRST ITERATIONS

An emphasis on the proliferation of generative demonstrations raises the question: How does the first instantiation of a generative demonstration come into existence? Originary objects belong to the world of custom design and artistic production, but even here nearly all architectural works have some basis in prior works. In conventional architectural practice, a new project is founded on the economies of custom design in which prior details, approaches, materials, and assemblies are redeployed. The new project—tailored to its particular owners, sites, lenders, architectural staff, commissions, and their unique chemistry— produces an original solution even though not all of its pieces are new.

In artistic production, a theory of originality was succinctly posited by the art historian George Kubler in 1962 in *The Shape of Time*.[10] There, he venerates the "prime object" from which derive later replications, mutants, and forgeries (as he names the subsequent artistic productions). Creativity, according to Kubler, is a search in the dark with the artist blind to precedent and art history. From the

FIGURE 5.9

Albert Kahn's six-story Ford Factory, Highland Park, Michigan (1914). Courtesy of the Bentley Historical Library.

FIGURE 5.10

Construction photo of the Soviet Chelyabinsk Tractor Plant (1930) shows fundamental similarities with Albert Kahn's earlier Ford factories in Michigan. Courtesy of the Chelyabinsk Tractor Plant Museum.

FIGURE 5.11

Soviet tanks were later mass-produced in Albert Kahn's Chelyabinsk Tractor Plant (1943). Courtesy of the Chelyabinsk Tractor Plant Museum.

chemistry of specific conditions and creative genius comes what Kubler calls a new "prime object." The fetish surrounding the prime object persists in architecture, despite the fact that architecture lives in an economic reality different from the other arts. In architecture's economy, original works depend on large investments of trusting and patient capital. The financial risk tied to that capital pushes toward previously tested experiments or conventions, making an original work all the more rare and difficult to achieve. All contributors look for ways to reduce uncertainty under such conditions, hence the reliance on convention and redeployment of past strategies.

But the design demonstration and its proliferation are nothing like Kubler's prime object and its mutants or Walter Benjamin's work of art in the age of mechanical reproduction. Nor does the design demonstration implicate Baudrillard's simulacra. Rather than working from art or media theory, with their emphases on creative production and consumption, design demonstrations take their cue from industrial prototypes. As such, a demonstration can look backward and forward simultaneously, referencing the prototype but refashioning it to perform in a specific context. In some cases, a second instantiation itself becomes the next prototype, displaying new principles to consider and operations to test. In this sense, there is a form of legibility in the demonstration; because the work of architecture is a display or demonstration, it acknowledges it is an instance along an experimental path and attempts to make its logic intelligible to others. Albert Kahn is sometimes described as an architect who worked in this manner. He undertook a number of automobile factory commissions, most notably for Henry Ford, advancing his design strategies from reinforced concrete to steel frame systems and generalizing from American car manufacturing to Soviet tractor and tank production. The prolific "industrial architect" developed his firm in Detroit in the first quarter of the twentieth century, at a time when factory lines and industrial production provided the context for new architectural programs, construction systems, and even office practices in his firm. His early factories were multistory, as at Highland Park (1910), a model for assembly line production he reused at the six-story Fisher Body Plant 21 in Detroit in 1919. Kahn created representatives of a building type—the manufacturing shed—that morphed and evolved over the course of many iterations. His large professional office also evolved by integrating specialists, team-based design, and rationalized operations, breaking norms in the larger design-construction system (see figures 5.9 and 5.10).[11]

If the examples from Elemental and Albert Kahn are representative, early iterations of generative demonstrations arise from pervasive circumstances when conventional solutions no longer seem appropriate. A groundswell or movement can form around a new approach, building a constituency for the demonstration and its proliferation. By definition, a generative demonstration emerges when it is designed to proliferate, to become legible as a model, and to address the system of production. One aspect of the latter is the development of needed social, political, and economic support. At cityLAB, for example, we have no actual "clients," so we must work to establish the potential constituency that any fresh architectural undertaking will need in order to survive.

If architecture continues to invoke singular works on individual sites for specific owners, clients, and occupants, then architecture will remain out of reach for those who do not own property, do not have the resources to invest significant time and capital, do not have relationships with lending institutions or investors, or cannot access any of a myriad of strategies that are common within the building industry but otherwise obscure. To some extent, the design of generative demonstrations—rather than singular commissions—undermines the privilege intrinsic to conventional architectural practice.

But even when building opportunities are made more widely accessible, as was the case when granny flats were legalized and every backyard became a potential site, architecture itself was not "ready" to respond. The arcane nature of the building system was a real barrier to the production of ADUs when the new laws took effect in California at the start of 2017 (see chapter 2's opening case). Architects were unprepared to undertake numerous small projects with reduced budgets on a wide variety of sites. As a result, there was a great deal of early enthusiasm in the tech sector, which saw opportunities in this "space."[12] They built on digital technology that was already playing a role in the building system, from the computational coordination of construction documents to open records in city building departments. Platforms were founded to scrape online municipal data about sites, zoning regulations, and local building costs to assess whether a property could feasibly accommodate an ADU, what it might cost, and the limits of its footprint. Other start-ups used tech-sector investment strategies to fund, manage construction, lease up, and reap most of the rent for granny flats on other people's property, with plans to transfer them back to the owner after the return on investment was maximized in about twenty years. Even though homeownership is a privileged status, most homeowners—particularly middle- and working-class individuals—have no experience with architects, building departments, building regulations, or construction loans and do not want the additional stress of managing an uncertain construction project in their backyard. Few under-resourced individuals or groups are able to take even the first steps of an architectural project, such as feasibility or planning studies. However, with

FIGURE 5.12

Richard Neutra's open classroom, showing indoor–outdoor connection at the Kester Avenue School in Sherman Oaks California (1949). Getty Research Institute, Los Angeles (2004.R.10). Courtesy of the J. Paul Getty Trust.

generative prototypes, many of those up-front costs are shouldered by the first instantiation and as such overcome much of the uncertainty of later variants. The success and the problems at Quinta Monroy informed the next iterations of half-houses undertaken with public subsidy. The state of California eventually hired an ADU specialist to resolve policy-level problems that trickled up from municipal planning jurisdictions and homeowners. By shifting the investment burden from the economies of individual households to the economies of collectives like the state, generative demonstrations can intervene in the conventional, inequitable provision of architectural goods. Would Frank Gehry's Guggenheim building design or process have been different if he intended first to create a new model for urban museums and second to demonstrate that model in a specific instance at Bilbao? Of course it would, and that would have made the model clearer for others to follow. But his design intention was to create the unique and ineffable, and it was only the intention of others to copy it. Most of its copies missed their marks.

Economies of propagation can operate within a practice or extend outside individual offices and geographies, and those opportunities surface at times of increased production. The pressure to create generative demonstrations is most apparent in times when a particular building type is in high demand, described in chapter 7 as critical junctures. One final example helps further explain this phenomenon. In postwar American public school buildings, architects contributed to educational thought about new forms of learning that would suit the emerging future generation. In her study of American elementary school design, Amy F. Ogata notes, "these buildings were not designed as heroic statements. Instead, these schools and their architects quietly contributed to the development of normative, mass-produced solutions." They generated three basic school site plan types, all single story: open schools, compact clusters, and long, single-loaded corridors of classrooms. Richard Neutra effectively developed principles to govern classroom design through a series of experimental schools in the Los Angeles area. Opening classrooms by providing extensive windows and access to the outdoors, Neutra demonstrated postwar thinking about child-centered education and freedom of movement.

Ogata alludes to the problem of adopting such normative models acritically: "They were created primarily for white middle-class children, yet were promoted as model solutions to a nationwide crisis."[13] If elementary schools were ideally single-story, indoor-outdoor classrooms, where did that leave children in high-density cities, children living in very cold or very hot environments, or children attending neighborhood schools where security concerns trump indoor-outdoor connectivity? The modern schoolroom shows that a generative demonstration, and the diffusion of innovation more generally, depends on careful redeployment of the model. Identification of the circumstances where a new iteration might be appropriate is related to the legibility of the prior demonstration's approach. Is Neutra's model demonstrating the importance of linking each single classroom's interior with an exterior space or of connecting outdoor space to a school's collection of classrooms? Among single-story schools that followed, single-loaded corridors of classrooms took the first lesson and classroom clusters tried the second, while higher-density, nonsuburban schools were unable to participate in the typological variants.

The needs associated with a housing crisis, manufacturing boom, and postwar population boom led to growth in particular types of architectural commissions. In this sense, generative demonstrations are historically and culturally specific. The examples above—Aravena's half-houses, Kahn's factories, Neutra's schools, cityLAB's backyard homes—show how designers responded. The most fecund demonstrations provide solid foundations for reducing uncertainty via plausibility, iterability, and open access and are realized by architecture that displays its intention to proliferate and leverages design to that effect. These same qualities open possibilities for the critical review of each iteration so that subsequent offspring are improved over time.

LEGIBLE POLICY

PEATONIÑOS, LABORATORIO PARA LA CIUDAD, MEXICO CITY

In Mexico City, a series of projects called Peatoniños, or Pedestrian Kids, temporarily closed streets to cars and marked them for neighborhood children's play. Peatoniños took hold for several reasons. Mexico City is a young city, with over a quarter of its population under the age of fifteen. In addition, poorer neighborhoods with the highest population of children have the least green space or parks and almost no dedicated play space. Finally, the city is oriented around the automobile, making it dangerous for pedestrians. The number of cars in the city more than doubled in the first two decades of the 2000s. The author Juan Villoro wrote about his 1960s childhood in Mexico City: "I would spend long hours sitting on a bench waiting for a car to pass, like some unusual spectacle. . . . The city in those days was so different that it's almost shocking it has the same name." He returns again and again to traffic congestion: "For people in cars, the map is a conjectural landscape transmitted by radio. . . . The inhabitant of Mexico City finds an impassable tide with the radio advising him to take 'alternative routes,' a name we ascribe to the parallel reality we cannot enter."[1] Pedestrian deaths in Mexico City exceed Mexico's national average, and Mexico has twice the world average when taking into account all road deaths. The most telling metric is that traffic-related accidents are the primary cause of death for children between five and fourteen years of age.[2]

FIGURE 6.1

Peatoniños, gathered on Paseo de la Reforma during Mexico City's Ciclovía, or Muévete en Bici (2016). Courtesy of Brenda Vértiz.

Peatoniños is an event-based initiative that shows how to make residents' "right to the city" visible to the public at large. Created in waves like the initiatives described earlier, the origins of Peatoniños can be traced back to the election of Mayor Miguel Ángel Mancera Espinosa and his establishment of the Laboratorio Para la Ciudad (which I'll refer to as the Lab) in 2013. The Lab existed throughout his tenure as mayor, closing in 2018. Written into the city's new municipal constitution as an administrative unit, Mayor Mancera proposed: "Laboratorio Para la Ciudad will facilitate the interaction between citizens and government . . . to think about the city as a whole, generating a bank of ideas and solutions, to build a city that supports and stimulates the imagination, a creative city."[3] From the outset, it was an experimental space for incubating pilot projects that engaged Mexico City residents "revealing the city to itself."[4] It is no surprise that the concept of legible policy arose from the Lab, which had a uniquely systematic way of undertaking, evaluating, and learning from its initiatives.

When the Lab began under the directorship of Gabriella Gómez-Mont, one of its six prioritized focal areas was called Ciudad Lúdica—the Playful City—and another was Ciudad Peatón, or Pedestrian City. The Lab's agenda was explicitly

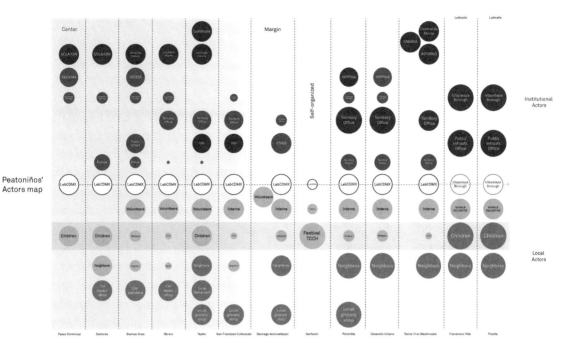

FIGURE 6.2

Data from twelve play street installations, including the five Peatoniños events with UCLA.
Courtesy of Brenda Vértiz, LabCDMX, INTORNO-Arquitectura, Urbanismo e Interconectividad S.C.,
Central de Muros.

guided by theory developed by French social philosopher and Marxist Henri Lefebvre about everyday life and residents' "right to the city." Extended by the geographer David Harvey, thinking about right to the city infused the Ciudad Lúdica focus. Building on the United Nations' landmark adoption of the Convention on the Rights of the Child on November 20, 1989, Mancera asserted a child's right to Mexico City. Given city conditions, Peatoniños, which began in the spring of 2016, combined children's play with safety, and its primary goal was protecting children while insuring that they thrive. It was expected that attending to the most vulnerable members of society would provide secondary benefits to all age groups. After twelve installations of play streets, Brenda Vértiz, leader of Peatoniños at the Lab and now a scholar of playful cities, confidently claims, "when children or adults are playing, they expose their most creative ways of living in and thinking about cities."[5]

Before Peatoniños, there was Peatonito (little pedestrian), a grown man dressed as an action hero. Data about traffic safety as well as personal experience motivated activist Jorge Cáñez to don the mask and cape of a traditional Mexican luchador. As Peatonito, Cáñez patrolled the streets of Mexico City with the goal of reducing traffic injuries and deaths to zero.[6] Cáñez, one of the "world's first pedestrian super-heroes,"[7] partnered with the Lab for several years in Mexico City, joining several Peatoniños street closures and adding another dose of playfulness.

For the pilot instantiation of Peatoniños, cityLAB, with the Lab's support, installed a Ciclovía station on Paseo de la Reforma on March 20, 2016. Mexico's Muévete en Bici (Move by Bike) began in 2007 and every Sunday takes over Mexico City's primary boulevard. Following Bogotá's 1974 bike activism, the Mexico City event has grown into one of Latin America's biggest government-sponsored open streets programs. Though the initiative was initially met with hostility, all twelve lanes of La Reforma and fifty-five kilometers of streets are now closed every Sunday morning with space dedicated for children's play and cycling lessons.[8] This public event prepared residents of the city for other temporary street closures, paving the way for Peatoniños. With little more than chalk, playground balls, matching T-shirts, questionnaires, and a sign, UCLA students and Lab members at Muévete en Bici began drawing on the street, inviting passing children to help

FIGURE 6.3

Jorge Cáñez, the superhero Peatonito, protects pedestrians against dangerous traffic. Photo by Hector Rios.

transform it into a play space. The team learned that a few more easily engaged and inexpensive props would be helpful: bubbles, empty cardboard boxes, jump ropes, crayons, balloons, hula-hoops, and soccer balls, along with chairs for the adults supervising the children. Signage and some overhead flags marked the space more clearly.

For the second, more formal iteration, again with cityLAB (and its sister program, the Urban Humanities Initiative), the Lab suggested a particular intersection in the Doctores neighborhood of Cuauhtémoc. The Peatoniños team fanned out through the community to talk to residents, shop owners, and children about their ideas for turning the street into a temporary play space and invited them to join. With help from the local police, who blocked traffic in the area, the auto body shop that provided power via extension cords, and Peatonito, who enlivened the group, this Peatoniños attracted many children and family members over the course of the day. The UCLA students and Lab team engaged children who came out to play, assisted by parents who played soccer with kids on a portion of the closed street and older women who sat in chairs watching their grandkids. Children made luchador masks and drawings at small tables, invented uses for cardboard boxes, played ball games, jumped rope, and generally ran wild. The most popular activity by far was chalk drawing. Very quickly, the double benefit of the activity became apparent: children "owned" the street by turning it into their own canvas, and their drawings made legible that something unique was occurring at the intersection, causing passersby to stop and inquire. The chalk drawings, Peatoniños signage on roadblocks, and team members in hot pink T-shirts all created a light framework of legible policy. Together these became part of a "toolkit for street closures." Observation and interview data collected by the cityLAB team during the Doctores street closure indicated that more than 90 percent of the children who came to play were under the age of eleven. All the parents felt that streets were generally not safe for play, and three-quarters of them wanted to see a weekly play street closed to traffic. About a third of the participants learned about the closure just by walking by, while half had seen a flyer posted in the neighborhood.[9]

Later iterations of Peatoniños, including three more with cityLAB members, occurred under the direction of Brenda Vértiz. Measured both in terms of the

FIGURE 6.4

Peatoniños and Peatonito in luchador masks on a play street in Mexico City (2016).
Photo by Gus Wendel.

FIGURE 6.5

Peatoniños in Mexico City. A few simple props like cardboard boxes and balloons can convert dangerous streets into imaginative play spaces (2018). Courtesy of INTORNO-Arquitectura, Urbanismo e Interconectividad SC.

number of children who came out to play and by the extent of community engagement, the most successful installations took place in the borough of Iztapalapa in suburban Mexico City. According to the Lab's summary of the Peatoniños initiative, eight more play streets were created by July 2018, averaging four hours with fifty children and seventeen adults and reaching the highest turnout of one hundred fifty children, thirty adults, and fifteen facilitators. In Iztapalapa, which has the most children and the least green space in Mexico City, Vértiz developed long-term partners in the municipal government and created a permanent play street.

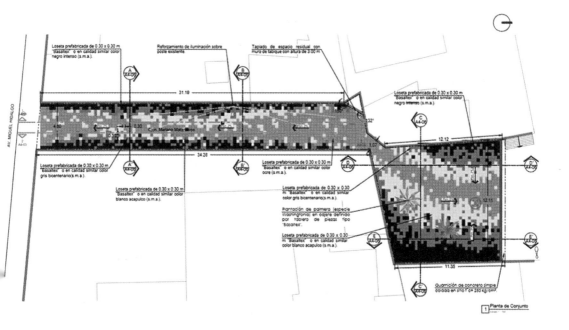

FIGURE 6.6

Plan for a permanent play street in Iztapalapa, showing paving patterns (2019). Courtesy of Brenda Vértiz, LabCDMX, INTORNO-Arquitectura, Urbanismo e Interconectividad S.C., Central de Muros.

FIGURE 6.7

Before: this street in Iztapalapa was selected to become a play street because it was uninviting to children and adults alike and could be closed to traffic. Courtesy of INTORNO-Arquitectura, Urbanismo e Interconectividad SC.

FIGURE 6.8

After: the same street, with paving plan and murals installed. Courtesy of LabCDMX, Central de Muros.

The Lab documented what it learned from the Peatoniños initiative, turning it into legible policy to be reproduced later and by other municipalities. The policy included sharing the vision of the project with neighbors, community leaders, and volunteers in advance; collaborating with a range of experts who can help translate, improve, and expand each street action; gathering metrics and documenting each intervention to improve the prototype; and creating a strategic plan of clear steps for replicating Peatoniños (including project stages, time frames, definition of roles, and indicators of success). Vértiz has since built a toolkit for the design of playstreets, which calls for adequate lighting, level surfaces for play, and shade (ideally from trees). In terms of siting, they must be located outside of hospital zones and without any intersecting streets. Beyond these few required elements, there are a range of design possibilities and recommendations in the toolkit, particularly about the processes of community engagement.

While Peatoniños models the development of legible policy, its design as a physical urban intervention has yet to fully evolve. Since the Lab was shuttered while it was still in its prime—when Mancera was voted out of office—there is no central agency to further the initiative outside of the Iztapalapa municipal government, and this too hinges on the reelection of the local mayor. Brenda Vértiz, who at the time of this writing is completing a PhD on urban play and spearheading a three-year implementation grant to install play streets, is now the primary force behind the initiative. When cityLAB and the Lab in Mexico City collaborated between 2016 and 2018, we imagined that Peatoniños would take place on an intermittent schedule on streets transformed with a branded identity to mark them as play streets. Following the modest design identity that began in Doctores, play streets would become familiar through patterned paving tiles at the points of closure, overhead signage, lamppost banners, and wall murals. A permanent set of play-props, such as the pop-up shade tents and chairs, would also be legible as part of the Peatoniños effort, wherever it was taking place. With a more advanced urban design strategy, the legibility of Peatoniños would be enhanced along with its urban impacts and participatory potential. While Peatoniños began as an event-based urban intervention much like Ciclovía, Vértiz concluded that permanent street closures were more effective—they could gather needed resources, follow good design guidelines, and be regularly maintained without requiring staffing, municipal support, and resources on an intermittent, impromptu basis.

Peatoniños demonstrated that when children's right to the city is exercised, they can reclaim some of its most dangerous spaces for their own play and for neighborhood socializing. The forcefulness of their reclamation, the commoning that play entails, and the joy expressed by the children are hardly captured by the term *legible policy*, and yet it was the unexpected urban imaginary of playing in dangerous streets that empowered Peatoniños. Its success hinged on the fact that those viewed as most vulnerable—the city's children—were the agents of transformation. Children destabilized modernist planning logics by taking over the space of heavy, deadly automobiles. "Disrupting established auto-centric understandings of street use transforms what collectively constitutes the largest amount of public space (that is, streets) as one where children actively have agency and authority."[10]

Legibility is another word for engaging the public.
—Sarah Whiting[11]

Policy shapes our built environment in ways that are usually described as incomprehensible or intrinsically complex, but such statements provide cover for rules that are followed without being understood. What if policy can be created, unpacked, and rematerialized in ways that put it back into public hands? If architecture and design can "translate" policy, laypeople would be able to participate in and argue about its ongoing evolution. This position is distinct from long-running arguments about whether architecture itself is legible, about the possibility of reading architecture as if it were a text, or about iconicity, historicism, or branding. The 2013 discussion published in *Log* between architect-educators Peter Eisenman and Sarah Whiting distills some of these debates, ending near the topic of this chapter. If some architects make buildings that speak primarily to fellow architects, while others make buildings for an attentive public, Whiting suggests these audiences are limited: "How do you form an audience . . . ? How do you have an impact? I think the interesting possibility is through policy and politics rather than through populism [and popular culture]."[12] For her, policy is created by politicians, and if architecture is to "intersect policy" it will do so by teaching politicians about architecture. I suggest instead that architecture can investigate policy, make it manifest, and evolve by learning from public engagement. Legible policy is cocreated with architecture.

Legible policy is defined as publicly accessible prototypes, pilot projects, or demonstrations that invite engagement via everyday life's informal processes as well as through formal political processes. Because it is observable, legible policy is a means to shape cities through public participation, partnerships, inclusion, and impacts and thereby to advance spatial justice. Prior chapters lay out guiding principles for architecture to grow more relevant to a wider public and build up to the notion of legible policy:

- Design is the lever that architects will use to create a more just built environment.
- The buildings most effective at advancing social goals will be designed to be radically public in that they are fresh, adaptable, and equitable.
- To suit this greater public, the design process and outcome will depend on partnerships of difference, within which debate and contestation are upheld.
- In turn, those partnerships will aim to create generative demonstrations that are intended to proliferate.

Such built demonstrations can sometimes be translated into policy that ensures ongoing public engagement. Though this may sound utopian, the case studies in each chapter show that the principles above emanate from architecture-in-the-making from around the world and from my own work at cityLAB. This chapter answers how it is that design can be leveraged into policy, which is an especially effective means by which prototypes can proliferate and subsequently evolve and improve.

With the right to the city as foundational for spatial justice, we can speculate about how that right can be enacted through public engagement in urban policy. But before taking that step, it is worth asking what—if any—role architecture plays in the right to the city. Is there also a right to the *architecture* of the city and, if so, what would that mean? At minimum it means that everyone is entitled to the aesthetic pleasure, accommodation, and dignity architecture brings. A concomitant right is embedded in our ability to effect change, or—put differently—to enact our agency. Performative theories of architecture argue that social practices, particularly by occupants, continuously reproduce the spaces of everyday life.[13] Buildings, once "completed," are inevitably adapted by their inhabitants. Within architectural history, the poster child for this view is Le Corbusier's Pessac development in southwestern France. The 1920s worker housing was not planned to be adaptable but, according to Philippe Boudon, was so stark that early residents were motivated to change it.[14] They used the buildings as a canvas for personalization, obscuring the clean modernist linearity by adding brickwork and do-it-yourself ornament, enclosing rooftop terraces and outdoor stairs. The process of transformation circles back to more recent residents who have instituted "preservation" regulations that peel decoration away to return to the original form. Occupants like those at Pessac are not passive recipients, consumers, or patrons of architecture as if it were a completed work of art—they are agents of ongoing engagement and self-expression.

For occupants and publics to be active agents rather than consumers, they must have the time, skills, money, and authority to manipulate their surroundings. Informal building depends on this, but the same practices in formal building systems are delegitimated by structures of property and ownership. Efforts like those at Pessac are undertaken by owners or tenants with long-term, secure tenure, primarily in the context of housing. Other building types like office buildings, schools, factories, and public institutions are essentially regulated by management. As a result, changes by occupants are more likely to be superficial. Office workers are "allowed" to display family photographs on their desks and school administrators may "approve" a mural by students. If factory workers want better ventilation, lighting, break rooms, or safety measures, they advocate through their unions or organize a protest. When it comes to architecture, agency is either a privilege tied to ownership and tenure or a form of resistance.

The notion of architecture as an aesthetic project realized through practical, legible policy represents an alternative to more common readings of buildings as lived-expression. Instead, as the Peatoniños initiative suggests, generative design demonstrations can go one further by inscribing into policy the means to make themselves available for public engagement and adaptation. An important lesson from Peatoniños is how fragile temporary generative demonstrations can be. Such interventions—and the complications of realizing them with a full complement of resources like local community support, funding, materials, expertise, and sites—are difficult to sustain. The lack of rigidity and investment is both a strength and a challenge of temporary design practices. Architectural activism by definition relies on a shifting base of support and, because of this, elevates the importance of policy as well as legislation as the means to carry an initiative forward. Legible policy extends the life of activist design practices, guarding against their collapse. Legible policy here represents the potential for an initiative to live on through continued public engagement codified in both material form as well

FIGURE 6.9

Pessac, Cité Frugès, Le Corbusier, 1926. In this row of houses, transformations by occupants are visible in the white facade compared to the units beyond, which reflect a more recent priority on the preservation of Corbusier's original design (2015). Photo by corno.fulgur75.

as through more conventional understanding of policies: as texts that explain the principles of action as well as their potential for future adaptation.

As explained earlier, if generative demonstrations are to proliferate intelligently, each iteration will learn from its predecessors. Public policies, enacted through laws and regulations, are intended for this purpose; they establish guidelines, goals, and rules for future projects. Policy documents outline the principles for collective action. Legible policy and its legislative results exist in places where governmental systems dominate, as in most of the developed world. In regions where informal urban growth is the rule, formal urban laws struggle to keep up with the extraordinary growth.[15] The Peatoniños projects in Mexico toggled between formality and informality, and the team at the Lab understood how to work effectively in both domains. There were regulations governing temporary street closures, but once these were followed and official permissions were granted, the participation of local police or neighboring business owners was more ad hoc. It is not surprising that legible policy as a concept arose from this context, where a progressive governmental organization like the Lab was structured around visible community and grassroots participation. Legible policy's applicability to even heavily bureaucratic urban regimes depends on the same principles; any successful participatory urban intervention must be made apparent to a wider public. Parklets and parking space dining areas that cropped up during the pandemic offer an American example. When they began to proliferate in different cities, the enabling policy was less apparent than their demonstrated logics and success. Many cities rushed emergency legislative reform to catch up with the parklets, searching for long-term strategies to keep them in place and ensure compatible design. Most of us—that is, the public—assume that laws have been put in place if the parklets remain.

Parallel to Hayden White's distinction between practical and professional knowledge, a practical policy would be legible to the public while professional policy is inscrutable to anyone but lawyers and planners. For example, because some residents of the incremental houses at Iquique built taller than the original structures were meant to safely grow, Elemental built physical limits on subsequent iterations. Above the second floor in the Constitución development the cap is shaped like a typical residential roofline. The outlined roof is a legible

FIGURE 6.10

Housing "caps" are legible policy, open for self-building (top) and filled in by residents (bottom).
Villa Verde in Constitución, Chile. Courtesy of Alejandro Aravena, Elemental.

policy quite directly showing the boundary of future additions. We could contrast that to professional policy, which is illegible to the public yet is ironically a written record of the rules. Such policy and legislation may be legally necessary and accessible to professional planners, but they are rarely read by do-it-yourself builders or the public. The practical form of legible policy might be called "indicative"—that is, it offers accessible evidence about itself to the public. Thus, while effective legislation is formally defined by professional policy, the principles of spatial justice add the goal of practical legible policy.

LEGIBLE POLICY IN ACTION

The term *legible policy* was coined and refined by Gabriella Gómez-Mont, director of the Lab in Mexico City. For the most part, the idea evolved through the Lab's actions, but in 2016, she and international colleagues authored a collection of essays on legible policy. Gómez-Mont's own contributions offer loose definitions: "I believe we have spent too much time thinking that policy begins and ends with laws or interventions on the physical infrastructure. . . . Unusual ideas and powerful metaphors can be so much more effective in making important changes within society. . . . True legibility begins when one is enticed into actively becoming part of the [city's] unfolding story. . . . The more deeply and creatively we understand what is at stake, the better decisions we can make as a society." Gómez-Mont wants to "prototype the city" so that open-access experiments abound, along with citizen engagement. Other contributors to the volume offer more conventional definitions, like this one from urban data expert John Lynch: "If a policy is actively discussed, before, during and after implementation, the relevant authority has at least demonstrated positive momentum towards policy legibility. . . . Beyond legibility . . . is true participation in the policymaking process, the adoption and implementation of policies, and the process of iterating policy over time in response to the changing needs of the city."[16]

Lynch's idea of policy and legibility is more limited than Gómez-Mont's, but both talk about "true" participation or legibility. In their use, truth implies direct lived experience, unmediated by government requirements and with the potential for political implications. Still, for Lynch, as for most planners and civic leaders, true participation is *about* some formal policy for the city and is legible when participants are continuously involved. For the Lab in Mexico City and in this book, participation is actively *within* the city, part of everyday life, and urban policies can materialize in physical prototypes. This type of legible policy can include a blockaded street for pedestrian use and not merely the written policy or rules that enable the closure. Playing in a street closed to traffic is then as true a form of participation as attendance at any meeting about urban transformation. With legible policy, the policymaking process looks more like everyday life than political wrangling in city hall. Like Peatoniños, the public is invited to cocreate places through use over the course of multiple demonstrations. Children do not need to attend a meeting in order to make their desires known, but they can play in a safe street and show us how it works. This is research-in-action, or participation *in* rather than participation *about*. Lived policymaking like this depends on actors' agency, in which participants make free choices in space and time.

Such active agency is clear evidence of exercising the right to the city. When residents opt in to particular ways of engaging their city, they are enacting their spatial rights. And if generative demonstrations embed legible ways for residents to actively engage unexpected urban changes, then subsequent iterations have the possibility of learning and improving. Ciclovía may be the best-known example of a global legible policy—the policy that cars can be removed from city streets to give them back to nonmotorized activities. Over four hundred cities worldwide, from Bangalore to Ottawa, temporarily close streets to traffic. On Sundays across Latin America, Ciclovía invites myriad possibilities, and its evolution—significant expansion from several blocks to a network of streets, the addition of city-sponsored booths where recreational gear is available, and the incorporation of street performances—has been guided by popular demand. Public legibility is measured directly by how many people come out, how long they spend, how much fun they are having, where they hang out, and whether people of all ages are engaged. Ciclovía street closures are legible policy in action. It was no coincidence that the Peatoniños experiment began at Mexico City's Muévete en Bici.

Although overlapping, we can distinguish legible policy from cities' open participation platforms by which citizens vote in some fashion for their desired outcome. For example, Mexico City crowdsourced part of its governance under the leadership of Mayor Mancera when in 2015 he began the process of engaging the public in the creation of the city's first constitution. Legible policy also involves open participatory processes, but in less formal and less governmental ways. It is probably only planners who imagine an ideal of citizen participation that involves the creation, implementation, and evolution of all policy. Most citizens would prefer not to expend time except when policies that are relevant to their own lives are taking shape. If legible policy makes people more aware of the rules that regulate their everyday life, then architects play a key role in designing publicly visible, intelligible spaces and buildings. By so doing, people gain agency over the tacit rules that govern our collective action. For Peatoniños, play streets evolved from temporary barricades, chalk, balls, and banners to permanent installations of tiled surfaces, painted walls, tree planting, lighting, and play structures. Permanent play streets legibly demonstrate that children have a right to the city, building expectations among all residents that streets can and should be safe.

Since practical legible policy is cocreated through public action, the role of planners, architects, and policymakers will take different forms. One obvious role in cocreation is to formalize legible policy when needed into professional, legislative language. But they can also reflect, challenge, instigate, and design spatial policy so that it becomes publicly accessible. Sometimes policy begins with legible flaws in the existing policy framework. That is, policies evolve to solve problems that have been identified in the real world.

In some cases, a social movement arises to transform unjust conditions by making them not only publicly visible but also intelligible. Legible policy has played a historically documented role within social movements as well as within policymaking and legislation.[17] The nineteenth-century housing reform movement of philanthropists and social advocates was substantially advanced with the publication of Jacob Riis's startling book of photographs, *How the Other Half Lives*, published in 1890. The book and subsequent housing policy comprise a perfect story about legibility. Riis was an early adopter of flashbulb photography, which allowed him to document the dark interiors of crowded tenement life otherwise hidden from public view. The autoethnographic book of photographs, along with Riis's explicit texts about smells and experiential qualities of tenement life from which he himself emerged, were considered factual evidence of the need for housing policy for the poor.[18] In letters, President Theodore Roosevelt told his photographer friend that the book substituted for in-person visits to places like sweatshops. Through powerful photo documentation, Riis made visible and legible immigrants' spaces of injustice.

Subsequent housing reform was created with the expectation that increasing habitability would also be increasingly apparent. Reformers who saw whole families living in rooms with no windows lobbied for early laws that specified every room needed light and ventilation, and they expected to see those windows in new residential buildings. But builders skirted the intent by creating tight "dumbbell" plans for tall buildings with minuscule light wells in order to comply. In 1901, the subsequent "New Law" specified building height, lot coverage, and minimum courtyard dimensions.[19] The loopholes around light and ventilation were closed (or at least tightened) because they were visibly in conflict with the intent of the regulation. Legislation intended to accomplish policy goals can produce loopholes, inadvertent oversights, and unintended consequences. Even though lawmakers create regulations to be flawless, they must watch what happens when a law is enacted to determine whether it met the policy goals. Tenement reform demonstrates how architecture intersects with legible policy, not unlike the lived-in Quinta Monroy housing.

LEGIBILITY IN GENERATIVE DEMONSTRATIONS

Those projects that are intended to proliferate hold the capacity—even the responsibility—to go further in their public orientation by incorporating ways to gather community partnerships and feedback as the prototype evolves. Legible policy is one such means insofar as the model broadcasts its intentions. Moreover, it becomes a sign toward possible futures that were previously difficult to imagine. A generative demonstration is intrinsically the kind of material outcome that should become legible policy. Perhaps the best-known legible policy, mentioned earlier, is the former New York City Department of Transportation Commissioner Janette Sadik-Khan's creation of over sixty pedestrian plazas. Starting with tactical temporary interventions like colorfully painted streets furnished with plastic chairs, food trucks, and traffic barriers, some spaces evolved into permanent public space. Nimble transformation allowed the city to test ideas, monitor community reaction, and adapt quickly. Evidence was collected in the form of traffic counts, accidents, public reaction, and the financial repercussions for local businesses, and the data was studied before permanently redesigning streets into plazas.[20] As material and procedural transformations, the temporary public space interventions were so evident—so legible—and so low-risk that cities around the world have implemented their own plaza programs.

New York's temporary street plazas are the kind of generative prototype that is well suited to become a legible policy. Like Peatoniños, the designed space is part of the public realm, visible to passersby who can join the activity and offer opinions about how it might be improved or where else it might be installed. The installations function as built or 3D diagrams because the basic ideas are communicated schematically, with the expectation that they can be transformed in subsequent projects. In practice, generative demonstrations invite viewers to investigate what is going on (that is, to "read" them) because they are by definition unconventional responses to some common condition. The colorful jellybean-like study pod for UCLA, described in the next chapter, is both shelter bed and library carrel, but it looks like nothing anyone has seen before, calling out to be explored and understood. The material form of a delightful temporary accommodation or streets reclaimed for play or plazas establishes a new spatial category. Other solutions are more easily imagined once legible policies have been established in real space and in our shared experience.

RAMPING AS LEGIBLE POLICY

Enacting architecture as both politics and form, engaged and autonomous, is at the heart of legible policy that goes beyond written guidelines. The proposition outlined here considers legible policy as a physical, open-access demonstration of those guidelines, such that political goals and rules are visible in an evolving built environment. The proposition is based first in the construct of legible policy and second in the concepts of *ramping* and *curb cutting* from critical disability studies. So that legible policy does not slip into easy narratives of reading material form, "curb cutting disrupts the concretized status quo through acts of rematerialization,"[21] while ramping explicitly implies moving from one existing reality to another, bridging and making connections for public access.

Legible policy defines a path to the intersection of architecture and policy through which architects and urban designers leverage design to make those policies and make the built environment available for subsequent adaptation. By so doing, architecture acknowledges its collusion with power and seeks to undo it. This can be subversive, as when designers knowingly deviate from formal and informal norms (e.g., by leaving half of an affordable housing unit unbuilt). Or it can be tactical, through interventions meant to call attention to an issue (e.g., painting asphalt green and blocking traffic). But to turn such practices into legible policy, the material artifact needs to be accountable in some way and mark its policy agenda. According to critical disabilities scholar Aimi Hamraie in a lecture at UC Berkeley, "even while technologies and material forms may promise justice or equity, their entanglement with systems of discrimination and domination also demand different forms of accountability."[22]

In its ideal formulation, legible policy anticipates future ramping by creating urban guidelines (rather than fixed rules) whose adaptability is apparent to residents in physical form. When residents experience the material shape of at least some part of urban legislation, they can also engage their agonistic agency to change it, support it, use it, or fight against it. Following Hamraie, unlike the liberal imaginary of a "seamless, smooth, a cross-cutting plane from point A to point B, paving over physical and attitudinal barriers," here ramping signifies friction, noncompliance, and the forceful building of connections to overcome political and physical blockades. Ramping, as a metaphor for political leverage in the built environment, references Parent and Virilio's oblique function in which sloped architectural surfaces produce destabilizing effects. Ramping adds to their theory the agency of inhabitants not just to adapt to existing inclined planes, but also to make and mark the metaphorical ramp.

The role of architecture in manifesting shared agreements embedded in policy is significant. All kinds of urban forms constitute legible policy. Building and planning codes, such as those dictating building height, entryway sizes, and stair treads, reflect norms about our common good. For example, the simple six-inch curb tells us a lot: who is considered an average pedestrian (someone who can readily negotiate a six-inch step), where pedestrians and vehicles are to be channeled, that the separation between them is one of mutual trust (since either could "jump" the barrier), that a public entity creates this standardized infrastructure, where stormwater is directed, and more. Over time, shared agreements grow stable and their underlying policies grow into tacit norms.

What is unclear, however, is how that curb might be renegotiated. Embedded in the now-familiar corner curb cut is the fraught history of a worldwide accessibility movement—the decades-long political activism that challenged just who was part of the "common" good. That movement resisted the stigmatized status of inclusion as *being in need*, and evolved into a civil rights initiative demanding full rights to the city. The critical disabilities movement's most visible challenge is told in the curb cut, which demonstratively invites personal wheeled vehicles to move smoothly across what had been a barrier. Lest the smooth narrative forget the radical "crip interventions" that occurred from the late 1960s until 1990, when the ADA was made into law, sledgehammer wielding activists cracked into curbs and made their own ramps where curbs blocked access.[23] Such a seemingly small formal gesture, just six inches of topography and its slope allowing universal access, makes implicitly legible a variety of shared agreements constituted in policy. The sidewalk's design also contains in-progress negotiations, such as textured markings of the transition from sidewalk to street for visually impaired pedestrians. In Japan, sidewalks are adorned with tenji blocks, bright yellow tactile paving for the visually impaired, establishing new practices that may turn into global standards much like road signage for traffic safety. The standard of accessibility continues to evolve toward universal design of the built environment to serve the widest range of bodies, stages in the life cycle, and mobilities.[24]

Legible policies can be read throughout cities, such as when a guardhouse marks the entrance to a gated community, when a wall is capped in concertina wire, or when a Confederate monument dominates a public park. One might

FIGURE 6.11

Disabilities activists undertook the Walk of Shame in March 1988 to protest Hollywood's inaccessible Walk of Fame after a man in a wheelchair who had no safe paths of travel was struck and killed by a motorist. Sledgehammers to the curbs made it clear that activists would wait no longer for ramping to begin. © Tom Olin Collection, MSS-294, Ward M. Canaday Center for Special Collections, The University of Toledo Libraries.

FIGURE 6.12

At the Walk of Shame in 1988, activists installed Hollywood Boulevard's first ramp, a piece of street theater but also a sign of the simple solution that had yet to be adopted by the city. This kind of resistance laid the groundwork for passage of the Americans with Disabilities Act in 1990. © Tom Olin Collection, MSS-294, Ward M. Canaday Center for Special Collections, The University of Toledo Libraries ask: If the built environment is susceptible to engaged adaptation, what happens when injustice predominates in communities with spatial histories of discrimination? We need only look around us to see what happens. Confederate monuments that have remained in public spaces for one hundred fifty years after the end of the Civil War are the target of political resistance; many have finally been removed. Historians of these monuments argue that the statues were not only memorials to a past cause but also messengers about an intended future. Since monuments donated to or created by a municipality become government speech, when displayed in a public place (itself a public forum) they legally and symbolically narrate the public point of view.[25] Likewise, racist suburban landscapes persist today, and their embedded injustices are proving difficult to redress. In urban sociologist Sharon Zukin's words, the built environment consists of "landscapes of power," where forces of economic might and White racial dominance create and destroy the built environment.[26]

To be clear: architecture, urban design, and infrastructure all manifest underlying policies. And like other forms of agonistic democracy, the results—in this case, the shape of the built environment—depend on ongoing contestation. If architecture is always in some way public, making the governing policies legible to its public is part of architecture's responsibility. As is made clear in the recent violence surrounding controversial monuments worldwide—from the memorial to General Baquedano in Plaza de la Dignidad in Santiago, Chile, to the deadly protests in Charlottesville, Virginia—the public plainly comprehends that material environments convey significant political messages. Consistent with this understanding of how we interpret the built environment, our public spaces, monuments, and buildings not only memorialize the past and configure the present but also point toward the future.

CRITICAL JUNCTURES

BRUINHUB AT UCLA, CITYLAB, LOS ANGELES

In California in the late 2010s nearly one-third of all higher education students were housing insecure and food insecure, and a full 20 percent of California's community college students had experienced homelessness in the prior year. Starting in 2020, the coronavirus pandemic worsened the housing crisis, and college administrators realized that when campuses reopened in the fall of 2021, their students would face even greater set backs. Few solutions were on the horizon.

The housing situation at the University of California Los Angeles (UCLA) in 2021 was particularly dire. The university is squeezed between wealthy neighborhoods to the north and east and a four-hundred-acre Veterans Affairs compound to the west, leaving UCLA's forty-six thousand students to compete for apartments crammed into a small residential zone adjacent to campus. Because that neighborhood serves a captive market, the rents are the highest in the state of California, and with the exception of Manhattan, in the nation.[1] Despite ambitious dormitory construction, fewer than half of undergraduate students live in university housing, with the rest renting private housing, many with long commutes to campus. In a 2019 cityLAB survey conducted with UCLA Transportation Services, 43 percent of commuting students said their commute took more than sixty minutes each way. After long days at school, rather than braving traffic to get home only to return the next morning, 42 percent of these students had remained overnight on or near campus.[2] From a series of focus groups, we learned the reasons for living far from campus were most often more affordable rent, living with family, or living near work, but every student had a unique reason. At the extremes were students like Christian, completing his PhD with a four-hour commute involving four intermodal transit shifts: a car ride to the train station at four in the morning, debarking an hour later at Union Station for a bus to West LA to catch another bus to campus. No wonder students were sleeping in their cars and in classroom buildings, renting the floor of a dorm room midweek, or couch surfing.

Los Angeles, including the UCLA vicinity, had reached a critical housing juncture. In that context, those who are housing insecure experience a precarious condition that wavers between being precipitously behind on bills to being evicted onto the street. Its roots are as complex as solutions must be, since the universal goal of permanent affordable housing is so distant. In Los Angeles, seventy thousand people sleep unsheltered on a given night, and although social services found homes for twenty-three thousand people in 2019, an even greater number became homeless that same year. At cityLAB, we had been questioning how architects might address the immense problems of unhoused Angelenos when we realized we could start right on our own campus. Because a student identity is temporary and their experience of housing insecurity is unstable, alternatives to long-term housing rose as worthy considerations. We formulated a *continuum of accommodation* with a place to nap at one end, a dorm somewhere in the middle, and an apartment at the other, and sought spaces along that continuum where design could be transformative. Student advocacy was growing for "safe parking," (parking areas where individuals can sleep overnight in cars, often including some forms of security, services, and assistance) viewed by campus administrators as a last resort they hoped to avoid.

Initially, the cityLAB team led by Gus Wendel partnered with UCLA's Housing Services to identify potential design-related cost efficiencies, since the least expensive dorms cost twice as much as living at home. The campus had experimented with higher-density dorms, but there was little demand for the eight-person, two-bedroom arrangement. Students had two principal complaints about the apartments: the ad hoc crush of bunkbeds with minimal storage or study space

EXTREME COMMUTES

Thousands of UCLA students experience long (60+ minutes) and extreme (90+ minutes) commutes. These students have diverse motivations for their commutes, and face a wide variety of challenges, but have proposed simple solutions to improve their academic life. Through a series of focus groups, we connected with these students to hear their stories and brainstorm solutions together.

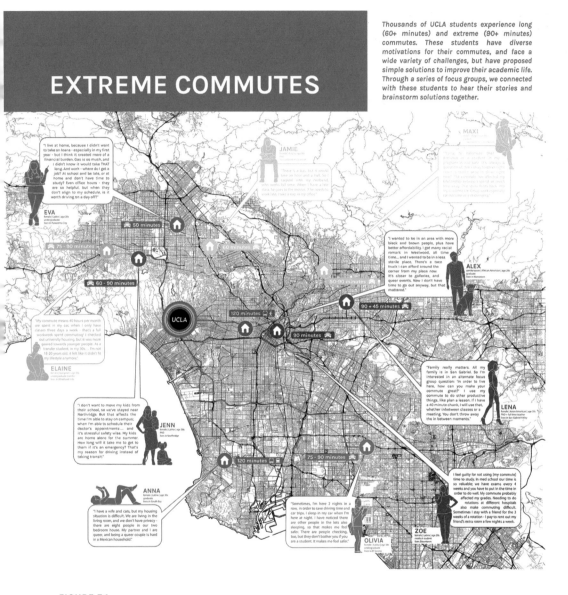

FIGURE 7.1

Map of Los Angeles showing a range of UCLA student commuter stories (2019). Image by Rayne Laborde Ruiz, courtesy of cityLAB.

Park Bench   PodShare   Dormitory   Cohousing   Apartment   House

FIGURE 7.2

In response to the housing crisis, cityLAB created the continuum of accommodation to define shelter as a typological range in which the mid-range options have been understudied (2020). Image by Melissa Peter Rovner, courtesy of cityLAB.

and the difficulty of finding eight compatible roommates. We intended to leverage design to find more creative, humane solutions to the ubiquitous problem of universities packing students into small rooms and the parallel overcrowding in private housing due to high rents. We collaborated with architect-educator Marta Nowak to generate furnishing schemes for compact dorm life and formed what seemed a fortuitous partnership with a global furniture maker. If Robert Probst's Action Office system could transform the workplace, perhaps a dorm room system could transform college residential life. Nowak's provocative ideas stimulated forward-looking conversations with Housing Services partners, but the industry group latched onto our most conventional ideas and quickly leaped into production issues, thwarting further research or student engagement. A primary reason this direction failed, in retrospect, was because we collaborated with industry prematurely—that is, prior to refining the concept in the form of a demonstration project. Early, radical ideas were summarily rejected in favor of more familiar solutions, like desks that fold down when beds stow away, which were promptly tested against industry's conventional construction systems.

Westwood Chateau

resident x8

bed x8

dresser w/ fold-out desk x8

folding chair x8

bathroom x2

Westwood Chateau 2-8 UCLA University Apartments	
number of residents:	8
approx square footage:	980
monthly cost per person:	$525.67
number of bedrooms:	2
number of bathrooms:	2
per person:	
approx square footage:	122.5
number of bedrooms:	.25
number of bathrooms:	.25

FIGURE 7.3

This axonometric drawing shows UCLA's existing high-density apartments with two bedrooms for eight roommates and crowded furnishing (2018). Image by Joshua Nelson, courtesy of cityLAB.

FIGURE 7.4

These three dormitory densification concepts invent room furnishings to ease the experience of overcrowding in typical college dorm rooms. The Minimum Module at left too quickly became the favorite of furniture industry partners. Designed by Marta Nowak of AN.ONYMOUS architects with UCLA Architecture and Urban Design students. Courtesy of cityLAB.

During our dorm densification studies, an underrepresented and poorly served group of students kept reappearing: long-distance commuters who spent very long days on campus, arriving early and leaving late to avoid traffic. With Nowak, we examined the ways that universities accommodate such students who need to nap on campus. Two images captured the inadequacy: the difficulty of finding ways to rest on Harvard Yard chairs and the uninviting cots in the University of Michigan's napping station. The first was, according to students of Harvard's Nap Space Project, a way to "embrace the springtime weather–lean back in a multicolored chair, lie down in the grass,"[3] pleasant if ad hoc; the second might be somewhat more comfortable, but far more stigmatized. In contrast to the uncomfortable chair and the shelter bed, there had to be better solutions. First, Nowak and her students drew up new lawn furniture that we scattered into photos of the UCLA campus. These over-scaled, fruit-like lounges effectively caught the imagination of students and administrators, and we found a small amount of funding to conduct a series of focus groups with long-distance commuters. In addition, the UCLA Transportation Services and cityLAB sent out the aforementioned questionnaire, the first of its kind, to learn more about commuter students' everyday experiences as well as their housing. In addition to the survey and focus groups, we used other means to reach out: exhibitions with publications like *My Commute is Hell*, multiple presentations to campus groups, media exposure, and ongoing collaboration with commuter student organizations. The design of the lawn lounge furniture was appealing enough to convince campus administrators to explore a dedicated commuter lounge, and attention turned to the Wooden Recreation Center at the heart of campus, with its 24/7 schedule, student health commitment, and access to infrastructure like showers, restrooms, and lockers, and security.

Relatively quickly, the coalition identified two adjacent squash courts that might become the BruinHub, and Nowak's team of students created alternatives that took advantage of the height of the courts. Input from students and administrators led to a surprising tower of study pods that rose up through the center of the courts. Still just a concept, an animated rendering showed students arriving at a check-in desk, chatting, and climbing the stairs to occupy individual pods (see figure 7.9). We kept the evolving design and its engaging renderings in

FIGURE 7.5

Harvard Yard's supply of metal chairs makes resting or napping rather uncomfortable. Courtesy of Management Consulted.

FIGURE 7.6

The Napping Station at University of Michigan is so bare-bones that it stigmatizes those who need a place to nap. Photo by Patrick Record, courtesy of the Ann Arbor News.

FIGURE 7.7

Rendering of an early version of strawberry and lemon study pods on UCLA lawn (2019). Image by Marta Nowak, AN.ONYMOUS architects, and UCLA students, courtesy of cityLAB.

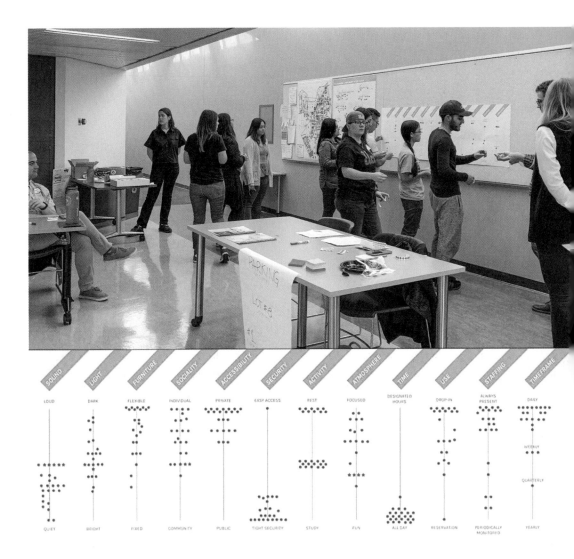

FIGURE 7.8

Student commuters in a focus group indicate their preferences for a future commuter lounge (top, 2019). Data from focus groups was rendered into a readily understood infographic (bottom, 2020). Courtesy of cityLAB.

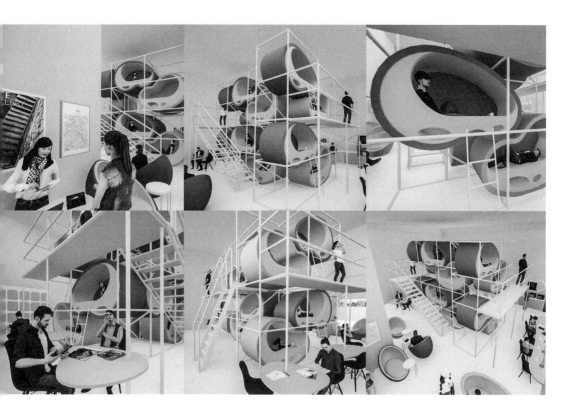

FIGURE 7.9

Clips from an animated rendering of the two-story, two-squash-court concept for the BruinHub (2020). Assembled by Miranda Hirujo-Rincon. Image by Marta Nowak, AN.ONYMOUS architects, and UCLA students, courtesy of cityLAB.

the public eye to remind participants that we were still hard at work, create constituencies, and, not least, gather input about the design direction. A steadfast team of administration advocates formed and met every three weeks for more than a year.

Nowak's pods were the perfect lure—optimistic, surprising, attractive, and accommodating—to form a coalition that weathered the long game from conception to implementation. Surprisingly, no one ever suggested the pods were impractical, which is a common response to design that does not *look* economical. In part, this was because senior administrators were advocates and because the pods were indeed functional, based on requests from students who would use them. And those students, primarily students of color who had been marginalized by the university, were widely deemed "deserving" as long-distance commuters. Another reason we met little resistance was because the giant jellybean-like pods are bespoke objects clearly designed for delight, and they arrived at a juncture after pandemic closures when delight was in a crisis of its own.

A set of critical factors aligned, or could be made to align, that would help push a well-meaning but conservative institution and its decision-makers toward an experimental solution. The housing crisis in California and around campus was the most significant. The coronavirus pandemic focused state legislative action on student needs. The Budget Act of 2019 (Assembly Bill 74) authorized $15 million in funding for the food and housing needs of students at UC campuses, a portion of which was allocated "to support rapid rehousing efforts assisting homeless and housing insecure students" and for "establishing ongoing emergency housing procedures, including on-campus and off-campus resources."[4] The BruinHub received a small grant from these funds and was awarded a competitive, UC-wide Innovation Grant for a "dedicated and safe 24-hour space on campus for long-distance commuting students to study, store belongings, and rest" bringing the total budget for implementation to $225,000.[5] The stature and amount of these funds were significant within UCLA and lent momentum to cityLAB's efforts. The funds produced ten study and napping pods, purchased the furniture and finishes to outfit a single squash court, and paid for minimal transformations that readied the squash court (including fire safety and electrical). Wooden and UCLA's Student Affairs division—both dedicated to student well-being in a broad sense—provided staff, necessary online platforms, and ongoing management.

A combination of factors within the architects' control and situated within powerful conditions framed by the pandemic and the deepening housing crisis created the critical juncture that sustained this unconventional project over time. First, the foundation for the BruinHub was systematically grounded in evidence about student needs as well as input from students about solutions. The team turned the research outcomes from the transportation survey and focus groups into infographics to present at every opportunity, always before showing the design solutions (figure 7.8). Second, the pods and their two-story structure within the squash courts always surprised viewers to whom we presented the project, and they were dedicated to students in need who were working hard to gain their degrees. Members of the commuting student group themselves became strong advocates for the project. Finally, cityLAB's design output—including the novel animation produced by Nowak's team, a full-scale prototype that we tested and showed widely throughout the pandemic, and the schematic design for a squash court—was intended to erode disbelief. With one actual pod and a real site, the BruinHub had an imaginable future that seemed plausible.

Many people pushed the project forward for more than two years, yet more hurdles remained. One restricted the lounge to just one court rather than two, which prevented a two-story solution from further design development. Another threatened overnight use of the lounge. Nevertheless, in September of 2021, just in time to welcome students back to campus after a year and a half of remote learning, the BruinHub launched with great fanfare. Since that time, the pods, study desks, and lounge areas have been full of commuters who register for free for a BruinHub pass online—the space remains reserved for those who need it most. Registration comes with a spate of services, and, for the first time, not only can the university identify students who may be on the brink of homelessness, but UCLA's commuter students have a home away from home at UCLA.

FIGURE 7.10

After building and testing the first prototype pod, a film scenery shop fabricated four more (2021). Photo by Gus Wendel, courtesy of cityLAB.

FIGURE 7.11

A typical day at the BruinHub in fall 2021. Photo by Dana Cuff, courtesy of cityLAB.

In cities around the world, new additions to any streetscape look surprisingly similar to those down the road. The protocols for schools, offices, big-box retail, multifamily housing, and other building types seem hard and fast. That is because the production of the built environment is highly constrained by structural conditions that form a stable pattern for reproducing architecture that is already known. Thus, in everyday circumstances the status quo prevails, and we get more of what we already have, with only slight variations. The evidence is pervasive: segregated cities reproduce themselves, commercial developers build basically the same office tower again and again, social housing units are interchangeable, and public institutions only hire architects who have a portfolio of similar buildings. Since architecture requires major capital and political investment, conservative tendencies are particularly potent.

Despite the pull toward convention, architectural and urban innovation characterizes each of the sites featured in this book. What enabled those projects to break from customary practices? In each case, the status quo was unsettled by some change in conditions, nowhere more dramatic than the Great East Japan Earthquake. Although the Japanese government intended to rebuild by relying on emergency engineering solutions, architectural collaboratives resisted by providing creative design alternatives. At the BruinHub, general recognition that students were facing dire housing and commuting conditions helped mobilize the coalition that implemented the project.

Innovative buildings, particularly those that require public engagement, often stem from what can be called *critical junctures*. A critical juncture involves some tangle of problematic forces that are widely shared and publicly understood. The recognition of these forces weakens the fundamental constraints that reproduce the status quo and heightens the contingencies leading to change. A critical juncture represents a change in the *context* for architecture, making possible the kinds of world-building transformations that spatial justice initiatives require. Such shared forces of change include economic shifts, catastrophes, social movements, powerful agencies, and even charismatic individuals. When design solutions untangle problematic conditions, not only making them clear but also overcoming some of them, architectural innovation is possible. For architecture, a critical juncture is defined by a destabilization of the intersecting networks that maintain the status quo where leveraging design can accelerate or redirect incremental environmental change into more sustained transformation. This final chapter about spatial justice discusses critical junctures as the context in which the other potentialities become effective. An appropriate critical juncture can lead to conditions that enable architects to leverage design and create radically public architecture, partnerships of difference, generative demonstrations, and legible policy.

Architects believe—and sometimes demonstrate—that ideas themselves, as well as their built results, have the power to catalyze collective action. Catalytic architectural ideas are self-consciously dependent on context, and they are not only shaped by that context but contribute to it, forming part of a critical juncture. Previously elaborated examples demonstrated how design supercharges desired outcomes during critical junctures. In eastern Japan, ArchiAid used architectural means to empower communities displaced by the tsunami. The BruinHub pods magnetized a coalition to persist through multiple barriers to implementation. Most surprisingly, the BIHOME became the poster child for secondary units even though it was only ever a full-scale mock-up. Architecture was a means to make a critical juncture effective in each instance, and powerful and optimistic design ideas fueled real transformation.

Because the built environment's status quo is characterized by social inequity in which race, economic power, and privilege are inscribed, by definition spatial justice advances through the breaking of conventions. This reasoning drives the influence of creative design visions that have both formal integrity and imaginative possibility.

The power of design ideas to catalyze a critical juncture as well as potential unforeseen or unacknowledged side effects is exemplified by the concept for Atlanta's BeltLine by Ryan Gravel, who was an architecture student at the Georgia Institute of Technology in 1999. In his thesis, Gravel illustrated how an abandoned industrial rail line could become a new, 33-mile, 6,500-acre linear park that encircled the city and linked together as many as forty mainly low-income, Black neighborhoods. A project as comprehensive as the BeltLine demonstrates that some critical junctures are activated by the project itself, which makes visible its own logic. As the decades-long work on the BeltLine progressed, its potential grew, as did its pitfalls (including significant gentrification and displacement of nearby residents). The first segment of Gravel's vision opened in 2012, and the ideas laid out in his thesis continue to be implemented decades later.

The vision for the BeltLine did not appear in a vacuum even as a concept; another rail line transformation, the High Line in Lower Manhattan, had opened in 2009. A primary component of any critical juncture is either evidence that the new proposal is possible or a suspension of disbelief. If the High Line already existed, then why not the BeltLine? In addition, the BeltLine crystalized forces of some permissive and productive critical junctures: the replacement of federal urban programs with municipal interventions in lower-income neighborhoods of color, the proven capacity of tax increment financing in Atlanta (the BeltLine was the sixth and largest such initiative), the voluminous coverage of the project in the local press, and the pent up demand by real estate speculators.[6] Atlanta's speculators and White boosters likely foresaw the displacement of poor, Black neighborhoods because it is a historically recurring consequence of such urban improvements. The residents of these neighborhoods also saw this coming and now face steeply rising home prices and rents in a process of gentrification that is displacing Black households at an alarming rate. The design concept did not resist this convention, implicitly exacerbating racial inequities in the city. To protect against further spatial injustices, in a long-term project like the BeltLine there must be continual course corrections. Atlanta has not done enough to protect naturally occurring affordable housing along the parkway or to build new affordable housing, nor was housing integral to the design concept. The BeltLine demonstrates the stamina and constant reevaluation required over the long duration of critical junctures that affect the built environment.

The BruinHub case opening this chapter is neither a disaster narrative nor a public open space undertaking—it is a new use type characterized as very-temporary housing, dignified shelter, or affordable hoteling. Housing has been a focus throughout this book, and while the BruinHub with its study-napping pods are not housing per se, they are at one end of the continuum of accommodation (figure 7.2). Starting with temporary, micro, and flexible formats and ending with more permanent multifamily or single-family housing, along the continuum are forms of shelter like hotels, dormitories, single-room occupancy units, and micro-apartments. All these constitute "housing" worthy of focus now, since the housing crisis continues to worsen worldwide, and in the United States these housing inequities are disproportionately borne by Black residents and people of color. For several reasons, a discussion of architecture and spatial justice keeps returning to housing and why housing design matters deeply. First, housing is widely viewed as a basic human right; second, housing has historically been a tool of racial and economic discrimination; third, housing is mass produced, so good (and bad) ideas multiply; and finally, there is a global housing crisis. The last of these reasons sets the backdrop for this chapter. Rather than the crisis discourse that brings with it opportunistic "shock doctrine" responses that Naomi Klein documents so vividly in her book of the same name, this chapter explains the critical junctures or confluence of forces that set the stage for innovative architectural solutions.

DESIGNING FOR CRITICAL JUNCTURES

Critical junctures are characterized by the convergence of a number of factors with spatial justice implications. To understand this convergence, three sources are useful: the logics of critical junctures as primarily theorized in political science, social movement history and theory, and the architecture that runs parallel with social movements. As such, critical junctures sit at the intersection of contingencies that feed a broad consensus about the necessity for change. When the histories of social transformation are told, these contingent factors figure prominently, but rarely has the connection to architecture been drawn. Examples illustrating the connections between broad transformation and the built environment include the *existenzminimum* rehousing effort in Germany between the two wars, the civil rights movement and rewriting of public history through the creation and destruction of memorials, and postwar anti-American Japanese art activism and the Metabolist architectural camp. Each social movement gives birth to a material culture, which continues to evolve in forms like monuments and public spaces, or even an aesthetic. The movements are public, gathering collectivities over time which themselves seek to mark in material terms their historic role. Architecture and the arts find their form in those movements. In the case of civil rights memorials, portrayals of violence, heroism, and everyday courageous acts are figured and named to redress their erasure. Sometimes architecture's participation in a critical juncture is characterized by a degree of remove, but, at other times, architecture finds the means to contribute more directly.

The political scientist Hillel David Soifer outlines a helpful set of qualities that describe the causal logic of critical junctures. Sets of permissive and productive conditions are necessary, respectively defined as those that change the underlying context to ease structural constraints and those that shape the divergent outcomes that will be reproduced after the juncture has closed. Together, the critical juncture is a space for possibility or window of opportunity marked by both permissive and productive conditions.[7] The changes comprise a shift that undermines a prior regime of norms so that contingency and agency play an expanded role, making for a situation marked by divergence and, when applied to design practices, innovation. After the introduction of divergent and innovative outcomes, a critical juncture ends and the mechanisms of reproduction take hold. New norms are set in place, a transformed status quo stabilizes, and the outcomes produced in the critical juncture fluidly proliferate. A causal framework for critical junctures includes permissive and productive conditions that are individually necessary and collectively sufficient to create a divergent outcome. Then, as the enabling conditions expire, the new norms and organizations allow for the outcome to spread.

There is a fitting parallel between the permissive conditions that allow for sociopolitical divergence outlined by Soifer and those that enable change in the built environment. Given the significant investment buildings require, for architecture to break with convention and for design agency to be effective, sufficient permissive conditions must be present. The incremental housing of Chilean architect Alejandro Aravena described in chapter 5 demonstrates how permissive and productive conditions yielded a new model of affordable housing that has since been reproduced. In the BruinHub example that opens this chapter, permissive conditions included the convergence of startlingly high rents around UCLA's campus and growing numbers of long-distance commuter students. These super-commuters, primarily students of color, undermined the university's long focus on establishing itself as an equitable, residential campus. The conditions forged an effective coalition between students, administrators, and our cityLAB team. Productive conditions included the availability of funding for innovative ideas to address housing insecurity and the recreation center's dedication of an underutilized squash court. The nonconforming BruinHub differs from napping capsules, commuter lounges, or overnight shelters on other campuses by its organization around the playful, individual study-napping pods collected into a lounge where the full range of students' daily needs are dignified by design and accommodated without stigma. Since this first divergent outcome opened in fall 2021, it remains to be seen whether destigmatizing centers for housing-insecure and commuting students will be reproduced on other campuses. There are early indications that proliferation has begun: other units on the UCLA campus are requesting pods and students across town at the University of Southern California are lobbying for their own version of a BruinHub.

The literature on crises related to disaster and emergency conditions is also relevant, but what has become apparent in recent decades is that crises—or catastrophes, disasters, and emergencies—are typically considered sporadic events when in fact they can be constant and steady. That is, a crisis can be either acute or chronic. Chronic crises like homelessness, racism, insufficiently clean water, police violence, the digital divide, or extreme weather require different forms of spatial response and thinking than episodic, recurring catastrophic events like earthquakes, flooding, excessive heat, or the excruciating nine-minute-long murder of a Black man captured on video. If a chronic crisis requires something like community resilience or protest, an acute crisis can bring chronic conditions to a breaking point and fuel a social movement. The murder of George Floyd was such a breaking point in 2020. A critical juncture was solidified when chronic, documented police murders of Black men, women, and children became acutely focused around monstrous violence, further fueling the Black Lives Matter liberation movement. The latter was founded in 2013 after Trayvon Martin's killer was acquitted. Widely circulated social media carried incontrovertible evidence to the public, bringing into all homes what Black households had long known about state-sanctioned racial violence. Effective social movements extend critical junctures over time and grow their membership, deepening the networks of their influence. At the time of this writing, the Black Lives Matter movement claims forty chapters around the world. So long as the movement and its coalitions continue to expand, the space of possibility or the critical juncture remains open. Black Lives Matter's critical juncture, built on more than four hundred years of brutal exploitation, is just beginning to implicate the physical environment. Evanston, Illinois began issuing housing subsidies to address the historical harm the city caused its Black residents in the twentieth century. Bruce's Beach in Manhattan Beach, California, is partially restored to the descendants of the Black family that was violently and illegally pushed out of their property. What some call the largest monument to slavery, General Robert E. Lee's statue, has been removed from Monument Row in Richmond Virginia.

What factors come together to form a critical juncture varies tremendously. Some factors are within the control of an initiative's instigators, but others are powerfully outside their control and potentially fleeting. After the Great East Japan Earthquake of 2011 or after Hurricanes Katrina and Rita in 2005 along America's Gulf Coast, the extensive environmental damage and destabilization of the status quo created permissive conditions for new and divergent practices of urban recovery. In both crises, architects were shut out of the formal recovery processes, but in Japan, architects built organizations that would form the productive conditions for design to play a role. In New Orleans, no such effective coalitions took shape, which left architects responding in piecemeal fashion. Even as the window of opportunity closed, which happens when permissive or productive conditions no longer pertain, architects from Homes for All and ArchiAid continued to engage in practices focusing on resilience in disaster, working closely with displaced and returning communities. Japanese architects organized, collaborated with communities, and pressured government agencies on what became a distinct agenda of designing and building communal processes and facilities that were not part of engineering-dominant emergency rehousing programs.

By contrast, a key problem for rebuilding post-Katrina New Orleans was thinking that architectural ideas could solve the hurricane's complex repercussions, from racial disparities and displacement to the permitting and construction processes. When Hurricanes Katrina and Rita struck the Gulf Coast in the fall of 2005, architects across the United States shared a heartfelt sense of duty to respond along with a recognition of the potential opportunity to design innovative post-disaster housing. One effort crystalized around some one hundred fifty New Urbanist architects (those who elevate traditional, local architectural and urban form) who descended on the Gulf Coast in the immediate aftermath to create design guidelines and plans for rebuilding in the region. Considerable work went into multiple reports that were handed over to local agencies for implementation. The New Urbanists' plans may have been based on established urban and environmental design practices, but they did not entertain crucial impacts of this disaster in this particular locale. For example, some two million residents were displaced by the storm and two hundred thousand were still living elsewhere after three years. The most likely to be displaced over the long term were New Orleans's poor, Black residents, in part because of the storm's disproportionate destruction of low-cost housing and the steep increase in land costs after the hurricane. Six months after Katrina, the Federal Emergency Management Agency delivered nearly one hundred thousand travel trailers for temporary accommodations, infamously referred to as "Katrina Cottages." In the rebuilding effort, neoliberal approaches emphasized economic recovery, the return of tourism, and poverty deconcentration. All these patterns favored "elite-driven relief, recovery, and redevelopment objectives."[8]

None of the more complex social factors played a significant role in the post-disaster architectural thinking, even though they were significant to any architecture or urban design that would evolve. Seeing that Black neighborhoods, particularly the Lower Ninth Ward, were still derelict two years after the hurricanes, another outsider architectural initiative formed under the Make It Right Foundation, led by the actor Brad Pitt. Founded in 2007, Make It Right enlisted twenty-one well-known architects from around the world to design affordable replacement housing, and by 2016, 109 houses had been built in the Lower Ninth Ward. There was little connection with the community, and those who were resettled "received" a house and mortgage. Moreover, the Make It Right neighborhood of individual houses included almost no attention to shared community

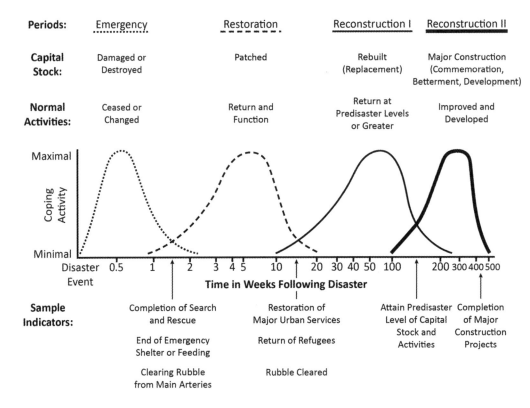

Periods:	Emergency	Restoration	Reconstruction I	Reconstruction II
Capital Stock:	Damaged or Destroyed	Patched	Rebuilt (Replacement)	Major Construction (Commemoration, Betterment, Development)
Normal Activities:	Ceased or Changed	Return and Function	Return at Predisaster Levels or Greater	Improved and Developed

Maximal

Coping Activity

Minimal

Disaster Event	0.5 1 2 3 4 5 10 20 30 40 50 100 200 300 400 500

Time in Weeks Following Disaster

Sample Indicators:	Completion of Search and Rescue	Restoration of Major Urban Services	Attain Predisaster Level of Capital	Completion of Major Construction
	End of Emergency Shelter or Feeding	Return of Refugees	Stock and Activities	Projects
	Clearing Rubble from Main Arteries	Rubble Cleared		

FIGURE 7.12

The timeline for disaster event recovery follows predictable patterns. Image by Miranda Hirujo-Rincon, modeled on graph from Lawrence J. Vale and Thomas J. Campanella, eds., *The Resilient City: How Modern Cities Recover from Disaster* (New York: Oxford University Press, 2005), 337.

facilities or infrastructure like sidewalks, parks, or day care. The neighborhood resembled some kind of housing exhibition. In 2018, a lawsuit was filed by residents against Make It Right alleging it built substandard houses, and that same year, Make It Right filed its own lawsuit against the New Orleans executive architect who oversaw the projects of the twenty-one design architects.[9] The critical juncture had surely closed by the time these legal battles erupted, and the conditions that characterized it did not lead to lasting, divergent practices.

Although the Gulf Coast and East Japan disasters both lent the permissive conditions needed to open a critical juncture, only the Japanese architects located their agency within the context of the crisis. While many differences characterized the productive conditions of the two scenarios, one of the most egregious was the relevant government organization. Municipal, state, and federal responses in the Gulf region were uncoordinated, while in Japan responses were tightly controlled at the national level. Both conditions essentially blocked architectural production, but rather than offering architecturally designed houses as in New Orleans, the Japanese architects rightly identified the productive conditions to design community spaces within emergency and replacement housing programs and to generate counterproposals to government town planning in partnership with displaced communities.

The comparison between the crises in eastern Japan and the American Gulf region demonstrates that these critical junctures blocked rather than invited architectural responses. For architects to become effective agents of change, they had to explicitly identify the context's structure and grapple with those conditions. Rather than automatically link crisis or disaster with reform, political theorists pull apart the facets of any crisis in order to be more precise about the conditions for experimentation. In other words, they are interested in the framework of the critical juncture. If we are instead interested in ways that a crisis might open a more spatially just path, then we should identify first where effective architectural agency is opened and second how we might shape the process to overcome inequities. In this sense, unlike political theory, a spatial justice analysis demonstrates that architectural agents do more than stand back and identify the productive conditions of a crisis. Instead, they actively help constitute them as did the Japanese architects.

The history of disasters demonstrates a predictable post-catastrophe pattern, from the immediate response and restoration of basic services to phased reconstruction. But not all disasters constitute a critical juncture where architecture can advance social justice goals, as the distinctly different outcomes in East Japan and New Orleans demonstrate. Every disaster that destroys the physical environment does set up the conditions for rebuilding. However, rebuilding is usually undertaken with a speculative real estate agenda rather than social goals. Architects and planners have famously participated in historic rebuilding efforts, such as in Skopje after the 1963 earthquake, Chicago after the Great Fire of 1871, Rotterdam after World War II, and Lower Manhattan after 9/11. Crises as well as other significant events, from World Cups to World's Fairs, bring an influx of resources to a particular place at a particular point in time. At such moments, the populace and government representatives may share an urgent desire for substantial change to open the way for transformative design. The necessary permissive conditions require additional productive conditions, which are both less predictable and require strategic intervention by agents, including architects. Rarely is that agential intervention undertaken without some larger social momentum, often built on popular reform movements.

SOCIAL MOVEMENTS AND ARCHITECTURE

Throughout history, wide swaths of people have sought transformative justice, as during the civil rights movement in the 1950s and 1960s and the disabilities rights movement in the 1970s in the United States. Spatial justice can progress through social movements when the mobilization is sustained, multifaceted, and unified, to loosely paraphrase political sociologist Charles Tilly's history of social movements.[10]

While determining the outcomes of social movements is notoriously difficult, studying their origins is much more straightforward. Historians examine the cycles of mass political protest that defined social movements in 1960s America to understand the structures of opportunity for mobilization as well as the subsequent implications for change. Social movement theory is largely based on this opportunity-outcome analytic, where outcomes can be further disaggregated, particularly between opportunities that sparked mobilization, resistance, or activism versus opportunities for public policy reform.[11] But nowhere in the social movement literature is there mention of architecture as a form of either activism or public policy. A perspective of critical junctures and design illuminates the intersection of some set of auspicious conditions and architectural activism. But this is only a rough parallel to the opportunity-outcome model. Consider the intertwined global crises of neoliberal capitalism, climate change, and housing access—existential crises of civilization itself, in which the opportunity-outcome framework feels decidedly inadequate. What can we *make* of shared threats of such immense proportions? Under these conditions, *every* potential action presents an opportunity. From an architectural perspective, every empty site is an opportunity to build housing, every building is an opportunity to address global warming, and every private commission is an affront to a more egalitarian economic order. Here, social theory lays the groundwork, but activist practices, including design, show the way forward.

When architectural practice is part of a social movement, it recognizes opportunities for design to redress harm, enhance spatial equity, and reimagine our shared world at critical junctures. A critical juncture is a precondition that provides fuel for architecture to break with convention and to keep an initiative alive. That fuel is normally capital, but since activist architecture stands outside conventional economic relationships, a shared crisis can provide all-important motivation. The BruinHub demonstrates that a broad concern like the housing crisis can be focused on a local instantiation like affordable student accommodation at UCLA to become an engine for architectural activism. The cityLAB coalition grew over several years, and its focus on housing-insecure students evolved from overcrowded dorm rooms to long-distance commuters who were sleeping in their cars. It is important to note that a primary force pushing to address the crisis was (and remains) students' demands for safe overnight parking. Their vocal and persistent calls for an immediate solution kept housing insecurity as a present problem to be addressed by the university. Along with resistance came visions for a future direction in the shape of a commuter lounge filled with study pods. No one implied it was an adequate or singular solution, but it welded together commuter students, UC administrators and staff, and cityLAB, who continue to expand the initiative. As an assembly of study pods and services, the BruinHub goes beyond a singular instantiation to stand as both a legible policy and a generative demonstration for other institutions serving housing-insecure populations. It remains to be seen whether this destigmatized form of shelter will contribute to a new norm, be adopted in new contexts, and strike one small path toward a new, more just status quo.

If the housing crisis is to have an appropriately scaled outcome, it will need a multipronged social movement. What took place at UCLA was a form of allyship. A particular type of coalition, transformational allyships can address injustices and advance equity by centering the voices of targets of oppression and by building social movements. Architecture can activate such allyships when it represents shared futures that coalitions have helped envision. The formal aesthetics in such instances are crucial; they must push past known models of design, respect and dignify the occupants, and locate an optimism that underlies new futures. Without inscribing some new direction in the built form, architecture literally maintains the status quo.

AUGMENTING CRITICAL JUNCTURES WITH DESIGN

This logic of formal innovation for activist architecture does not define the extent to which the design should vary from convention. When a new idea is put forward, even its champions will look for precedents to ward off inevitable skepticism. But precedents can be hard to find or inappropriate in certain contexts. In fact, what architects can bring to a movement for spatial justice is an optimistic vision for a world not yet seen. The architect's renderings open possible futures for discussion, radically or ever so slightly dismantling the disbelief that anything other than the status quo can exist. At root, the entire effort to advance spatial justice hinges on transformation that itself depends on collective belief undergirding actions toward a new future. The scale of first futuristic moves need not be utopian or comprehensive. Le Corbusier's success in creating a shared "machine for living in" was greater at La Tourette than at Ville Radieuse.

Nor need they be built—Cedric Price and Joan Littlewood's conceptual Fun Palace was more influential than his built InterAction Arts Project.

An inspiring example of seemingly subtle transformation is Priscilla Namwanje's Connective Infrastructure project for a neighborhood in Kampala, Uganda. Winner of the LafargeHolcim Next Generation first prize in 2021, Namwanje lays out an array of small, detailed interventions that together shape a network of shared, humane public spaces.[12] She suggests what these could look like, who would maintain them, how they would prevent flooding, and how they would bridge between socioeconomically fragmented subcommunities. The young architect's project is a clear example of how design can communicate a world as yet unseen, yet it is envisioned with enough care and intricacy to seem possible. If and when contextual pressures coalesce into a critical juncture for this imagined world to come, the conditions would exist to move from concept to action, from idea to implementation. A conceptual project like Namwanje's could also catalyze some of those conditions to mobilize implementation around just one public space, thereby strengthening productive opportunities to undertake the next steps. In this way, architects can not only take advantage of such conditions but also augment them.

Identifying, seizing, and augmenting the forces that come together to form a critical juncture are skills that architectural designers need. This means designing buildings in new ways, in terms of understanding not only the program, materials, and structure, but also the permissive and productive conditions that improve the odds a project will be realized. This requires adjusting professional expectations to go beyond the drawings for a building. For example, it is no small feat for an architect to design a small, inexpensive, easy-to-build house. As a single building, that small house does little to address homelessness until a prototype is constructed as the repetitive module on a site, with multiple units, managed by some agency. A number of "tiny house" villages in Oakland, California have done just this, largely without benefit of an architect. Oakland city councilmember Treva Reid says, "This is a model that will not end here. This is a model we believe in." That model involves using city land to empower youth-led design-build and local artists. It also involves extensive outreach, services, resident assistance, directing the housing toward unhoused youth between the

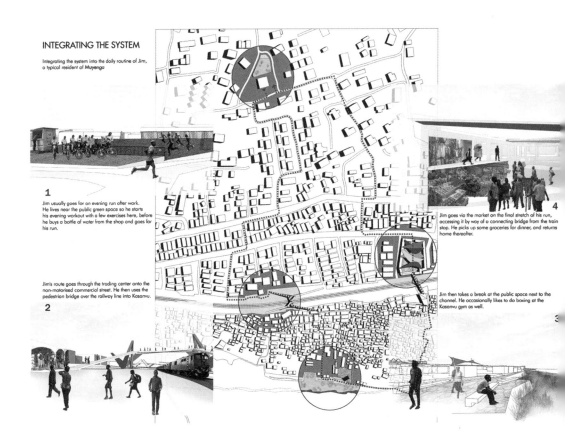

INTEGRATING THE SYSTEM

Integrating the system into the daily routine of Jim, a typical resident of Muyenga

1
Jim usually goes for an evening run after work. He lives near the public green space so he starts his evening workout with a few exercises here, before he buys a bottle of water from the shop and goes for his run.

2
Jim's route goes through the trading center onto the non-motorised commercial street. He then uses the pedestrian bridge over the railway line into Kasanvu.

3
Jim then takes a break at the public space next to the channel. He occasionally likes to do boxing at the Kasanvu gym as well.

4
Jim goes via the market on the final stretch of his run, accessing it by way of a connecting bridge from the train stop. He picks up some groceries for dinner, and returns home thereafter.

FIGURE 7.13

Designer Priscilla Namwanje inserts small, acupuncture-like infrastructural transformations in the Muyenga-Namuwongo neighborhood in Kampala, Uganda (2021). Courtesy of Priscilla Namwanje.

FIGURE 7.14

Tiny House Empowerment Village in Oakland, where twenty-six eight-by-ten-foot homes as well as public rooms and bathrooms are sited on a city-owned lot (2021). Photo by Michael Dear.

ages of eighteen and twenty-five, and very small, detached dwellings for single individuals. The buildings are crucial, but their design ingenuity is limited to the flexible interior furnishings and the colorful exterior art programming. The same goes for the six other "community cabin" villages installed in Oakland by January of 2020.[13] All those supplementary arrangements convert a tiny house into a broader, more impactful solution. Such projects await the contributions architecture could make beyond paint, furnishings, and siting. Most important is the recognition that tiny house projects are only interim solutions while agencies build dignified, permanent housing.

When architects accept present conditions and expectations, their designs are unlikely to augment the critical juncture. Responses to disaster, as political theorists Eric Cazdyn and Naomi Klein argue from their different perspectives, intrinsically embed an acceptance of present conditions.[14] In cities experiencing disaster, the cascading forces of destruction and repair readily lead back to the most powerful or corrupt actors, because to create something better requires years of preparatory effort, political leadership, partnerships of difference, and visionary imagination. This last requirement is what creative, experienced designers can bring to a critical juncture. But without the other elements of long-term endurance, committed leadership, and deep partnerships, a designer's visions can be reduced to caricatures. This was abundantly and tragically apparent in the efforts described earlier of New Urbanist architects after Katrina. It was exactly this observation of misplaced agency that motivated me to found cityLAB in 2006, but it was only years later that I would learn the lessons recounted here. Case in point: it took a decade of research, political allyship, community engagement, fieldwork, site studies, and design to grasp the granny flat as a generative demonstration and to understand how to write effective state legislation. At the outset, it was a less robust solution that could help curtail suburban sprawl and make housing more affordable in Los Angeles. It should not be surprising that a long game was essential to achieve the goal of doubling the density of the entire state of California's suburbs. The Backyard Homes long game also raised the next challenges addressed through subsequent cityLAB initiatives including Schoolyard Homes, our ongoing research into how to design infill apartments for teachers and staff with protected affordability by siting the housing on public school land.

8

CONCLUSION: ARCHITECTURE'S PRACTICAL FUTURE

Architecture is an aesthetic practice. It is also an expensive undertaking. Those facts have been the building blocks of the profession's historic dependence on privilege. But architecture is also and always has been a political practice. The last time that the intersection of form, economy, and politics came forcefully together was within modern architecture, but just because the modern project was not sustained does not mean that its fundamentals of aesthetics, finance, and social agenda failed. The mixture was meant to evolve, and the critical juncture facing contemporary architecture in cities worldwide provides the opportunity—or mandate—to chart a change of course. Global warming and income inequality, as I have argued, are directly linked to the work we do as architects. Recognizing that dire conditions demand a powerful response, this book lays out in explicit examples just how an insurgent architecture is already taking action grounded in spatial justice.

The book shines a light on professional advances to forge architecture's optimism, pleasures, and dignity more broadly. Realizing that potential requires setting aside conventional thinking about commissions, projects, and publics so that architecture is framed in a new context. It means respecting not just disciplinary knowledge and history but also practical, lived experience, pushing Hayden White's concept of a practical past toward a practical future. This is the ground on which we will build the world we want to live in.

Architecture, sitting as it does at the precise intersection of culture and economy, may be the last bastion of imperialism. Wrapped in a beautiful cloak of aesthetic production, we are seduced into seeing architecture as separate from politics. Le Corbusier's Chandigarh, a government center, is indeed a formal triumph intended to house democratic practices universal to modern man. That such notions of governance and humanity were transported from Europe adds little nuance to our understanding of Chandigarh or of Western imperialism in India. Yet the ways that settlements grew in and around the government complex—and the ways in which Corb's residential grid was overwhelmed, resisted, and remade by local inhabitants—are not considered part of Chandigarh's architectural story. Thus, the colonial project is maintained.

Postcolonial theorist Edward Said's critique of the ways in which the novel has been detached from colonial histories and relegated to "culture, culture being the elevated area of activity in which they 'truly' belong and in which they did their 'really' important work"[1] also illuminates the ways in which architecture is viewed and practiced. Those among us who see the politics of all architecture need not be blind to its aesthetic power, but neither do we need to set aside politics in order to appreciate its beauty. If the project of autonomy in architecture did much to advance its theoretical possibilities, it simultaneously buried criticism of its cultural hegemonies, associations with global finance, roles in displacement, and participation in global warming. Far more so than the novel, architecture is deeply, undeniably rooted in the economic structures needed for its production. As such, its material condition commits to the advancement of existing power relations, with all their concomitant subjugations and spatial geographies. But to see this as inevitable is to maintain the imperial stance. Instead, these pages excavate forms of practice that resist the idea that architecture's ties to power are inescapable, not to discard aesthetics but to pull back and appreciate that cloak simultaneously. In some cases, this means leveraging design's aesthetic power for the powerless—as when architects stepped into the post-tsunami breach in East Japan—or lending that power's compelling optimism where hope needs rekindling. These are qualities attributed not to autonomous objects or external works of architecture but to works of architecture resulting from humanistic practices of engagement, resistance, and inclusivity.

Tellingly, it may be easier to grasp that such lofty goals will require real labor than that they require an equal if not greater measure of creativity. The legacy of associating aesthetic production with privilege is ready for subversion.

Located between the discipline and the profession of architecture are the practices that shore up this reading of design as a form of activism. This book's opening pages raised this question: Can architecture embody principles of spatial justice? The answer: Not without a systemic transformation of its relationship to the public, to capital, and to privilege. Structural changes are already underway in the practices of architects included in this book. Architecture schools are reevaluating their own histories and present commitments, with students pressuring administrations to advance equity through actions and to dedicate real resources to the effort. The professional organizations and licensing bodies, thoroughly dominated in North America by White men, are publishing their own unflattering data about the participation of women and people of color. Architecture's history of social and racial exclusion is structural, and while exaggerated in North America, it is not geographically constrained there. Anti-migrant policy and discourse have racialized immigrants and refugees in the European Union; religious minorities are persecuted in China; "Japanese-only" practices of discrimination are common in Japan; women's empowerment remains distant despite the global ratification of the Convention for the Elimination of Discrimination Against Women; and, as of May 2021, sixty-nine countries (half in Africa) criminalize homosexuality, an extreme form of LGBTQ persecution. In the face of such injustices, architecture always plays a role and has many opportunities to cultivate more ethical, inclusionary practices. Since nations in the Global North dominate the architectural market for services, their practices bear a commensurate burden to challenge inequality along with professional imperialism. And in all places where racism, discrimination, and injustice prevail, spaces of resistance, agonism, and creativity arise. In these spaces, the DNA of emancipatory social relations will propagate.

The tactics of transformation will vary globally, but some common principles have been proposed in these pages. These point to the labor necessary for effective change. First, ethical projects in architecture are never complete. Linked together into justice initiatives, a series of projects can be transformative.

When singular works are conceptualized as part of ongoing, long-term efforts, their radically public potential increases. Next, the designer occupies a position of power to be mediated and mitigated by knowledge, collaboration, immersion, and advocacy. Symmetries of both ignorance and expertise characterize architectural processes, providing fertile ground for partnerships of difference. Third, and a corollary to the preceding principle, spatial justice initiatives are built by constituencies rather than by individual clients or architects. A good deal of antagonism exists among these constituencies, partnerships, and publics, and our architectural work must live in the midst of the contestation without searching for consensus. An uneasy agonism is fundamental to ethical practices of design. Fourth, leveraging design on behalf of spatial justice requires resources that are always insufficient. There will never be adequate money, talent, labor, allyship, or time, and so these cannot stand in as constraints. Part of the design process for architects and their partners is to shore up resources that are lacking. In Chile, build only half the house, making sure the occupants have the means to complete it. Without public funds for affordable housing in California, use design demonstrations to unlock the underutilized land in private backyards. Finally, justice projects carry a burden of legibility so that initiatives are made public and can be built on by others. A work of architecture can be a material manifestation that renders underlying policy open to contestation and evolution, giving architecture a degree of malleability and responsiveness.

These principles do not storm the disciplinary core but instead flourish in the borderlands that divide architecture from is close relatives urban design and social arts practices. If architecture is to rise to the tasks at hand—the existential threats of global warming, income inequality, racial injustice, and homelessness—the action will take place in these borderlands, where conventions hold less sway and architectural practices can expand to establish spatial justice as a fundamental part of every architectural effort—not as a goal per se but as a central principle on par with the Vitruvian triumvirate of commodity, firmness, and delight. Like civil rights, such a comprehensive ethic advances slowly and is punctuated by critical junctures that catalyze more significant progress. The Trump presidency, Black Lives Matter movement, and the coronavirus pandemic have catalyzed what began with the Occupy movement, setting up the present as one of those junctures. If architecture's agency is to fundamentally transform to embrace and lift up spatial justice, it will do so by building on lessons from activist practices that have experimented, failed, and occasionally succeeded. cityLAB is one such practice. Each chapter opens with other such practices, and within each chapter numerous built projects offer incontrovertible evidence that architecture-as-activism is already in the works.

To conclude, we can speculate about the future of architecture for spatial justice. What would it mean for our practices to recognize that all communities deserve architectural dignity, not just those privileged by power, wealth, race, and geography? It means beginning the process of undoing architecture's Whiteness and dismantling the disciplinary and professional structures that perpetuate power imbalances. It means critically revisiting conventional definitions of architecture, client, project, and office. It also means actively seeking ways to work outside capital's driving inequalities. I have repeatedly examined two primary lenses through which architecture's realignment might become visible: the public and capital. What appears to be a radical thought experiment about a future with new relations between capital, the public, and architecture is actually an empirical project. The real-world practices and projects offered in each chapter provide hard evidence that systemic structures are already being challenged. There are already multiple paths for just such a realignment that imagine and engage publics in new ways and create projects that give back to other projects, sites, publics, and architects. Activist projects, characterized by more inclusive relations to the public and less dependence on capital, are built around enduring values of form and aesthetics and nestled within new norms that honor partners, long-term processes, and generative capacity. Without conventional commissions, fees, or clients, the sustenance of activist practices depends on the creativity and conviction of practitioners and the broadening of institutional platforms like universities, foundations, civic agencies, nonprofits, and museums. In a progressive scenario, activist engagement sets standards for all architectural practices. If that seems implausible, we can see that sustainability goals have begun to do just that. Something that was radical when it began in 1995, the LEED green building rating system, has heavily influenced the construction industry and the whole notion of design performance standards.

Activist architecture for spatial justice has already recast a segment of the field's practices that will continue to permeate the discipline's core. New models like cityLAB are signposts on the road ahead.

A conviction that the architect's agency is the key to spatial justice probably strikes skeptical readers as a contradiction. But I do not view architects as the problem. Some architects, maybe, but the structural problems lie beneath the actors. If economies and publics—that is, constituencies, partners, collaborators, and civic leaders—can be unconventionally figured, new agency becomes possible. The same skeptics will note that architecture's transformative potential is not a new topic but one populated by zealots and marked by a series of failed historical experiments. Even if that is true, we are condemned to experiment again, with more intelligence and energy, given the confluence of historically unprecedented crises we face today.

As we look to a future in which the optimism of an equitable, sustainable, and beautiful built environment is broadly shared in society, we will need an optimistic cohort of young designers that celebrates its Black, Indigenous, Brown, Asian, female, LGBTQ, differently abled members and works within schools and offices to open up more vibrant environments. That is not a future to be defined by conventional norms, disciplinary strictures, or professionals alone; it is a practical future that respects the wide array of stories that compose it. My goal in writing this book was to pry open architecture's form and politics to make room for the creativity, study, and optimism of the next generation.

ACKNOWLEDGMENTS

This book began a long time ago, perhaps as far back as when I began my own architectural career. Over the past four decades, I've watched the numbers of women grow in a male-dominated profession, and I am proud to have mentored many young women in the field. But the numbers of people of color, particularly Black and Indigenous architects, remain stubbornly and unacceptably low. Related to this and despite a growing archive of design works outside the North American-European axis, architectural history's canon resists expansion because the very definition of architecture is tied to hegemonic conventions. And contemporary journals filled with overlarge homes for wealthy White owners and oxymoronically exclusive public buildings do the discipline a disservice. For me, a profound love of architecture—its formal elegance, its complex materiality, its structural logics, its optimism, its palimpsest of the lives lived within—can appear to contradict ethical commitments to make the world we want to live in. More than practically any other field of study or profession, architecture holds that transformative capacity.

My own actions to resolve this contradiction center around reconstructing a corner of the field from within by doing architecture in new ways with new constituencies and partners. I have been able to use my own privilege of being tenured at one of the world's best public universities in one of the most dynamic cities to push architecture in alternative directions. And so was born cityLAB in 2006 in UCLA's Architecture and Urban Design Department. The only resources available at first included time carved from my full-time appointment, rarely used offices that colleagues didn't mind sharing, and a motivated labor pool of smart students. Basically, we were squatters with a telephone.

Given the exploitation of interns in architecture and the inequities furthered by unpaid internships, I resolved to pay all cityLAB student workers a living wage, which meant seeking financial resources. Throughout the lab's life, our support has come from enlightened, powerful women who shared my beliefs about architecture's unmet capacities. Without this metaphorical "old girls' network" there would be no cityLAB. Sarah Jane Lind wrote the first check with a generosity and faith that seems astonishing on reflection. We met in a feminist think tank organized by Betty Friedan in the late 1980s, where I was naturally curious about Sarah Jane's early career as a residential builder in Los Angeles. Her intelligently articulated expectations for cityLAB's work were coupled, when we met the challenge, with further support. Another incredible woman, Cindy Miscikowski, stepped in more recently. A former LA city councilmember with sophisticated aesthetic sensibilities, Cindy saw cityLAB as a site where architecture and politics merged to guide our city in innovative directions. She offered her network of LA's most productive activists along with consistent annual support, forming the platform to launch our second-generation initiatives.

Just five years into cityLAB's life, Hilary Ballon and Mariët Westerman at the Mellon Foundation invited me to a brainstorming session about bringing together architecture, urbanism, and the humanities. They opened the door for cityLAB to invent an interdisciplinary academic program called the Urban Humanities Initiative (UHI) with colleagues Anastasia Loukaitou-Sideris, Todd Presner, and Maite Zubiaurre. The inspiring, open-minded intelligence of these people paired with their commitments to social justice form the foundations of the most creative and promising teaching in the university to date. The diaspora of our UHI students and alums from architecture, planning, and the humanities is spreading new versions of cityLAB and UHI across the world.

Over the years, cityLAB has grown in terms of thoughtfulness, design demonstrations, academic rigor, community outreach, and influence. What began as a "stone soup" effort where promise far outweighed results has matured into a bona fide design research laboratory. There has never been a stronger core staff at cityLAB, consisting of Rayne Laborde Ruiz, Gustavo Leclerc, and Gus Wendel. Their brainpower, commitment to our collective work, and friendship turns every day at cityLAB into a rewarding reunion. By now we have awarded a dozen graduate cityLAB fellowships and a half dozen undergrad fellowships to a group of UCLA's finest students who continue to amaze. Along with our research associates, these BIPOC, first-generation, and exceptionally talented folks are the power of cityLAB and provide facts on the ground that architecture's future is bright. They include Heidi Alexander, Nallely Almaguer-Rodriguez, Jonathan Banfill, Jacqueline Barrios, Evan Breutsch, Cate Carlson, Aaron Cayer, Roya Chagnon, Katie Chuh, Jonathan Jae-an Crisman, Per-Johan Dahl, Will Davis, Anna Drew, Carrie Gammell, Anatoli Georgiadou, Gavin Guo, Riley Hammond, Miranda Hirujo-Rincon, Cassie Hoeprich, Marco Icev, Akana Jayewardene, Yessenia Juarez, Felix Lam, Ben Leclair, Louie Leiva, Kara Moore, Joshua Nelson, John Northrup, Dami Olufowoshe, Paolo Ovando, Melissa Peter Rovner, Emmanuel Proussaloglou, Xiuwen Qi, Sai Rojanapirom, Linda Samuels, Bianca Siegl, Emmanuel Soriano, Nan-Tse Su, Pablo Subiotto Marqués, Katherine Taylor-Hasty, Dexter Walcott, Kenny Wong, Yang Yang, and Kevin Yeoh. Some undertook our accounting or graphic design, others were instrumental partners on Backyard Homes, some led the building of the BIHOME, others are still shepherding the BruinHub along, and many helped research, write, design, and produce our publications. My appreciation for these individuals and so many more who graced cityLAB is unbounded. Two women, Miranda Hirujo-Rincon and Rayne Laborde Ruiz, have worked beyond my expectations to help complete this book. Their dedication represents their own convictions, sure to flourish in the years ahead, about architecture's spatial justice potential.

Cultivating a garden like cityLAB depends on the terroir of the Architecture and Urban Design Department at UCLA, where I am surrounded by colleagues who make their living turning novices and skeptics into architectural proponents. Roger Sherman cofounded cityLAB before moving into new territory, Neil Denari read the prospectus for this book, architect-teachers Kevin Daly and Marta Nowak led design of the BIHOME and BruinHub respectively, department chairs Hitoshi Abe, Sylvia Lavin, and now Mariana Ibañez gave cityLAB a home, and fellow faculty Diane Favro, Craig Hodgetts, Greg Lynn, Thom Mayne, Michael Osman, and Mohamed Sharif offered critical insights from their wildly different perspectives. In the dean's office, David Rousseve and Brett Steele, along with their staffs, have amplified cityLAB's capacities. In UCLA's wider world, I'm grateful for the activist intelligence of colleagues in the Urban Planning Department: Anastasia Loukaitou-Sideris, Kian Goh, Vinit Mukhija, Ananya Roy, and Gary Segura.

The projects that kick off each chapter have their own crowds of collaborators, many of whom have been named above. For the Backyard Homes project, I add thanks to Assemblyman Richard Bloom and his staff who invited us to co-author the ADU bill that became law in 2017. Jane Blumenfeld, a senior fellow at cityLAB, was our partner on this bill and everything related to turning good ideas into good policy. The BruinHub would not exist without its effective, committed team: Amber Brown, Mick Deluca, Rudy Figueroa, Carmen Garcia-Shustari, and Erinn McMahon. The industrial designer Don Chadwick made us believe that a giant jelly bean could turn into a good piece of furniture. In Japan, I am grateful for the generosity of Hitoshi Abe, Yasuaki Onoda, and the studio of Toyo Ito. In Mexico, activist-scholars Brenda Vértiz and Gabriella Gómez-Mont have been collaborators of the finest sort. I am fortunate to have Walter Hood as a friend and guide and I appreciate all the help offered from his studio. Thanks also to Elemental, Alejandro Aravena's office in Chile. At the MIT Press, I was exceptionally lucky to fall into the spheres of Beth Clevenger and Victoria Hindley who recognized the promise of the book and to benefit from the editorial finesse of Kathleen Caruso and Liz DeWolf, with Yasuyo Iguchi's graphic vision.

I am indebted to colleagues and friends with whom I have shared many good conversations, questions, projects, suggestions, coffees, lectures, travels, and more: Abby Arnold, Eric Avila, Eve Blau, Teddy Cruz, Michael Dear, Fonna Forman, Mario Gandelsonas, Frank Gruber, Christopher Hawthorne, Catherine Ingraham, Janet Levin, Lisa Lowe, Jennifer Schab, Bob Somol, Sarah Whiting, Mabel O. Wilson, and Jennifer Wolch. I am fortunate to have an extended family that gets together often for long dinner debates: Penny Cuff, Pam Cuff, Maura Daly, Tracy Lewis, Abby McNulty, Bob McNulty, and Maria McNulty. And, most of all, my life, loves, and thoughts are intertwined with those of my husband Kevin Daly and children Amelia and Julian Cuff Daly. I write from the bounty of our days passed together, often in the unfamiliar spaces and company of others, scrutinizing curious architectural phenomena and the workings of the world. This book is yours too.

NOTES

CHAPTER 1

1. Celine McNicholas and Margaret Poydock, "Who Are Essential Workers?," *Economic Policy Institute Working Economics Blog*, May 19, 2020, https://www.epi.org/blog/who-are-essential-workers-a-comprehensive-look-at-their-wages-demographics-and-unionization-rates/.

2. See Kyle Chayka, "How the Coronavirus Will Reshape Architecture," *New Yorker*, June 17, 2020, https://www.newyorker.com/culture/dept-of-design/how-the-coronavirus-will-reshape-architecture; Lee Billington, "Understanding the Touchless Workplace," *Gensler* (blog), April 15, 2020, https://www.gensler.com/blog/understanding-the-touchless-workplace; Kay Sargent, "COVID-19 and the Case for a Hands-Free Workplace," *HOK News and Events*, March 26, 2020, https://www.hok.com/news/2020-03/covid-19-and-the-case-for-a-hands-free-workplace/.

3. Charles Moore, "You Have to Pay for the Public Life," *Perspecta* 9/10 (1965): 57–97, https://doi.org/10.2307/1566912.

4. Simon Sadler, "You (Still) Have to Pay for the Public Life," *Places Journal*, January 2016, https://placesjournal.org/article/you-still-have-to-pay-for-the-public-life/?cn-reloaded=1; see also Bruno Latour, "From Realpolitik to Dingpolitik or How to Make Things Public," in *Making Things Public: Atmospheres of Democracy*, ed. Bruno Latour and Peter Weibel (Cambridge, MA: MIT Press, 2005), 14–43; Bonnie Honig, *Public Things: Democracy in Disrepair* (New York: Fordham University Press, 2017).

5. Edward Soja, *Seeking Spatial Justice* (Minneapolis: University of Minnesota Press, 2010); Henri Lefebvre, *Writings on Cities* (Cambridge, MA: Wiley-Blackwell, 1996). First published in 1968 by Anthropos.

6. Michael Sorkin, "Afterword: Architecture without Capitalism," in *Architecture and Capitalism: 1845 to the Present*, ed. Peggy Deamer (New York: Routledge, 2014), 217–220; Richard Sennett, "New Ways of Thinking About Space," *Nation*, September 5, 2012, 24–26, https://www.thenation.com/article/archive/new-ways-thinking-about-space/.

7. bell hooks, *Feminist Theory from Margin to Center* (Boston: South End Press, 1984); Gloria Anzaldúa, *Borderlands/La Frontera* (San Francisco: Aunt Lute Books, 1987).

8. John Ruskin, *The Seven Lamps of Architecture* (London: J. M. Dent & Sons Ltd., 1969). First published in 1849 by Smith, Elder & Co.

9. See, for example, Spiro Kostof, "Architecture, You and Him: The Mark of Sigfried Giedion," *Daedalus* 105, no. 1 (Winter 1976): 189–204, https://www.jstor.org/stable/20024393.

10. Sir Bannister F. Fletcher, *A History of Architecture on the Comparative Method* (London: B. T. Batsford, 1905). The tree appears in the front matter, above the statement that it should be "taken as suggestive only."

11. The racist implications of Fletcher's tree are articulated in Irene Cheng, Charles L. Davis II, and Mabel O. Wilson, eds., *Race and Modern Architecture* (Pittsburgh: University of Pittsburgh Press, 2020).

12. Eric Cazdyn, "Anti-anti: Utopia, Globalization, Jameson," *Modern Language Quarterly* 68, no. 2 (June 2007): 333, https://doi.org/10.1215/00267929-2006-041.

13. Bernard Rudofsky, *Architecture Without Architects* (New York: Museum of Modern Art, 1964).

14. See Anastasia Loukaitou-Sideris and Tridib Banerjee, *Urban Design Downtown: Poetics and Politics of Form* (Berkeley: University of California Press, 1998); Bonnie Honig, *Public Things* (New York: Fordham University Press, 2017).

15. See David de la Peña, Diane Jones Allen, Randolph T. Hester Jr., Jeffrey Hou, Laura J. Lawson, and Marcia J. McNally, eds., *Design as Democracy: Techniques for Collective Creativity* (Washington, DC: Island Press, 2017); Mary C. Comerio, "Community Design: Idealism and Entrepreneurship," *Journal of Architecture and Planning Research* 1, no. 4 (December 1984): 227–243, https://www.jstor.org/stable/43028704.

16. Toni L. Griffin, Ariella Cohen, and David Maddox, eds., *The Just City Essays: 26 Visions for Urban Equity, Inclusion and Opportunity* (New York: The J. Max Bond Center, Next City, and The Nature of Cities, 2015), https://static1.squarespace.com/static/5b5dfb72697a9837b1f6751b/t/5b7d8b5a88251b1adad06c60/1534954340 713/JustCityEssays.pdf.

17 Mary McLeod, "Architecture and Politics in the Reagan Era: From Postmodernism to Deconstructivism." *Assemblage* 8 (February 1989): 22–59, https://doi.org/10.2307/3171013.

18. Debate about Rural Studio's depiction of poverty is captured in Anna G. Goodman, "The Paradox of Representation and Practice in the Auburn University Rural Studio," *Traditional Dwellings and Settlements Review* 25, no. 2 (Spring 2014): 39–52, https://www.jstor.org/stable/24347716.

19. Peter Blake, "The Modern Movement: What Went Wrong?" *Wilson Quarterly* 3, no. 1 (Winter 1979): 127, https://www.jstor.org/stable/40255568.

20. Gilles Deleuze, Félix Guattari, and Robert Brinkley, "What Is a Minor Literature?," *Mississippi Review* 11, no. 3 (Winter/Spring 1983): 13–33, https://www.jstor.org/stable/20133921.

21. Joan Ockman, "Consequences of Pragmatism: A Retrospect on 'The Pragmatist Imagination,'" in *The Figure of Knowledge: Conditioning Architectural Theory, 1960s-1990s*, ed. Sebastiaan Loosen, Rajesh Heynickx, and Hilde Heynen (Leuven, Belgium: Leuven University Press, 2020), 292.

22. Sarah Whiting and Peter Eisenman, "I Am Interested in a Project of Engaged Autonomy," *Log* 28 (Summer 2013): 112, https://www.jstor.org/stable/43630873.

23. Milton S. F. Curry, "Toward an Architecture Race Theory," in *Reconstructions: Architecture and Blackness in America*, ed. Sean Anderson and Mabel O. Wilson (New York: The Museum of Modern Art, 2021), 166.

24. Joyce Chen and Rachel Wallace, "57 Design Shows to Watch Now," *Architectural Digest*, November 25, 2021, https://www.architecturaldigest.com/story/design-shows-to-binge -over-the-holidays.

25. Hayden White, *The Practical Past* (Evanston, IL: Northwestern University Press, 2014); Hayden White, "A Reply to Dirk Moses," *History and Theory* 44, no. 3 (October 2005): 335, https://www.jstor.org/stable/3590819.

26. Dan Cameron, "Cocido y crudo," in *Cocido y crudo*, ed. Jerry Saltz, Mar Villaespesa, Gerardo Mosquera, Jean Fisher, and Dan Cameron (Madrid: Museo Nacional Centro de Arte Reina Sofía, 1994), 325; Sarah Suzuki, "Post: Notes on Art in a Global Context: Kingelez Visionnaire," *MoMA*, September 12, 2018, https://post.moma.org/kingelez-visionnaire/? _ga=2.188401710.726127972.1640048838-408500485.1639506617&gac=1.195993054.1639507668 .CjoKCQiAnuGNBhCPARIsACbnLzoEeuWReol6rPuQoj5WQwoIHNTTqWnHu50MXks _6pxRqGpCLT6IoE4aAv6_EALw_wcB.

27. Richard Rothstein, *The Color of Law* (New York: Liveright Publishing, 2017).

28. Dana Cuff, *The Provisional City* (Cambridge, MA: MIT Press, 2000); Dana Cuff and Rodger Sherman, eds., *Fast Forward Urbanism* (New York: Princeton Architectural Press, 2011).

29. Rosalind Krauss, "Sculpture in the Expanded Field," *October* 8 (Spring 1979): 30–44, https:// doi.org/10.2307/778224.

CHAPTER 2

1. Becky M. Nicolaides, *My Blue Heaven: Life and Politics in the Working-Class Suburbs of Los Angeles, 1920–65* (Chicago: University of Chicago Press, 1992).

2. Vinit Mukhija, Dana Cuff, and Kimberly Serrano, *Backyard Homes and Local Concerns: How Can the Concerns be Better Addressed?* (Los Angeles: UCLA Luskin School of Public Affairs and cityLAB, April 2014), 153, https://static1.squarespace.com /static/58e4e9705016e194dd5cdc43/t/58fb35bf20099eb9a7159970/1492858335968/2014 _BYH+Report+cityLAB+UCLA.pdf.

3. Timothy Pershing, senior field representative, Office of Assembly Member Richard Bloom, AD 50, email message to author, October 26, 2015.

4. Alysia Bennett, Dana Cuff, and Gus Wendel, "Backyard Housing Boom: New Markets for Affordable Housing and the Role of Digital Technology," *Technology|Architecture+Design: Urbanizing* 3, no. 1 (March 2019): 76–88, https://doi.org/10.1080/24751448.2019.1571831.

5. bell hooks, "Architecture in Black Life: Talking Space with Laverne Well-Bowie," *Art on My Mind* (New York: The New Press, 1995), 159.

6. bell hooks, "Black Vernacular: Architecture as Cultural Practice," *Art on My Mind* (New York: The New Press, 1995), 150.

7. Cornell West, "A Note on Race and Architecture," *Keeping Faith: Philosophy and Race in America* (New York: Routledge, 1993), 46.

8. bell hooks, "Art on My Mind," *Art on My Mind* (New York: The New Press, 1995), 4–9.

9. Horst W. J. Rittel and Melvin M. Webber, "Dilemmas in a General Theory of Planning," *Policy Sciences* 4 (1973): 155–169, https://doi.org/10.1007/BF01405730.

10. Robin Pogrebin, "Retire? Gehry's Got No Time," *New York Times*, April 13, 2021, https://www.nytimes.com/2021/04/13/arts/design/frank-gehry.html.

11. For innovative, low-cost housing design concepts, see Ron Rael's 3D-printed mud structures (Eleanor Gibson, "Rael San Fratello 3D Prints Earth Structures to Demonstrate Potential of Mud Architecture," *Dezeen*, October 3, 2019, https://www.dezeen.com/2019/10/03/mud-frontiers-rael-san-fratello-3d-printed-low-cost-construction/; Sophia Choi, "Feel the Squeeze: 7 Skinny Houses in Tokyo," *Architizer*, accessed November 22, 2020, https://architizer.com/blog/inspiration/collections/japan-tokyos-skinny-homes/; Emily Young, "We Asked Top Architects for Bold Solutions to LA's Homeless Crisis," *Los Angeles Magazine*, October 1, 2020, https://www.lamag.com/citythinkblog/housing-solutions-los-angeles/).

12. The Star Apartments are positively regarded, but the development's prefab system is considered impractically expensive. Such experimentation, as with the mass timber project, is part of the long game of trying to find more effective construction systems to bring costs down. See Steven Sharp, "Skid Row Housing Trust Plans Mass Timber High-Rise in DTLA," *Urbanize Los Angeles*, March 23, 2020, https://urbanize.city/la/post/skid-row-housing-trust-plans-mass-timber-high-rise-dtla.

13. Christine Serlin, "Infill Development Creates Supportive Housing for Homeless," *Housing Finance*, July 7, 2017, https://www.housingfinance.com/developments/infill-development-creates-supportive-housing-for-homeless_o.

14. Dickson Lam, *Paper Sons: A Memoir* (Pittsburgh: Autumn House Press, 2018); Janet McDonald, *Project Girl* (Berkeley: University of California Press, 1999).

15. Ruth Wilson Gilmore, "Organized Abandonment and Organized Violence: Devolution and the Police," The Humanities Institute at UCSC, November 9, 2015, Vimeo video, 1:41:44, https://vimeo.com/146450686.

16. Teddy Cruz and Fonna Forman, "cityLAB Opens House Panel 02: Activist Paths for Architects," *UCLA Urban Humanities Initiative,* October 20, 2020, YouTube video, 56:46, https://www.youtube.com/watch?v=11Bytw7ejoc&ab_channel=UCLAUrbanHumanitiesInitiative.

17. Dana Cuff, *Architecture: The Story of Practice* (Cambridge, MA: MIT Press, 1991).

18. Lisa Findley, "Building Future: Tjibaou Cultural Centre," in *Building Change: Architecture, Politics and Cultural Agency* (New York: Routledge, 2005), 43–78; James Thompson, "Antipodal Architecture: Traces of the 'Other Tradition' in Piano's Tjibaou Cultural Centre," in *102nd ACSA Annual Meeting Proceedings, Globalizing Architecture / Flows and Disruptions*

(2014), 250, https://www.acsa-arch.org/proceedings/Annual%20Meeting%20Proceedings /ACSA.AM.102/ACSA.AM.102.29.pdf.

19. Marcus Ferraz, "The Making of SESC Pompéia," *Lina Bo Bardi: Together*, August 3, 2012, https:// linabobarditogether.com/2012/08/03/the-making-of-sesc-pompeia-by-marcelo-ferraz/.

20. Ferraz, "The Making of SESC Pompéia."

21. Elizabeth Fazzare, "UVA's New Memorial to Enslaved Laborers Confronts the School's History," *Architectural Digest*, September 9, 2020, https://www.architecturaldigest.com /story/uva-memorial-to-enslaved-laborers.

22. United Nations, *Fact Sheet No.21, The Human Right to Adequate Housing*, https://www .un.org/ruleoflaw/files/FactSheet21en.pdf. The United Nations specifically identifies adequate housing as a cornerstone of basic human rights: "Adequate housing is defined within the Global Strategy as meaning: adequate privacy, adequate space, adequate security, adequate lighting and ventilation, adequate basic infrastructure and adequate location with regard to work and basic facilities–all at a reasonable cost."

23. Diana Favro, "Was Man the Measure?," in *Architects' People*, ed. Russell Ellis and Dana Cuff (New York: Oxford University Press, 1989), 15–43.

24. "By and large, we have only dealt with large or significant symbolic monuments: the traditional objects of academic scrutiny. We have not painted a picture of vernacular and other nonmonumental architecture, such as domestic space." Francis D. K. Ching, Mark M. Jarzombek, and Vikramaditya Prakash, *A Global History of Architecture* (Hoboken, NJ: Wiley, 1995), xii.

25. Lisa Findley, *Building Change: Architecture, Politics and Cultural Agency* (New York: Routledge, 2005), 3.

26. Black histories in America, such as Saidiya Hartman's *Wayward Lives, Beautiful Experiments*, have caused extensive disciplinary debate on multiple grounds, particularly around archives and methodologies for establishing narratological evidence.

27. Barbara Miller Lane, "Architects in Power: Politics and Ideology in the Work of Ernst May and Albert Speer," *Journal of Interdisciplinary History* 17, no. 1 (1986): 283–310, http://www .jstor.org/stable/204134.

28. One clear exception is the architect Shaun Donovan, who was appointed Secretary of Housing and Urban Development from 2009 to 2014. Donovan worked to establish New Urbanism as the dominant style of public housing in mixed income developments under the Hope VI program as it evolved into Choice Neighborhoods, a program he created.

29. Cruz and Forman, "cityLAB Opens House Panel 02: Activist Paths for Architects."

30. Design Resources for Homelessness: An Online Knowledge Solution, accessed June 28, 2021, http://designresourcesforhomelessness.org/. This initiative is run by Dr. Jill Pable at Florida State University.

31. Ivan Abreu, Jon Ardern, Roberto Ascencio, Sofia Bosch, Jorge Camacho, Sergio R. Coria, Laura Ferrarello, et al., *The Pursuit of Legible Policy: Agency and Participation in the*

Complex Systems of the Contemporary Megalopolis (Mexico City: Buró–Buró, 2016). Documentation of the Peatoniños interventions can be found in Brenda Vértiz, "Peatoniños: Liberating Streets for Kids and Play," in *Urban Humanities: New Practices for Reimagining the City*, Dana Cuff, Anastasia Loukaitou-Sideris, Todd Presner, Maite Zubiaurre, and Jonathan Jae-an Crisman (Cambridge, MA: MIT Press, 2020), 30–35; "The Peatoniños of Mexico City: Liberating the Streets for Kids and for Play," UCLA Urban Humanities Initiative, accessed June 28, 2021, https://www.urbanhumanities.ucla.edu/peatoninos; and "Laboratorio de Datos," Laboratorio Para la Cuidad, accessed June 28, 2021, https://labcd .mx/experimentos/laboratorio-de-datos/.

32. Linnéa Moore and Nadine Maleh, eds., "Live/Work for the Workforce," *Institute for Public Architecture* (New York: The Printing House, ca. 2017), https://de2a8e75-04d0 -4a0e-a817-2bd8893b003c.filesusr.com/ugd/9c1902_25d4d289f6aa4835b2639a57a625d256 .pdf?index=true.

33. See the organization's website: https://designcorps.org/.

34. Patrick Sisson, "LA-Más is Building a More Equitable Los Angeles," *Curbed*, November 15, 2017, https://archive.curbed.com/2017/11/15/16635056/la-mas-architecture-timme -leung-groundbreakers-2017.

35. See Katharine Keane, "Gensler Details the Future of Cities in Annual Design Forecast," *Architect Magazine*, November 5, 2018, https://www.architectmagazine.com/practice /gensler-details-the-future-of-cities-in-annual-design-forecast_o.

36. But because nonprofits cannot be the architect of record in some states, MASS Design Group has created for that purpose a subsidiary called Model of Architecture Serving Society, LLC. The information about MASS Design Group comes from Alan Ricks, "cityLAB Opens House Panel 02: Activist Paths for Architects," *UCLA Urban Humanities Initiative,* October 20, 2020, YouTube video, 56:46, https://www.youtube.com/watch?v=11Bytw7ejoc&ab _channel=UCLAUrbanHumanitiesInitiative; and Michael Murphy and Alan Ricks, *Justice Is Beauty* (New York: Monacelli Press, 2019).

37. Ricks, "cityLAB Opens House Panel 02: Activist Paths for Architects."

38. In its 2016 report, the National Committee for Responsive Philanthropy reported that in 2013, 31 percent of foundation giving benefitted underserved communities, a rise of just 5 percent (from 26 percent) since 2003. Ryan Schlegel, *Pennies for Progress: A Decade of Boom for Philanthropy, A Bust for Social Justice* (National Committee for Responsive Philanthropy, 2016), 20, https://bjn9t2lhlni2dhd5hvym7llj-wpengine.netdna-ssl.com/wp -content/uploads/2016/11/Pennies-for-Progress-highres.pdf.

39. Rebecca Meejoo Choi, "Black Architectures: Race, Pedagogy, and Practice, 1957–68" (PhD diss., University of California, Los Angeles, 2020), https://search.proquest.com/openview /74bea8c38248680cece8dc7111abb022/1.pdf?pq-origsite=gscholar&cbl=18750&diss=y.

40. Susan Henderson, "The Resilient Community," in *From the Ground Up*, ed. Peggy Tully (New York: Princeton Architectural Press, 2012), 31. The difference in cost was subsidized by Syracuse University, a sponsor of the competition.

41. Martha Pskowski, "Mexico's Housing Laboratory Shows Off 32 Low-Cost Proto-types," *Architect's Newspaper*, October 8, 2019, https://www.archpaper.com/2019/10/mos-mexican-housing-laboratory/.

42. Presidencia de la República EPN, "INFONAVIT is the main Mexican state institution for ensuring that families can exercise their constitutional right to decent housing," Gobierno de Mexico, April 26, 2016, https://www.gob.mx/epn/prensa/infonavit-is-the-main-mexican-state-institution-for-ensuring-that-families-can-exercise-their-constitutional-right-to-decent-housing-epn.

43. Zoe Ryan, *As Seen: Exhibitions that Made Architecture and Design History* (Chicago: Art Institute of Chicago, 2017).

44. Rixt Woudstra, "Exhibiting Reform: MoMA and the Display of Public Housing (1932–1939)," *Architectural Histories* 6, no. 1 (2018): 11, https://doi.org/10.5334/ah.269.

45. Rebecca Greenwald, "Black Landscapes Matter: Q&A with Landscape Designer Walter Hood," *Metropolis Magazine*, November 3, 2020, https://www.metropolismag.com/architecture/landscape/walter-hood-black-landscapes-matter/; Walter Hood and Grace Tada, eds., *Black Landscapes Matter* (Charlottesville: University of Virginia Press, 2020).

46. Rittel was not especially concerned about what wicked problems meant for architectural practice. He often joked with his Berkeley architecture students, of which I was among, that after taking his course we might never be able to pick up a pencil again.

47. Françoise Choay, *The Rule and the Model: On the Theory of Architecture and Urbanism* (Cambridge, MA: MIT Press, 1997). First published 1980 by Seuil.

48. Bryan Stevenson, founder of the Equal Justice Initiative, quoted in Katie Couric, "The Blood of Lynching Victims Is in This Soil," *National Geographic: The Race Issue*, March 12, 2018, https://www.nationalgeographic.com/magazine/2018/04/race-lynching-museum-katie-couric-alabama/#close.

CHAPTER 3

1. Maria Cristina Didero, "Toyo Ito: Re-building From Disaster," *Domus*, January 26, 2012, https://www.domusweb.it/en/interviews/2012/01/26/toyo-ito-re-building-from-disaster.html.

2. Takuya Sekiguchi, Yoshihiro Hagiwara, Yumi Sugawara, Yasutake Tomata, Fumiya Tanji, Yutaka Yabe, Eiji Itoi, and Ichiro Tsuji, "Moving From Prefabricated Temporary Housing to Public Reconstruction Housing and Social Isolation After the Great East Japan Earthquake: A Longitudinal Study Using Propensity Score Matching," *BMJ Open* 9 (May 2019): e026354, http://dx.doi.org/10.1136/bmjopen-2018-026354; Elise Hu, "Five Years After Japan 'Disasters,' Temporary Housing Is Feeling Permanent,"

Morning Edition, National Public Radio, March 11, 2016, https://www.npr.org/sections
/parallels/2016/03/11/469857023/5-years-after-japan-disasters-temporary-housing-is
-feeling-permanent.

3. Yasuaki Onoda (architectural planner, ArchiAid), in interview with author, July 28, 2021.

4. Pablo Bris and Félix Bendito, "Impact of Japanese Post-Disaster Temporary Housing Areas' (THAs) Design on Mental and Social Health," *International Journal of Environmental Research and Public Health* 16, no. 23 (November 2019): 4757, https://doi.org/10.3390 /ijerph16234757.

5. See the excellent article in English by Yasuaki Onoda et al., "Complexities and Difficulties Behind the Implementation of Reconstruction Plans After the Great East Japan Earthquake and Tsunami of March 2011," *Advances in Natural and Technological Hazards Research* 47 (2018), https://doi.org/10.1007/978-3-319-58691-5_1.

6. Yuki Sumner, "Japan After the Storm," *Architectural Review,* July 19, 2013, https://www .architectural-review.com/places/japan/japan-after-the-storm.

7. Hitoshi Abe (founder, ArchiAid), in interview with author, July 27, 2021.

8. Hitoshi Abe (founder, ArchiAid), in interview with author, July 27, 2021.

9. Bris and Bendito, "Temporary Housing Areas."

10. "Soma City HOME-FOR-ALL / Toyo Ito and Associates + Klein Dytham architecture," *ArchDaily,* September 18, 2017, https://www.archdaily.com/879747/soma-city-home-for-all -toyo-ito-and-associates-plus-klein-dytham-architecture.

11. Letter published in full in Justine, "Designing Housing After Fukushima—'Home for All,'" *Spoon and Tamago,* September 12, 2012, https://www.spoon-tamago.com/2012/09/12 /design-housing-after-fukushima-home-for-all/.

12. Toyo Ito, "AD Interviews: Toyo Ito," interview by David Basulto, ArchDaily, September 6, 2012, YouTube video, 5:40, https://www.youtube.com/watch?v=Rcuhcanp -Wo&ab_channel=ArchDaily.

13. Michael Kimmelman, "A City Rises, Along With Its Hopes," *New York Times,* May 18, 2012, https://www.nytimes.com/2012/05/20/arts/design/fighting-crime-with-architecture -in-medellin-colombia.html; Jason Corburn, Marisa Ruiz Asari, Jorge Pérez Jamarillo, and Anibal Gaviria, "The Transformation of Medellin Into a 'City for Life': Insights For Healthy Cities," *Cities & Health* 4, no. 1 (2020): 13–24, https://doi.org/10.1080/23748834.2019 .1592735.

14. Renny Granda and Juan D. Machin-Mastromatteo, "Medellin Library Parks: A Model for Latin American Libraries and Urban Equipment," *Information Development* 34, no. 2 (2018): 201–205, https://journals.sagepub.com/doi/pdf/10.1177/0266666918755642.

15. "UCSD Community Stations: Public Spaces that Educate," UCSD Center on Global Justice, accessed June 28, 2021, http://gjustice.ucsd.edu/ucsd-community-stations/; Estudio Teddy Cruz + Fonna Forman, "Mexus," in *Critical Care: Architecture for a Broken Planet,* ed.

Angelika Fitz and Elke Drasny (Vienna: Architekturzentrum Wien; Cambridge, MA: MIT Press, 2019), 206–213.

16. "Rudy Bruner Award: Congo Street Initiative, 2013 Silver Medalist," Rudy Bruner Foundation, accessed June 28, 2021, http://www.rudybruneraward.org/winners/congo-street -initiative/; "Congo Street Initiative—Phase 2," bcWorkshop, December 23, 2016, https://www .bcworkshop.org/posts/tag/Congo+Street; "Dallas, Texas: Congo Street Green Initiative Provides Important Lessons in Community Revitalization," U.S. Department of Housing and Urban Development, accessed June 28, 2021, https://www.huduser.gov/portal /casestudies/study_04152013_1.html; "Jubilee Park and Community Center," T. Boone Pickens Foundation, November 17, 2014, http://tboonepickensfoundation.org/jubilee -park-and-community-center/. The Congo Street Initiative won the 2013 Rudy Bruner Award for Urban Excellence. The project relied on close collaboration with residents and became Dallas's first "green street," since all the houses are at least LEED gold certified.

17. Claude Parent, *The Function of the Oblique: The Architecture of Claude Parent and Paul Virilio 1963–1969* (London: AA Documents, 1996).

18. Josephine Minutillo, "Rolex Learning Center by SANAA," *Architectural Record*, June 19, 2010, https://www.architecturalrecord.com/articles/8237-rolex-learning-center-by-sanaa?oly _enc_id=9052I9930023F1D. The author critically notes that the ramping disappointingly does not make the building accessible.

19. Jürgen Habermas, *The Structural Transformation of the Public Sphere*, trans. Thomas Burger and Frederick Lawrence (Cambridge, MA: MIT Press, 1989).

20. Marshall Berman, *All That is Solid Melts into Air: The Experience of Modernity* (New York: Penguin Books, 1988). Of particular note are his comments about Baudelaire's poem "Eyes of the Poor."

21. Nancy Fraser, "Rethinking the Public Sphere: A Contribution to the Critique of Actually Existing Democracy," *Social Text* 25/26 (1990): 56–80, https://doi.org/10.2307/466240.

22. Michael Warner, *Publics and Counterpublics* (Princeton: Princeton University Press, 2002); Elijah Anderson, *The Cosmopolitan Canopy: Race and Civility in Everyday Life* (New York: WW Norton, 2011).

23. Charles "Chip" P. Linscott, "All Lives (Don't) Matter: The Internet Meets Afro-Pessimism and Black Optimism," *Black Camera* 8, no. 2 (Spring 2017): 104–119, https://www.jstor.org /stable/10.2979/blackcamera.8.2.06.

24. Jeremy Waldron, "Superseding Historic Injustice," *Ethics* 103, no. 1 (1992): 4–28, https:// www.jstor.org/stable/2381493.

25. Ann Markusen and Anne Gadwa, *Creative Placemaking* (National Endowment for the Arts, 2010).

26. Clare Mullaney, "Reading Lists: Disability Studies: Foundations and Key Concepts," *JSTOR DAILY*, April 13, 2019, https://daily.jstor.org/reading-list-disability-studies/.

27. Douglas Baynton, "Slaves, Immigrants, and Suffragists: The Uses of Disability in Citizenship Debates," *PMLA* 120, no. 2 (March 2005): 564, www.jstor.org/stable/25486185.

28. Bess Williamson, *Accessible America: A History of Disability and Design* (New York: NYU Press, 2019): 131.

29. Williamson, *Accessible America*, 138.

30. Heather McGhee, *The Sum of Us: What Racism Costs Everyone and How We Can Prosper Together* (New York: One World, 2021).

31. The ramps have generated some controversy about whether they are safe. See, for example, Jesse Johnston, "The Robson Square Steps are Beautiful but Are They Safe?" *CBC News*, August 22, 2019, https://www.cbc.ca/news/canada/british-columbia /robson-square-accessibility-1.5255477.

32. Karin Bendixen and Maria Benktzon, "Design for All in Scandinavia—A Strong Concept," *Applied Ergonomics* 46, Part B (January 2015):248–257, https://doi.org/10.1016/j .apergo.2013.03.004.

33. Jacques Derrida, *On Cosmopolitanism and Forgiveness* (New York: Routledge, 2001), 16; Jacques Derrida, *Of Hospitality: Anne Dufourmantelle Invites Jacques Derrida to Respond*, trans. Rachel Bowlby (Stanford: Stanford University Press, 2000).

34. Janette Sadik-Khan and Seth Solomonow, *Street Fight: Handbook for an Urban Revolution* (New York: Viking, 2016).

35. Russell Ellis and Dana Cuff, eds., *Architects' People* (New York: Oxford University Press, 1989).

36. Don Mitchell, *The Right to the City: Social Justice and the Fight for Public Space* (New York: Guilford Press, 2003), 2.

37. Dianne Harris, *Little White Houses: How the Postwar Home Constructed Race in America* (Minneapolis: University of Minnesota Press, 2013).

38. KangJae See Lee, "Public Space, Park Space, and Racialized Space," *Project for Public Spaces*, January 27, 2020, https://www.pps.org/article/public-space-park-space-and-racialized-space; Elijah Anderson, "'The White Space,'" *Sociology of Race and Ethnicity* 1, no. 1 (January 2015): 10–21, https://doi.org/10.1177/2F2332649214561306.

39. Raphael W. Bostic, Annette M. Kim, and Abel Valenzuela Jr., "Contesting the Streets: Vending and Public Space in Global Cities," *Cityscape* 18, no. 1 (2016): 8, https://www.jstor.org /stable/e26328235.

40. "2020 Greater Los Angeles Homeless Count Results," *Los Angeles Homeless Services Authority*, June 12, 2020, https://www.lahsa.org/news?article=726-2020-greater-los-angeles -homeless-count-results.

41. Don Mitchell, *Mean Streets* (Atlanta: University of Georgia Press, 2020), xi.

42. Moms 4 Housing, accessed February 8, 2021, https://moms4housing.org/.

43. Sarah Jaffe. "Reclaim Our Homes," *Dissent Magazine*, March 20, 2020, https://www.dissentmagazine.org/online_articles/reclaim-our-homes.

44. See Zoie Matthew, "Homeless Families Who Occupied Vacant El Sereno Homes Will Now Move into Them Legally," *LAist*, November 16, 2020, https://laist.com/2020/11/16/el_sereno_caltrans_homeless_families_reclaimers.php.

45. Sandra McNeill, "The Threat of Mass Evictions and Opportunity to Rethink Housing" (lecture, Luskin Center for Innovation, University of California Los Angeles, February 10, 2021).

CHAPTER 4

1. Walter Hood and Grace Mitchell Tada, "Lifeways," in *Black Landscapes Matter*, ed. Walter Hood and Grace Mitchell Tada (Charlottesville: University of Virginia Press, 2020), 35.

2. Princeton University, "University, Students Reach Agreement on Campus Climate Concerns," news release by the Office of Communications, November 19, 2015, https://www.princeton.edu/news/2015/11/19/university-students-reach-agreement-campus-climate-concerns.

3. Wilson Legacy Review Committee, *Report of the Trustee Committee on Woodrow Wilson's Legacy at Princeton* (Princeton University, 2016), 10–11, https://www.princeton.edu/sites/default/files/documents/2017/08/Wilson-Committee-Report-Final.pdf.

4. Walter Hood, "Senior Loeb Scholar Lecture: Walter Hood, 'When Memory Is Not Enough,'" Harvard GSD, February 24, 2021, YouTube video, 45:07, https://www.youtube.com/watch?v=cQxIBnwJuvM.

5. Quote from Hood, "Senior Loeb Scholar Lecture: Walter Hood, 'When Memory Is Not Enough.'" See also Benjamin Ball, "U. Inaugurates Installation on Woodrow Wilson's Legacy with Discussion, Dedication," *Daily Princetonian*, October 6, 2019, https://www.dailyprincetonian.com/article/2019/10/u-inaugurates-installation-on-woodrow-wilsons-legacy-with-discussion-dedication.

6. From the video announcement of the *Wrestling with History* exhibition lecture: "Woodrow Wilson: Wrestling with History," Woodrow Wilson School of Public and International Affairs, October 1, 2019, YouTube video, 0:30, https://www.youtube.com/watch?v=nO4uvxcrWlY.

7. Hood, "Senior Loeb Scholar Lecture: Walter Hood, 'When Memory Is Not Enough.'"

8. Oliver Effron, "Q&A With Walter Hood, 'Double Sights' Architect," *Daily Princetonian*, October 7, 2019, https://www.dailyprincetonian.com/article/2019/10/walterhood-q-a; Walter Hood, "How Urban Spaces Can Preserve History and Build Community," TED2018, April 2018, TED video, 14:05, https://www.ted.com/talks/walter_hood_how_urban_spaces_can_preserve_history_and_build_community?language=en.

9. James Midgley, *Professional Imperialism: Social Work in the Third World* (Farnham, UK: Ashgate Publishing, 1981).

10. Cathleen McGuigan, "Interview with Walter Hood on History and Race in Landscape Design," *Architectural Record*, August 4, 2020, https://www.architecturalrecord.com/articles/14749-interview-with-walter-hood-on-history-and-race-in-landscape-design.

11. Laura Mirviss and William Hanley, "No Retroactive Prize for Denise Scott Brown, Pritzker Jury Says, but She Remains Eligible for the Award in the Future," *Architectural Record*, June 14, 2013, https://www.architecturalrecord.com/articles/2906-no-retroactive-prize-for-denise-scott-brown-pritzker-jury-says-but-she-remains-eligible-for-the-award-in-the-future.

12. The conflation of gender and collaboration in architecture has roots in theory, discriminatory practices, and demographics. See, for example, Ann Forsyth, "In Praise of Zaha: Women, Partnership, and the Star System in Architecture," *Journal of Architectural Education* 60, no. 2 (November 2006) 63–65, https://www.jstor.org/stable/40480694. There are only two cases between 1979 and 2021 when the Pritzker was awarded to women only: Zaha Hadid in 2004, and Grafton Architects' principals Yvonne Farrell and Shelley McNamara in 2020. Note: There are forty-three prizes awarded in forty-two years because, in 1988, the Pritzker jury gave a shared prize to two individuals who did not practice together: Gordon Bunshaft and Oscar Neimeyer.

13. David Owen, "The Anti-Gravity Men," *New Yorker*, June 18, 2007, https://www.newyorker.com/magazine/2007/06/25/the-anti-gravity-men.

14. Horst W. J. Rittel and Melvin M. Webber, "Dilemmas in a General Theory of Planning," *Policy Sciences* 4, no. 2 (June 1973): 155–69, https://doi.org/10.1007/BF01405730. For Rittel, *planning* is the umbrella term for design thinking in architecture as well as the planning professions.

15. David Harvey, *Spaces of Hope* (Berkeley: University of California Press, 2000).

16. Sherry R. Arnstein, "A Ladder of Citizen Participation," *Journal of the American Institute of Planners* 35, no. 4 (July 1969): 216–224, https://doi.org/10.1080/01944366908977225.

17. John Gaber, "Building 'A Ladder of Citizen Participation,'" *Journal of the American Planning Association* 85, no. 3 (June 2019): 188–201, https://doi.org10.1080/01944363.2019.1612267; John H. Strange, "Citizen Participation in Community Action and Model Cities Programs," *Public Administration Review* 32 (October 1972): 655–669, www.jstor.org/stable/975231.

18. Anthony J. Kline and Richard Le Gates, "Citizen Participation in the Model Cities Program—Toward a Theory of Collective Bargaining for the Poor," *National Black Law Journal* 1, no. 1 (1971): 68–69, https://escholarship.org/uc/item/0fxok3r8.

19. Sherry Arnstein, *Technical Assistance Bulletin No. 3: Citizen Participation in Model Cities* (U.S. Department of Housing and Urban Development: 1968), 23.

20. Markus Miessen, ed., *The Nightmare of Participation: Crossbench Praxis as a Mode of Criticality* (Berlin: Sternberg Press, 2011); Ammon Beyerle, "Participation in Architecture: Agonism in Practice" (PhD diss., University of Melbourne, 2018), http://hdl.handle.net/11343/225579.

21. Beyerle, "Participation in Architecture," 19.

22. Nikolaus Hirsch and Markus Miessen, eds., *The Space of Agonism: Markus Miessen in Conversation with Chantal Mouffe* (Berlin: Sternberg Press, 2012); Chantal Mouffe, *Agonistics: Thinking the World Politically* (London: Verso, 2013).

23. Eric W. Orts and Alan Strudler, "Putting a Stake in Stakeholder Theory," *Journal of Business Ethics* 88 (2009): 605–615, https://doi.org/10.1007/s10551-009-0310-y.

24. Pierre Bourdieu, *The Logic of Practice* (Stanford, CA: Stanford University Press, 1990). Anthropologists have begun to break free of the single-sited, geographically bound notion of field in order to sidestep methodological barriers to multi-local and online fields for fieldwork; see, for example, Máiréad Nic Craith and Emma Hill, "Re-locating the Ethnographic Field: From 'Being *There*' to '*Being* There,'" *Anthropological Journal of European Cultures* 24, no. 1 (2015): 42–62, https://www.jstor.org/stable/26355934.

25. Andres Lepik, "Transformation of Tour Bois-le-Prêtre," audio interview, MoMA, 2010, accessed June 28, 2021, https://www.moma.org/interactives/exhibitions/2010/smallscalebigchange/projects/transformation_of_tour_boise_le_pretre.html.

26. Robin Pogrebin, "Affordable Housing Earns French Couple the Pritzker Prize," *New York Times*, March 16, 2021, https://www.nytimes.com/2021/03/16/arts/design/pritzker-prize-anne-lacaton-jean-philippe-vassal.html; Michael Kimmelman, "At Edge of Paris, a Housing Project Becomes a Beacon," *New York Times*, March 27, 2012, https://www.nytimes.com/2012/03/28/arts/design/renovated-tour-bois-le-pretre-brightens-paris-skyline.html.

27. See, for example, Harvey, *Spaces of Hope*.

CHAPTER 5

1. See David O'Brien and Sandra Carrasco, "Contested Incrementalism: Elemental's Quinta Monroy Settlement Fifteen Years On," *Frontiers of Architectural Research* 10, no. 2 (June 2021): 263–273, https://doi.org/10.1016/j.foar.2020.11.002; see also Peter Rowe and Har Ye Kan, "Urban Intensities: Housing Special Populations," *Building Types Online* (Berlin: Birkhäuser, 2016), https://www.degruyter.com/document/database/BDT/entry/BDT_06_035/html.

2. Sandra Carrasco and David O'Brien, "Revisit: Quinta Monroy by Elemental," *Architectural Review*, January 4, 2021, https://www.architectural-review.com/buildings/housing/revisit-quinta-monroy-by-elemental.

3. Michael Kimmelman, "Alejandro Aravena, the Architect Rebuilding a Country," *T: The New York Times Style Magazine*, May 23, 2016, https://www.nytimes.com/2016/05/23/t-magazine /pritzker-venice-biennale-chile-architect-alejandro-aravena.html; see also Amiee Ground-water, "A Case for the Incremental: Quinta Monroy," *ArchitectureAU*, November 26, 2015, https://architectureau.com/articles/a-case-for-the-incremental-quinta-monroy/; Rowe and Kan, "Urban Intensities"; Rodrigo Salcedo, "The Last Slum: Moving from Illegal Settlements to Subsidized Home Ownership in Chile," *Urban Affairs Review* 46, no. 1 (May 2010): 90–118, https://doi.org/10.1177/1078087410368487.

4. Mark Foster Gage, "Killing Simplicity: Object-Oriented Philosophy in Architecture," *Log* 33 (Winter 2015): 95–106, https://www.jstor.org/stable/43630853.

5. For a critical review of the debate, see John Kaliski, "Master Johnson's House of Education," *Cite Magazine* (Summer 1986): 16–18.

6. Michael Speaks, "After Theory," *Architectural Record* 193, no. 6 (2005): 72–75; Patrik Schumacher, "The Historical Pertinence of Parametricism and the Prospect of a Free Market Urban Order," in *The Politics of Parametricism: Digital Technologies in Architecture*, ed. Matthew Poole and Manuel Shvartzberg (London: Bloomsbury, 2015), 19–44.

7. Patrik Schumacher, "Watch Patrik Schumacher's Keynote Presentation on Housing Live," Dezeen, November 18, 2016, Facebook video, 1:10:06, https://www.facebook.com /watch/?v=10154712724688674.

8. See, for example, Toshiko Mori's VisionArc research for Singapore, described in Mimi Zeiger, "Systems Thinking in Architecture," *Architect*, April 27, 2011, https://www .architectmagazine.com/practice/systems-thinking-in-architecture_o.

9. Herbert Muschamp, "The Miracle in Bilbao," *New York Times Magazine*, September 7, 1997, https://www.nytimes.com/1997/09/07/magazine/the-miracle-in-bilbao.html; Rowan Moore, "The Bilbao Effect: How Frank Gehry's Guggenheim Started a Global Craze," *Guardian*, October 1, 2017, https://www.theguardian.com/artanddesign/2017/oct/01 /bilbao-effect-frank-gehry-guggenheim-global-craze.

10. George Kubler, *The Shape of Time* (New Haven: Yale University Press, 1962).

11. Claire Zimmerman, "Albert Kahn in the Second Industrial Revolution," *AA Files* 75 (2017); Sonia Melnikova-Raich, "The Soviet Problem with Two 'Unknowns': How an American Architect and a Soviet Negotiator Jump-Started the Industrialization of Russia, Part I: Albert Kahn," *IA. The Journal of the Society for Industrial Archeology* 36, no. 2 (2010): 57–80, https://www.jstor.org/stable/41933723; Charles K. Hyde, "Assembly-Line Architecture: Albert Kahn and the Evolution of the U.S. Auto Factory, 1905–1940," *IA. The Journal of the Society for Industrial Archeology* 22, no. 2 (1996): 5–24, https://www.jstor.org/stable/40968351.

12. Alysia Bennett, Dana Cuff, and Gus Wendel, "Backyard Housing Boom: New Markets for Affordable Housing and the Role of Digital Technology," *Technology|Architecture+Design: Urbanizing* 3, no. 1 (March 2019): 76–88, https://doi.org/10.1080/24751448.2019.1571831.

13. Amy F. Ogata, "Building for learning in Postwar American Elementary Schools," *Journal of the Society of Architectural Historians* 67, no. 4 (December 2008): 562–591, https://doi.org/10.1525/jsah.2008.67.4.562.

CHAPTER 6

1. Juan Villoro, *Horizontal Vertigo: A City Called Mexico* (New York: Pantheon Books, 2021), 12, 13, 21, 31.

2. Aaron O'Neill, "Mexico: Age Distribution from 2010 to 2020," *Statista*, July 7, 2021, https://www.statista.com/statistics/275411/age-distribution-in-mexico/; David Bartels et al., "Incidence of Road Injuries in Mexico: Country Report," *International Journal of Injury Control and Safety Promotion* 17, no. 3 (February 2010): 169–176, https://doi.org/10.1080/17457300903564553; *Informe sobre la Situación de la Seguridad Vial, México 2019* (Secretaría de Salud/Consejo Nacional para la Prevención de Accidentes [CONAPRA], Mexico, 2019), https://drive.google.com/file/d/1Y3jBmQqFBDuMOk5rTGgO_87S4nVMIdRQ/view.

3. "Experimentación y Creatividad en la Ciudad de México (Archivo 2013–2018)," Laboratorio Para la Cuidad, https://labcd.mx/#descripcion-lab. Because the Lab is no longer in existence, documentation exists primarily in web archives and is written primarily by the Lab itself. Critical reflections on the Lab's life and effectiveness were gained through interviews by the author with participants.

4. Laboratorio Para la Cuidad.

5. Brenda Vértiz (leader of the Peatoniños initiative at Laboratorio Para la Cuidad), in interview with author, May 26, 2021.

6. Nathaniel Janowitz, "Mexico's Pedestrian Activists Are Waging a Battle for Safer Streets," *Bloomberg CityLab*, April 16, 2019, https://www.bloomberg.com/news/articles/2019-04-16/the-activists-behind-mexico-s-new-road-safety-law.

7. Peatonito came after Peatón Man in Quito and the 420 mimes that Bogotá mayor Antanas Mockus hired to control traffic after he himself dressed in a superman costume; see Mara Cristina Caballero, "Academic Turns City into a Social Experiment: Mayor Mockus of Bogotá and his Spectacularly Applied Theory," *Harvard Gazette*, March 11, 2004, https://news.harvard.edu/gazette/story/2004/03/academic-turns-city-into-a-social-experiment/.

8. Jeremy Shepherd, "17k Bike Tour Will Celebrate Bicycle Month in Mexico City," *Mexico News Daily*, June 14, 2019, https://mexiconewsdaily.com/mexicolife/bicycle-month-in-mexico-city/.

9. The participating UCLA students—Heidi Alexander, Maricela Becerra, Kenton Card, Ryan Hernandez, Devin Koba, Paola Mendez, Maria Teresa Monroe, and Jeannette Mundy—documented their research in a paper entitled "The Power of Play in Reshaping Public

Narratives," in *Urban Humanities in the Borderlands: Engaged Scholarship from Mexico City to Los Angeles*, ed. Jonathan Crisman (Los Angeles: UCLA Urban Humanities Initiative, 2016), 83–89, https://static1.squarespace.com/static/5d5c5d00fd05ea000147ebee/t/5de803d588321 b3df06de0b0/1575486438849/URBAN-HUMANITIES-IN-THE-BORDERLANDS-download. compressed+%281%29.pdf.

10. Alexander et al., "The Power of Play," 89.

11. Sarah Whiting and Peter Eisenman, "I Am Interested in a Project of Engaged Autonomy," *Log* 28 (Summer 2013): 114, https://www.jstor.org/stable/43630873.

12. Whiting and Eisenman, "Project of Engaged Autonomy," 117.

13. See, for example, Mark Llewellyn, "Polyvocalism and the Public: 'Doing' a Critical Historical Geography of Architecture," *Area* 35, no. 3 (September 2003), 264–270, www.jstor.org/stable/20004320.

14. Philippe Boudon, *Lived-In Architecture: Le Corbusier's Pessac Revisited* (Cambridge, MA: MIT Press, 1972).

15. Stephen Berrisford and Patrick McAuslan, *Reforming Urban Laws in Africa: A Practical Guide* (Cape Town: African Centre for Cities; Brussels: Cities Alliance, and Nairobi: UN-Habitat, 2017), 60, https://unhabitat.org/sites/default/files/2020/05/ulr-report_final_lr.pdf.

16. Gabriella Gómez-Mont, "Prototyping the City," and John Lynch, "Legible Policy in the Participatory City," in Iván Abreu, Jon Ardern, Roberto Ascencio, Sofía Bosch, Jorge Camacho, Sergio R. Coria, Laura Ferrarello et al., *The Pursuit of Legible Policy: Agency and Participation in the Complex Systems of the Contemporary Megalopolis* (Mexico City: Buró–Buró, 2016), 9–12, 42–52, https://labcd.mx/wp-content/uploads/2018/10/Legible-Policies_BB.pdf.

17. On the three elements of social movements, see Emahunn Raheem Ali Campbell, "A Critique of the Occupy Movement from a Black Occupier," *The Black Scholar* 41, no. 4 (Winter 2011): 42–51, https://doi.org/10.5816/blackscholar.41.4.0042.

18. Nihad M. Farooq, "Of Science and Excess: Jacob Riis, Anzia Yezierska, and the Modernist Turn in Immigrant Fiction," *American Studies* 53, no. 4 (2014): 73–94, www.jstor.org/stable/24589398.

19. Robert W. De Forest, "Recent Progress in Tenement-House Reform," *The Annals of the American Academy of Political and Social Science* 23 (March 1904): 103–116, www.jstor.org/stable/1009986.

20. Janette Sadik-Khan and Seth Solomonow, *Street Fight: Handbook for an Urban Revolution* (New York: Viking, 2016).

21. Aimi Hamraie, "Sloped Technoscience: Curb Cuts, Critical Frictions, and Disability (Maker) Cultures," in *Building Access: Universal Design and the Politics of Disability* (Minneapolis: University of Minnesota Press, 2017), 101.

22. Aimi Hamraie, "Aimi Hamraie on 'Making Access Critical: Disability, Race, and Gender in Environmental Design,'" Othering & Belonging Institute, uploaded March 4, 2019,

YouTube video, 47:21, https://belonging.berkeley.edu/aimi-hamraie-making-access-critical
-disability-race-and-gender-environmental-design.

23. Hamraie, "Sloped Technoscience."

24. This notion too is debated among critical disabilities scholars. The language of Design
for All universalizes bodies despite their differences. The liberal ideal that spaces can
accommodate everyone erases the friction that particular bodies experience.

25. Mary Jean Dolan, "Why Monuments are Government Speech: The Hard Case of Pleasant
Grove City v. Summun," *Catholic Law Review* 58, no. 1 (Fall 2008): 8–58, https://scholarship
.law.edu/cgi/viewcontent.cgi?article=3150&context=lawreview.

26. Sharon Zukin, *Landscapes of Power: From Detroit to Disney World* (Berkeley: University of
California Press, 1991).

CHAPTER 7

1. Brittany Martin, "The Priciest Neighborhood in Los Angeles is Now the Most Expensive
Place for Renters to Live Outside Manhattan," *Los Angeles Magazine*, October 12, 2019,
https://www.businessinsider.com/westwood-los-angeles-most-expensive-neighborhood
-outside-manhattan-2019-10.

2. cityLAB, *Experiments in Student Housing: A Preliminary Report* (Los Angeles: cityLAB, 2018),
https://static1.squarespace.com/static/58e4e9705016e194dd5cdc43/t/61d9e75f11883623bf
970f40/1641670501619/cityLAB_Experiments+in+Student+Housing.pdf; Dana Cuff and
Gus Wendel, *"My Commute is Hell": UCLA Students, Extreme Commutes, Impacts, Solutions* (Los Angeles: cityLAB, 2019), https://static1.squarespace.com/static/58e4e970
5016e194dd5cdc43/t/5d8bb03f597be3780c8542bd/1569435766654/19-0924+MCiH_Final
_Update.pdf; Gus Wendel, "My Commute Home: Students at the Intersection of Long-
Distance Commutes and Housing Insecurity" (unpublished paper, December 2021),
Microsoft Word file.

3. Maddie Sewani, "The Nap Map," *Harvard Crimson*, April 27, 2013, https://www.thecrim-
son.com/flyby/article/2013/4/27/nap_space_map/; Steven S. Lee, "Petitions Address Nap
Space, Brain Break," *Harvard Crimson*, February 20, 2013, https://www.thecrimson.com
/article/2013/2/20/us-petitions-nap-space/?page=single.

4. AB-74 Budget Act of 2019, State of California Office of Legislative Counsel (approved
June 27, 2019), 95, https://leginfo.legislature.ca.gov/faces/billTextClient.xhtml?bill_id
=201920200AB74.

5. Office of the President, *University of California Basic Needs Legislative Report: June
2019-June 2020* (Oakland: University of California, 2020), 12–13, https://www.ucop.edu
/operating-budget/_files/legreports/20-21/uc_basic_needs_leg_report-92220.pdf.

6. Dan Immergluck, "Large Redevelopment Initiatives, Housing Values and Gentrification: The Case of the Atlanta Beltline," *Urban Studies* 46, no. 8 (July 2009): 1723–1745, www.jstor.org/stable/43198502.

7. Hillel David Soifer, "The Causal Logic of Critical Junctures," *Comparative Political Studies* 45, no. 12 (December 2012): 1586, https://doi.org/10.1177/0010414012463902.

8. Jeffrey S. Lowe and Todd C. Shaw, "After Katrina: Racial Regimes and Human Development Barriers in the Gulf Coast Region," *American Quarterly* 61, no. 3 (September 2009): 807, www.jstor.org/stable/27735020.

9. Kaitlyn Menza, "Where Did Brad Pitt's Make It Right Foundation Go Wrong," *AD Pro: The Report*, January 18, 2019, https://www.architecturaldigest.com/story/brad-pitt-make-it-right-foundation-new-orleans-katrina-lawsuit.

10. Charles Tilly, *Social Movements: 1768–2004* (Boulder, CO: Paradigm Publishers, 2004).

11. See, for example, David S. Meyer, "Protest and Political Opportunities," *Annual Review of Sociology* 30 (2004): 125–145, http://www.jstor.org/stable/29737688.

12. "Global and Regional Holcim Awards 2021," Holcim Foundation, November 13, 2021, YouTube video, 15:16, https://www.youtube.com/watch?v=ySRGTVVhgl8&ab_channel=HolcimFoundation; Joseph Kizza, "Priscilla Namwanje: Ugandan Architect Wins Sustainable Design Top Prize," *NewVision*, June 17, 2021, https://www.newvision.co.ug/articledetails/106291.

13. Marisa Kendall, "Oakland Opens New Cabins for Homeless, Funded by Community Donations," *Mercury News*, January 20, 2020, https://www.mercurynews.com/2020/01/28/oakland-opens-new-community-cabins-for-homeless-with-resident-donations/.

14. Eric Cazdyn, "Anti-anti: Utopia, Globalization, Jameson," *Modern Language Quarterly* 68, no. 2 (June 2007); Naomi Klein, *The Shock Doctrine: The Rise of Disaster Capitalism* (Toronto: Knopf Canada, 2007).

CHAPTER 8

1. Edward Said, *Culture and Imperialism* (New York, Vintage Books, 1994), xiv. First published in 1993 by Knopf.

INDEX

Page numbers followed by f refer to figures;
page numbers followed by t indicate tables.

transformation impacted by, 255–256
Prophetic aesthetics, hooks on, 32, 34
PropX (design competition), 19
Prototypes. *See also* Models
 for affordable housing, 63f
 of car, 174f
 demonstrations compared with, 173, 183
 of pods, 227f, 232f
 policy from, 212
 precedents distinguished from, 173
Provisional City, The (Cuff), 15
Public, the, 119f. *See also* Radically
  public architecture
 agency of, 204
 architecture defining, 136
 in built environment, 92
 counterpublics contrasted with, 106–107
 engagement by, 153
 history of, 105
 legible policy and, 202, 210
 Raumlabor imagining, 121
Public housing, 8, 40, 81f, 267n28
 community emphasized by, 80f, 82f
 by Neutra, 52–53
 shared spaces in, 79–81
Public spaces, 91. *See also* Shared spaces
 anti-racism in, 65, 96–98
 homelessness in relation to, 123
 Medellín funding, 93–95, 94f
 in New York City, 212
 open-endedness of, 98–100
 race and, 106–107
 racism in, 111–12
 rights to, 121–122
 thick maps of, 153–154, 155f
Public sphere, 2. *See also* Commons
 Habermas defining, 105–106
 history missed by, 11
 spatial justice catalyzed by, 137

Queer theory, 106
Quinta Monroy, Santiago, Chile, 162–63

evaluations of self-building at, 164–66
 extension beyond plans at, 166f
 half-houses at, 159, 160f, 161f, 186
 transformation of, 167f

Race. *See also* Whiteness
 inequity and, 14–15
 injustice and, 127
 privilege and, 6–7, 10, 122
 public spaces and, 106–107
 redlining and, 14, 124
 segregation and, 14–15, 41, 111–112
Race and Modern Architecture (Sutton), 15
Racism, 16, 49, 122
 anti-, 7, 11, 65, 96–98
 anti-Black, 32, 127–128, 142
 in public spaces, 111–112
 of Tree of Architecture, 264n11
Radically public architecture
 defining, 92–98
 freshness in, 100–103
 after Great East Japan Earthquake, 85–86
 Home for All as, 91
 hospitality embedded in, 114
 objects in, 179–182
 as open-ended, 154
 beyond practices, 115
 spatial justice in, 96
 status quo destabilized by, 95
Ramp, stairway-with-, 112, 113f, 272n31
Ramping, in disability movement, 212–217,
  215f, 216f
Raumlabor (practice), 115–216, 117f, 119f, 121
Real estate
 architecture in relation to, 171
 basic human needs contrasted with, 49
 markets, 49
 speculation in, 41, 244
 theory embracing, 170–171
Reality shows, design, 11–13
Reclaiming Our Homes (organization), 123
Reconstructions (Curry), 11